FROM THE UNTHINKABLE
TO THE UNAVOIDABLE

D1566027

FROM THE UNTHINKABLE TO THE UNAVOIDABLE

American Christian and Jewish Scholars Encounter the Holocaust

Edited by
CAROL RITTNER AND JOHN K. ROTH

Westport, Connecticut
London

The Library of Congress has cataloged the hardcover edition as follows:

From the unthinkable to the unavoidable : American Christian and
  Jewish scholars encounter the Holocaust / edited by Carol Rittner
  and John K. Roth
       p.   cm. — (Contributions to the study of religion, ISSN
  0196–7053 ; no. 48. Christianity and the Holocaust—Core issues)
     Includes bibliographical references (p.   ) and index.
     ISBN 0–313–29683–9 (alk. paper)
       1. Holocaust, Jewish (1939–1945)—Influence.   2. Holocaust
  (Christian theology)   I. Rittner, Carol Ann.   II. Roth,
  John K.   III. Series: Contributions to the study of religion ; no.
  48.   IV. Series: Contributions to the study of religion.
  Christianity and the Holocaust—Core issues.
  D804.3.F76   1997
  940.53'18—dc20   96–28057

British Library Cataloguing in Publication Data is available.

A hardcover edition of *From the Unthinkable to the Unavoidable* is available from
Greenwood Press, an imprint of Greenwood Publishing Group, Inc. (Contributions
to the Study of Religion, Number 48: ISBN: 0–313–29683–9).

Library of Congress Catalog Card Number: 96–28057
ISBN: 0–275–95764–0 (pbk.)

First published in 1997

Praeger Publishers, 88 Post Road West, Westport, CT 06881
An imprint of Greenwood Publishing Group, Inc.

Printed in the United States of America

The paper used in this book complies with the
Permanent Paper Standard issued by the National
Information Standards Organization (Z39.48–1984).

10 9 8 7 6 5 4 3 2 1

To
GEORGE D. SCHWAB
"He who is a friend is always a friend . . ."
—*Proverbs* 17:16

Contents

Series Foreword

The Holocaust did not end when the Allies liberated the Jewish survivors from Nazi Germany's killing centers and concentration camps in 1945. The consequences of that catastrophic event still shadow the world's moral, political, and religious life.

The *Christianity and the Holocaust—Core Issues* series explores Christian complicity, indifference, resistance, rescue, and other responses to the Holocaust. Concentrating on core issues such as the Christian roots of antisemitism, the roles played by Christian individuals and groups during the Holocaust, and the institutional reactions of Christians after Auschwitz, the series has a historical focus but addresses current concerns as well.

While many of the series' authors are well-known, established Holocaust scholars, the series also features young writers who will become leaders in the next generation of Holocaust scholarship. As all of the authors study the Holocaust's history, they also assess its impact on Christianity and its implications for the future of the Christian tradition.

From the Unthinkable to the Unavoidable is a collection of essays by well-known American Christian and Jewish scholars who have been writing for many years about the Holocaust and its impact on our moral landscape. Thanks in large part to their efforts, our awareness of the Holocaust has changed. It is no longer possible for a thoughtful person to avoid confronting the "unthinkable." But what about these scholars? Over the years, have they changed, have their questions changed? In a world scarred by the Holocaust, hope is engendered by people who are not afraid to confront radical evil and who encourage others to do likewise. The essays in *From the Un-*

thinkable to the Unavoidable: American Christian and Jewish Scholars Encounter the Holocaust reveal the profound effect life stories and personal experiences have had on the way these scholars think and on the issues and questions that engage them. The scholars *have changed;* some of their questions *have changed;* but, as each writer makes clear, one thing *has not changed:* the formidable challenge facing us to heal and transform our fragile world.

Carol Rittner and John K. Roth

Acknowledgments

Between the lines of every book there are countless feelings of gratitude, and we are pleased to have an opportunity to thank all those who encouraged, assisted, and cooperated with us as we brought this particular volume to fruition. Editing a book reminds us once again how much we depend on the generosity of others.

First and foremost, we thank our contributors—scholars all—who took time from already crowded schedules to respond to our request for an essay. They thoughtfully and clearly responded to all of our questions, wrote insightfully and creatively, met our deadlines—sometimes more promptly than we did—and allowed us to include their essays in *From the Unthinkable to the Unavoidable: American Christian and Jewish Scholars Encounter the Holocaust*. Without their generosity, cooperation, and confidence in us, our book would have remained only an idea, albeit a good one. We thank each and every one of them.

Dr. George D. Schwab, Professor of History at City University of New York (Graduate Center and City College), to whom our book is dedicated, also deserves our thanks. In a conversation with Carol Rittner some years ago, Professor Schwab encouraged her to talk to John K. Roth about developing a series of books focusing on Christianity and the Holocaust—Core Issues. We are pleased to acknowledge our debt of gratitude and delighted to dedicate this volume to him.

There are others we also want to thank, people who often were behind the scenes, but who helped us as we wrote and edited *From the Unthinkable to the Unavoidable*. Our thanks to the secretarial staff in the Division of Arts and Humanities at The Richard Stockton College of New Jersey (especially Margaret Simons), all of whom extended every courtesy as we accomplished our tasks. In Oslo, Norway, the staff at the Fulbright office helped with the long-distance fax communications between us while John was on sabbatical from Claremont McKenna College during the 1995–96 academic year. They provided support in numerous other ways as well. We are grateful to them for their cooperation and courtesy. On countless occasions, the library staff at Stockton College helped us track down unclear bibliographical references, dates, and other information as well. We thank them for their assistance.

We have been fortunate to enjoy the encouragement of Dr. James T. Sabin, Executive Vice President, Greenwood Publishing Group, and privileged to have the support, encouragement, and good advice of Nina Pearlstein, our gracious editor at Greenwood Publishing Group. Their ever faithful understanding motivated us to do our best, and we trust they will be pleased with the result of our efforts. We also want to thank Arlene Belzer, our production editor, and Susan Sunderman, our copyeditor, who performed their work in a careful, wise, and gentle manner.

Finally, we thank our families and friends at home and abroad. John especially thanks his wife, Lyn, who made his long-distance work with Carol easier; and Carol offers special gratitude to the Sisters of Mercy in Dallas, Pennsylvania, and Derry, Northern Ireland, who cheered her on as she worked. Likewise, we thank our colleagues and friends in Oslo, Norway; in Claremont, California, at Claremont McKenna College; and in New Jersey at The Richard Stockton College. Because of their steadfast support and encouragement, we have the strength to engage in the work of *tikkun olam*— mending the world.

Introduction: Memories, Encounters, and Challenges

Carol Rittner and John K. Roth

> What happened, happened. But *that* it happened cannot be so easily accepted.
>
> —Jean Améry, *At the Mind's Limits*

The Holocaust was the systematic, state-sponsored persecution and murder of nearly 6 million Jews by Nazi Germany and its collaborators. During this slaughter, which the Nazis called *die Endlösung* (the Final Solution), two-thirds of Europe's Jews and one-third of the world's Jewish population were murdered. More than half of the dead came from Poland, where the Nazi annihilation effort was 90 percent successful. The Hebrew word *Shoah*, which means catastrophe, is also frequently used for this immense destruction. One result of the *Shoah* was that almost 1.5 million of its victims were Jewish children under the age of fifteen. Of the European Jewish children alive in 1939, only 11 percent survived.

Although Jews were the primary victims, Nazi Germany's genocidal policies also destroyed millions of other defenseless people. Roma and Sinti (Gypsies), the handicapped, and Poles were targeted for destruction or decimation for racial, national, or ethnic reasons. Millions more, including homosexuals, Jehovah's Witnesses, Soviet prisoners of war, and political and religious dissidents were also oppressed and put to death under Nazi tyranny.

Holocaust, the Final Solution, or *Shoah*—whichever name is used to identify this watershed event—there was a time when it was unthinkable. The necessary technology, political organization, and economic calculation, as well as the requisite imagination, intentionality, and will to power, were not yet available or adequately coordinated to produce this particular disaster. A certain lack of "progress" provided protection. The world had not yet become a place where everything was permitted. Unfortunately, that condition would not last. The unthinkable did become thinkable, and then the unthinkable happened.

Holocaust, the Final Solution, or *Shoah*—whichever name is used—a time arrived when this catastrophe became unavoidable. It could have been avoided, however, especially if Christians in Europe and the United States had responded differently, for the Holocaust was not inevitable. The void opened at Auschwitz and the abyss produced by Treblinka were ruptures that emerged from decisions and institutions of ordinary human beings. They were responsible for their actions. They could have acted differently and better than they did.

Time ran out. Too many people failed to act differently and better than they usually did. For those caught in the maelstrom—perpetrator, bystander, victim, rescuer—the Holocaust became not only thinkable but also unavoidable. Avoidable though it had been, the Holocaust became unavoidable because from start to finish Nazi Germany insisted that its so-called "Jewish problem" must be solved.

How to solve that "problem" was not crystal clear, however, since its size changed as more and more Jews came under Nazi control. Thus, policies evolved as circumstances changed. First, the Nazis segregated the Jews and tried to make them emigrate. Then, after World War II began in 1939, ghettoization and mass shooting occurred. Finally, Jews were deported to extermination camps equipped with gas chambers and crematoria.

The unthinkable happened. Long after it happened, the Holocaust still remains unavoidable, or at least it should, because the Holocaust is not over and never will be. It scarred heaven and earth too much for that. True, the Holocaust's slave labor ceased and the killing stopped, but Auschwitz and Treblinka linger as sites of memorialization and warning. The Holocaust's survivors age; their numbers dwindle. Yet their stories are being preserved, and their witness remains. Whenever its history is recounted, wherever the testimony of its victims is heard, the Holocaust compels attention. Even as it recedes into the past, the Holocaust invades the present. It is still unavoidable.

After Auschwitz, a complication is added to the unavoidability of the Holocaust. Paradoxically, as the Holocaust moved from being unthinkable to being thinkable and then to being unavoidable, it also became unthinkable all over again, although in ways very different than it was before the disaster took place. Philosopher Jean Améry, a survivor of Auschwitz, put the point well in his understated way. "What happened, happened," he wrote of the

Holocaust. "But *that* it happened," he added, "cannot be so easily accepted."[1]

Try as we may to comprehend it—historically, philosophically, religiously—the Holocaust leaves unanswered and perhaps unanswerable questions in its wake. Understanding does not, must not, come cheaply. Every effort to inquire and to understand the catastrophe must be made. Otherwise, what can be known is obscured by mystification. But few indeed are those who excavate the Holocaust's destruction and find the explanations that thinking can devise to be entirely acceptable.

Both thinkable and unavoidable, the Holocaust persists as unthinkable because it was avoidable. It did not have to happen. That recognition leaves humankind, morality, religion, and even God on trial.

All of the writers represented in this book are Americans who have made significant contributions over the years to research, teaching, and writing about the Holocaust. Some of them are Christian; others are Jewish. They embody different strands of experience within those two traditions. Differences of generation and gender, emotion and emphasis, can also be heard in their voices. As a group, these essayists are distinguished by their concern about the roles of and implications for religion and ethics that emerge from the Holocaust's history.

Emerging from diverse backgrounds, oriented by the particularities of their lives, each author has felt the Holocaust's impact in personal ways. For some the initial impact was immediate and direct; for others it took place at a distance from the actual events of the Holocaust and almost by accident. These contrasts are an important part of this book's story, for no one can tell in advance how, where, or when the Holocaust may become unavoidable for them. In varied but decisive ways, the Holocaust has permanently changed the lives of these American writers. It directs their work. An event that was once unthinkable has become unavoidable for each of them. That outcome leaves each one to wrestle with the question of how to think and feel about a history whose realities are at the mind's limits.

We sensed that the contributors to this book would have moving, compelling, and insightful stories to tell about how the Holocaust became—and continues to be—personally unavoidable. We wanted them to tell those stories so that others could benefit by reading them. Fifty years after the end of World War II seemed a good time to ask these writers to take stock of their own development as Holocaust scholars and to let their narratives speak in public.

We invited the writers to respond to a series of questions. We encouraged them to approach the questions in personal ways and to craft essays that would reveal their individual writing styles, scholarly perspectives, and spiritual outlooks as well as the most relevant details of their lives. What we wanted were reflections on questions such as these: What led you to start writing about the Holocaust? What were the fundamental problems and issues that made the Holocaust unavoidable for you? Has there been a persistent and consistent focus in your thinking and writing about the Holocaust? How has your thinking changed and why? What do you regard as your most important contributions to the interpretation and understanding of the Holocaust? Where is your thinking and writing heading now? What, in your view, remains to be done?

The writers did all that we asked and more as they explored the memories, encounters, and challenges that make the Holocaust unavoidable for them. We have used those three categories to organize the book. Each author's contribution involves all three of those dimensions, but some essays emphasize one strand more than the other two. As they do so, the memories are about experiences the authors have had and the people they have met. The encounters are with the traditions that the essayists have known and the events they have witnessed. The challenges are formed by beliefs they have tested and questions that will not go away. The writers explore in depth how the Holocaust has affected their understanding of Christianity and Judaism and the theological and ethical dimensions of those religions in particular.

As the book's editors, we do not need to say more by way of introduction. The writers introduce themselves eloquently, explore their ideas clearly, and express their feelings candidly. From the unthinkable to the unavoidable—what follows is the story of how fifteen dedicated Holocaust scholars are making that journey. If this book encourages even a few others to make a similar voyage of their own, it will accomplish all that we hope for it.

NOTE

1. Jean Améry, *At the Mind's Limits: Contemplations by a Survivor on Auschwitz and Its Realities,* trans. Sidney Rosenfeld and Stella P. Rosenfeld (New York: Schocken Books, 1986), xi.

Part One

MEMORIES

1

Voices for Change: Chapters in the Post-Holocaust Dialogue

Abraham J. Peck

Family history is an obstacle to both Germans and Jews. For Germans it remains the great divide between silence and dialogue. It is a diseased branch on the pages of far too many family trees, what the Germans call *Stammbäume.*

Every well-meaning German wishing to engage in a frank discussion of German-Jewish relations (and there are quite a number) is nearly always reduced to tears or to silence when the inevitable question is asked: "What did your father or grandfather do during the Second World War?" To argue that he was in the German *Wehrmacht,* the military, is no longer much of a rejoinder: the collaboration of the frontline troops with the racial ideologues of the SS in the murder of the Jews was established beyond a doubt, as a 1995 Hamburg exhibit and a number of new books have clearly established.

Perhaps even more disarming is the question: "What did your parents or grandparents know about the Final Solution, the planned destruction of European Jewish life?" Often the answer is one of genuine ignorance. German families in the main did not discuss this particular issue in the years after 1945. But we are beginning to learn that many more knew what was happening than have let on. Many more knew what was happening to the Jewish family that suddenly disappeared from their apartment building one fine day and never returned. Many more knew because their fathers, husbands, sons, and brothers could not keep a *Reichsgeheimsache,* a state secret, which the Final Solution was always intended to be. In letters from the front or from the concentration camp, or in drunken, sometimes terribly guilt-ridden confessions while home on leave, these men told a great part of the home front just what was happening in the "East" to the Jews of Nazi-occupied Europe.

But family history is also a problem for the children of Holocaust survivors. They have often lived in the eye of a hurricane, surrounded by the shadows of the Holocaust. They have grown up knowing that the Holocaust is a part of their being, but often do not know why. Many have asked next to nothing about the suffering of their parents during the Holocaust years or the absence of grandparents, uncles, and aunts. These children of Holocaust survivors fear the trauma inherent in their parents' reply.

I am one of those children. Born in a Jewish displaced persons' (DP) camp in the Bavarian town of Landsberg am Lech in May 1946, I was one of the first of the postwar survivor "miracles."

Both of my parents were the sole survivors of families with a combined total of sixteen brothers and sisters. They met and married in the Lodz, Poland, ghetto, renamed Litzmannstadt by the Nazis, in September 1943. The ceremony was a civil one, presided over by the head of the Jewish council (*Judenrat*), Mordechai Chaim Rumkowski. They were married in a religious ceremony shortly thereafter by my father's roommate, an orthodox rabbi. Separated in March 1944, my father and mother spent the next fourteen months not knowing whether each other had survived.

But they did survive. And unlike many children of survivors, I did ask about their experiences during the Holocaust. My mother could not discuss her suffering. She would begin to weep before any words could emerge and refer only to the terrible deaths of several of her brothers in the Lodz ghetto, two of whom died in her arms. Her only wish, she would then tell me, was to join them.

My father was obsessed with the events of his own years during the Holocaust, from his time in the Lodz ghetto from 1940–44 to his imprisonment in camps such as Skarzysko-Kamienna, Buchenwald, and, finally, to his liberation from Theresienstadt. I developed an unusual knowledge, at a very early age, of who my father's tormentors had been.

In a way, this macabre cast of Nazi guards, commandants, and physicians became more real to me than the shadowy figures who had been the murdered members of my family.

There was Paul Kuhnemann, a lame, dwarf-like man who, as commandant of Skarzysko-Kamienna Factory Camp A, would shoot Jewish prisoners for amusement, or allow his German shepherd to tear them to bits. There was a camp physician in Buchenwald who was decent to my father. When my father felt comfortable enough to ask him why the Germans were destroying the Jews, this SS doctor shook from head to toe in an angry rage and replied, "because the Jews and Judaism are superfluous, a people and a religion forgotten by God!"

I imagine that my father felt compelled to balance these tales of horror, the kind that would often give me nightmares, with less gruesome stories. He told me about some of the decent Germans he met, mostly older men who were his guards. They sometimes gave him extra rations and a reason to believe in survival.

He also told me stories about my birthplace, Landsberg am Lech. He told me how he and my mother had found each other in May 1945. My mother had survived Auschwitz, Stutthof, the firebombing of Dresden, and a sub-camp of Mauthausen, to be reunited with my father at Theresienstadt. They had made their way to the American zone of occupied Germany and arrived in Landsberg on August 22, 1945. My parents and I lived in the Jewish DP camp at Landsberg until November 1949, when we immigrated to the United States.

And it was from this Jewish DP camp that I found my substitute Jewish family. Although they were only names mentioned at bedtime, I knew them intimately: Dr. Nabriski, who delivered me into this world; Jacob Olejski, who headed the ORT (Organization for Rehabilitation and Training) school in Landsberg; Dr. Samuel Gringauz, the head of the camp council, respected for his brilliant intellect, and the American Jewish military commander of the Landsberg camp, Major Irving Heymont, who my father thought was a Christian, but who, my father told me, had a "Jewish heart."

In one form or another, I would write about all of these events and individuals. My published work on the Holocaust has centered on events prior to, during, and after the years of the Final Solution. It has focused on three major areas of inquiry, and I like to think that my father's oft-repeated story of his encounter with the Nazi doctor at Buchenwald influenced those choices. It is worth repeating this racial fanatic's reply to my father's question of why the Germans were destroying the Jews: because the Jews and Judaism were superflous, a people and a religion forgotten by God! In that answer was formed my interest in the relationship of Jews and Christians after the Holocaust; in the efforts of survivors in the immediate years after the Holocaust to teach the world about the nature of their survival, and, in the course of doing so, to change the nature of our world; and in the relationship of Germans and Jews after the Holocaust.

I became a child of Holocaust survivors long after I had grown into an adult. It was an overnight metamorphosis, almost as if that child in me had been waiting to emerge for a very long time. Helen Epstein has called it the opening of a "black box," the internal sense that children of survivors have of being different, of having grown up in a home with survivors, but without grandparents, uncles and aunts, or cousins.[1]

I remember, during those rare instances when I would be allowed to have a friend visit my home, my father entertaining (?) my friends of eleven and twelve with full-fledged stories of the ghettos and the camps. My friends would sit in shock, perhaps in grief, looking first at my father, and then at me, with the question, "Why is he telling me this?" on their faces and in their eyes. They rarely returned to hear part two.

I also questioned the purpose of my father's need to bear witness. I wanted desperately to hear about his childhood days playing baseball or playing hooky from school, even if these stories were fabrications.

But deep down I knew that it was my duty to listen to the Holocaust stories, not only because it allowed my father to fulfill a desperate need to tell them, but because they would one day become my stories to pass on to the next generation. They would become my legacy and my mission.

It was not an easy legacy. For years, I felt alone, believing that only I lived in the eye of the hurricane, surrounded by the shadows of death and destruction.

And it was not until 1977, when I joined one of the first therapy groups to be founded by children of survivors that I was able to realize that an entire generation of children had shared my experiences. That realization led to the publication of my first piece on Holocaust survivors and their children in the pages of the *Cincinnati Enquirer,* and reprinted a few years later in Allon Schoener's *The American Jewish Album: 1654 to the Present.*[2]

A short time before this publication, I had come to the Hebrew Union College–Jewish Institute of Religion in Cincinnati to help direct the American Jewish Archives, perhaps the premier institution in the world devoted to research and publication on the Western Hemispheric Jewish experience.

Almost immediately, I befriended a marvelous group of Christian graduate students at the College-Institute, participants in a unique and important program which had been sponsored by the Hebrew Union College since 1947. The program allowed Christian graduate students, many of them ordained clergy, the opportunity to learn about Judaism from a distinctly Jewish perspective and to understand Judaism as a living, creative faith community, not one that they often understood from their own traditions as a fossilized, first-century A.D. predecessor to the "truth" of Christianity.

So many of these Christian students had come with limited knowledge of what Jews believed or what they had endured during two thousand years of persecution at the hands of Christendom. Yet they also came with certain doubts and questions about the history of Christianity and what it taught about Judaism and the Jewish people.

I met and discussed the history of Christian-Jewish relations with strongly conservative Missouri Synod Lutherans, perhaps even more conservative Southern Baptists, liberal Methodists and Lutherans, and radical Catholic priests. The more we debated and discussed, the more convinced I became that these Christians could not be the same ones that were a part of my father's world in prewar Poland or during the Holocaust.

All of the Christian students knew that the churches of Europe and America had said or done little about the destruction of European Jewish life by the Nazis. They also understood that this shameful lack of action had been preceded by centuries of both teaching about and viewing Jews and Judaism with a kind of contempt that clearly had stood in the way of much positive action during the Holocaust years. They understood further that the Holocaust turned the one obsessive factor that united Christendom for centuries, namely the "Jewish question," into a "Christian question." They understood that the questions posed by the Holocaust for Jews are fundamentally different from those posed for Christians. Jews ask: "How do we survive in a world that watched silently while we were being killed? And what do we teach our children about this world?"

I wanted to know from my Christian friends how could they speak about an authentic Christianity or an authentic Christian until they understood and acknowledged that the Holocaust was a "Christian" catastrophe and how, in its wake, could the killers and the bystanders still call themselves Christians?

When I discussed informally my ongoing dialogue with the Christian fellows with members of the Hebrew Union College–Jewish Institute of Religion administration, including its then-president, Alfred Gottschalk, they immediately insisted that such an exchange should be broadened to include seminarians from other Christian institutions in the region.

It was thus with a special sensitivity and with a special commitment that I accepted the invitation of President Gottschalk to plan and organize a symposium called "Religion in a Post-Holocaust World." The symposium was held at the Hebrew Union College in November 1980. Over twelve hundred people attended the various sessions, including seminarians and their professors from over a dozen Catholic and Protestant seminaries in Ohio, Indiana, and Kentucky. This particular aspect of our symposium led to two evenings of intense dialogue, perhaps for the first time in history, between male and female students of Christian and Jewish seminaries.

In 1981 I edited and introduced the essays that were read at the major sessions of the symposium. The volume, entitled *Jews and Christians after the Holocaust,* featured a foreword by Elie Wiesel, and essays by, among others, the distinguished Catholic thinker, David Tracy, who confronted the issue of the Holocaust and Christianity for the first time in print, and the Jewish historian, Yaffa Eliach, who wrote about her Lithuanian birthplace Eisysky (Eisyshok), over a decade before it would be memorialized in the United States Holocaust Memorial Museum.[3]

The essays in the volume concerned themselves with what one American Christian theologian called "the death-knell for at least a certain kind of Western civilization,"[4] the most telling consequence of the Holocaust. This death knell discredited many of our accepted values—religious, secular, and intellectual. The essays challenged the complacency of Christians and Jews in accepting the Holocaust without giving thought to the fact that it may only have been a foreshadowing of what is yet to be.

Two sentences in my own preface to the volume strike me as having a continued relevance over a dozen years later, especially in the cases of Africa and Bosnia: "In light of continuing brutalities by individuals against individuals and nations against nations, does the Holocaust mark the decline of our Western culture and its systems of moral thought and belief? Can our religious institutions in fact shape human behavior and society to a future state of redemption that transcends both Christians and Jews?"

It was not long after the symposium that I began to notice a growing fascination with Holocaust survivors and their stories. The 1980s and the 1990s became "decades of the survivor," when they were asked to speak in classrooms and into the cassette recorder. The genius of the American soul allowed survivors and their children to occupy a unique role in the evolution of the Jewish presence in history. The Holocaust and its observance has become, in its rites and rituals, an American concern: witness the growth of local Holocaust centers and, of course, the creation of the United States Holocaust Memorial Museum, which places the events and its victims and perpetrators directly into the middle of American history and sacredness on the Washington Mall.

And when the texts of survivor voices are analyzed, when testimonies given by survivors in the 1980s and 1990s are studied, when "memory's encounters with a disintegrating time" is one of the "seminal themes of these testimonies," that memory is described in the words of Lawrence Langer as "tainted memory." For Langer, this memory is neither "uncontaminated" nor "heroic." It lacks both "self-esteem" and a "moral vision." And because it is "tainted" by time and age, it is rejected by historians who must reconstruct causal sequences and explain events by their antecedents.[5]

But neither Professor Langer nor most historians know or understand that this is not the first time that the survivors sought to present their testimonies.

Whenever I view oral testimony of survivors of the Holocaust on video or in another medium, there is a noticeable lack of attention paid to the period 1945–52, a period of time in which many of the survivors spent their days and years in displaced persons' camps in Germany, Austria, and Italy. But question a survivor about the events of this period and a glimmer of recognition arises. Those were exciting times, the survivor will tell you: We had a message that we wanted to give to the world.

They called themselves the *she'erith hapletah* (Hebrew for the surviving or saving remnant). They were survivors of the death camps, partisans in the forests and refugees from Hitler who took refuge in the deepest reaches of Russian Siberia. It was an identity that ultimately would give birth to a revolutionary ideology created from the inner being and experience of the *she'erith hapletah*.

The Jewish DP camps in those years were in a state of permanent frenzy. Koppel S. Pinson, who visited the Jewish DP camps in 1946–47, described those times as years of "constant movement—*men geyt*. Not all the motion is purposeful motion. Very much of it is emotional restlessness that arises from the situation in which these people find themselves."[6]

The situation consisted of blocked immigration to America and Palestine, overcrowded housing, and continuing antisemitism.

But the survivors, as I discovered in my research, resolved to create a new beginning. With the support of Jewish and international relief associations, the Jewish camps became centers of Jewish cultural and political life.

Yet other problems persisted. One of them lay in the truth of another of Koppel Pinson's observations about the survivors, that "for the Jewish DPs the war has not yet ended, nor has liberation in the true sense really come as yet. Their problems still unsolved, their future not in their own hands, they still consider themselves at war with the world and the world at war with them. . . ."[7]

One weapon in that war, the one that was entirely in the hands of the survivors, was memory. For the survivors, memory went beyond their desire to remember the dead. It also included the firm belief that in retelling the story of their catastrophe they would and could prevent future generations of Jews and non-Jews from being dragged into the same dilemma, because theirs was the first, and hopefully the last, generation to have endured such suffering in such magnitude, such evil.

One of the most important DP camps in which the survivor ideology was crystallized was Landsberg, the very camp in which I was born. Without a doubt, the most far-reaching thinker in the camps was Samuel Gringauz, who also headed the Landsberg DP camp committee.

Gringauz stressed the need for European Jews to say adieu to the discredited continent but to do so with dignity: "We no longer believe in progress; we no longer believe in the 2000 year old Christian civilization which created for them the Statue of Liberty in New York and the Westminster Abbey by the Thames, but created for us the Spanish Inquisition, the pogroms of Russia and the gas chambers of Auschwitz."[8]

Gringauz realized that the European era of Jewish history was over and that the Holocaust had created a situation where America and Palestine would be the new focal points of the Jewish future. "Our tragedy," Gringauz maintained, "must become the starting point of a new humanism," one that would seek to close the gap between the technological advances of the twentieth century, which had built the ovens of Auschwitz, and its moral development, which had suffered terribly in the era of Nazism.[9]

What Lawrence Langer and others differentiate as text and subtext in survivor testimonies is really all subtext. It is testimony addressed to the entire world, Jew and non-Jew alike. It is the effort to reflect on life at the end of life through the mirror and the shadow of the *Shoah*. It is in many cases devoid of self-esteem and perhaps lacks moral vision.

In my research and writings on the Jewish DP camps and the survivor ideology I have tried to understand the place of survivors in the years after

1945. I have tried to make clear that not only was there self-esteem, not only was there a moral vision and heroic memory of a kind that died an all-too-early death at the hands of an uncaring and unbelieving world, but that the survivor's call for "never again," meant "never again," for anyone, anywhere and not just for the Jewish people.

My father would often tell me stories of his time as a peddler in the region around Landsberg. He would sometimes have to spend the night with a German family, and he would be unable to sleep a wink after seeing a swastika hanging in a closet or a copy of *Mein Kampf* still sitting on a living room shelf.

For my father, as with most survivors, Germans would and could never be anything but Nazis, new or old. For me, the idea of speaking to a German, much less befriending one, seemed for the first twenty-one years of my life, an impossible idea. Now, many year later, I am aware that those Germans and children of survivors born after 1945 have both gone through the process of confronting what we have become and that we need to develop an understanding of who we are to be.

For me the beginning of this realization came when I was in my early twenties and a university undergraduate. At the American University in Washington, D.C., I met Petra Kelly.

She was the first German with whom I was able to speak about the Holocaust. Even at that time, in the late 1960s, Petra Kelly was an idealist whose great skill was in turning this idealism into practical results. She would never accept a situation of social injustice and knew only a desire to overcome it.

Such an attitude was admirable, especially for a German. And Petra was especially frank about the failures of her nation to confront, in the years after 1945, the murder of European Jewry during the war. It was from Petra Kelly that I first learned about a generation of German youth who would not accept their parents' crimes during the Holocaust nor their silence when their children confronted them with the facts.

I especially remember a conversation we once had in which we discussed our particular legacies as children of survivors and of oppressors. Petra would not be satisfied with simply acknowledging our individual burdens. She wanted to know what we would do with them, how we would use them to make the world a better place.

She went on to become one of the major forces in German and international society and politics. She cofounded a political party (the Greens), struggled on behalf of the oppressed of all nations, and sought to change the silence of her parents' generation into a roar of protest against the then-increasing danger of nuclear annihilation. Her short life, ended in a murder-suicide, was an extraordinary one.

In my friendship with Petra Kelly, it struck me that she and I had more in common than I did with my American-born friends, both Jewish and Christian.

However, it was not until much later that I learned just how much we really had in common. As Sabine Reichel, a young German woman born in 1946, has written: "I also began to discover some startling behavioral similarities between my generation and some of my Jewish peers. I learned that many children of Holocaust survivors grew up with a throttling silence and an inexplicable fear of a secret box that contained explosive materials and shouldn't be tampered with. These impressions, in turn, reminded me of my own upbringing. The inability of both groups of parents, in my case, an entire generation, to speak about the past—one because of pain, the other because of guilt—caused similar symptoms for their offspring."[10]

In the process of running away from their identity as Germans, and in the process of running toward their identity as children of Holocaust survivors, post-Holocaust Germans and Jews can meet somewhere in the middle. What they have to say to each other is, for the moment, not as important as the fact that they believe the possibility for dialogue is important.

I was never certain of this until I met Gottfried Wagner. Since 1991, this great-grandson of the nationalist German composer, Richard Wagner, great-nephew of the English-German antisemitic author, Houston Stewart Chamberlain, and grandson of Adolf Hitler's friend, Winifred Wagner, and I have been engaged in a wide-ranging dialogue, what we call the Post-Holocaust Generations Dialogue.

Gottfried Wagner has turned his back on a legacy and a family inheritance that could have been his. He has denounced the Wagner clan as a "Nazi family," and has highlighted in lectures and writings the anti-Jewish nature of Richard Wagner's literary and operatic works. For this, he has been banned by his father from the family villa at Bayreuth.

For me, Gottfried Wagner represents the beginning of Germany's efforts to recapture its sense of a "humane orientation." This phrase, first used by Ralph Giordano in his brilliant work, *The Second Guilt*,[11] must be understood as the real indictment of the Third Reich. Indeed, the Nazi state should be seen as a continuation of the symptomatic dehumanization of the German people and not its beginning.

That beginning may be tied to the generation of Wagner's great-grandfather Richard, and to Richard Wagner himself. What more appropriate representative of the need to reclaim for Germany its humane orientation than the great-grandson of the man who helped to lose it?

Where will our efforts, Gottfried Wagner's and mine, lead? Will we be able to leave our status as children of the event and live our lives as the adults we long ago became? Perhaps that depends on the world and on our own children. Will the voices that make up our dialogue convince enough people that the consequences of the Holocaust are all around us, in the brutalities that occur in national and international conflict, in the apathy with which we can view the victims of war, both young and old, and in our lack of trust in law, religion, and technology as important foundations of our civilization?

What purpose did the suffering of my parents and the murder of all of my uncles and aunts serve? To simply catapult survivors and the American Jewish community into the status of supervictim—but still a victim group in this age of collective American suffering and collective American victim-hood—wallowing in the bathos of the painful past? That surely is not enough.

My hope is that the teachings and the voices of the *she'erith hapletah,* the saving remnant, which I have sought to rediscover and renew, will help to correct the imbalance in our world between the past and the future, between constantly looking backward toward the sufferings of this most murderous century and rarely looking forward to a future of hope and shared optimism. We need to teach that suffering can lead to moral vision, to the heroic memory, to the redeeming myth necessary to change reality. For behind the voice of the *she'erith hapletah* and its prophetic vision lay the Jewish striving for *tikkun olam*—a desire to repair the world. Perhaps at the end of the next century there will have emerged a new collective world memory, one that remembers a world and a time of racial, religious, and ethnic hatred, of state-sponsored genocide and injustice, but that can pause to observe a new reality and a new future and in the process realize that soon such destructive realities will be no more.

NOTES

1. Helen Epstein, *Children of the Holocaust* (New York: G. P. Putnam's Sons, 1979).

2. Abraham J. Peck, "The Children of Holocaust Survivors," in *The American Jewish Album: 1654 to the Present,* ed. Allon Schoener (New York: Rizzoli, 1983), 309–10.

3. Abraham J. Peck, ed., *Jews and Christians after the Holocaust* (Philadelphia: Fortress Press, 1982).

4. Eva Fleischner, ed., *Auschwitz: Beginning of a New Era?* (New York: KTAV, 1977), x.

5. Lawrence L. Langer, *Holocaust Testimonies: The Ruins of Memory* (New Haven: Yale University Press, 1991), chapter 4, "Tainted Memory: The Impromptu Self" and chapter 5, "Unheroic Memory: The Diminished Self."

6. Koppel S. Pinson, "Jewish Life in Liberated Germany: A Study of the Jewish DP's," *Jewish Social Studies* 9:2 (1947): 110.

7. Ibid., 114.

8. Samuel Gringauz, "Der Geistiger Herzspiegel fun groisn Hrbn," *Landsberger Lager-Cajtung,* December 31, 1942, 2 (Yiddish).

9. Ibid.

10. Sabine Reichel, *What Did You Do in the War, Daddy? Growing Up German* (New York: Hill and Wang, 1989).

11. Ralph Giordano, *Die Zweite Schuld oder Von der Last Deutscher zu sein* (Hamburg: Rasch und Ruehring, 1987).

2

A Door that Opened and Never Closed: Teaching the *Shoah*

Eva Fleischner

My work in the field of Holocaust studies is so closely related to my personal journey that a brief sketch of how I came to confront the *Shoah* may be helpful at the beginning of this chapter.

Born in Vienna of a Catholic mother and Jewish father (who converted to Catholicism when I was eleven), I grew up with a strong sense of being Catholic, though fully aware of my father's Jewishness and that of his entire family. I was in my third year at a Dominican sisters' high school when Hitler annexed Austria in March 1938. Sent to England for safety by my parents, I spent the next six years in a high school run by a French order of nuns. Only with college at Radcliffe at the age of eighteen did I enter the world of secular education.

I had known Jews all my life, beginning with members of my own family. Like many middle-class Viennese Jews, they were all assimilated. I had no knowledge of Judaism as a faith.

This ignorance was to persist for many years, until my graduate studies at Marquette University. By then I was forty, enrolled in a doctoral program of Christian historical theology. Except for a deep love of the Scriptures, which had been instilled in me twenty years earlier during my years at Grail-ville,[1] I had no special interest in Judaism, let alone the *Shoah*. My deep concerns all related to Christianity and the Catholic Church, which was going through the exhilarating renewal of Vatican II at that time.

Two doctoral seminars and a book were to change this lack of interest, starting me on a road that eventually led to my life's work. One seminar was on the church fathers, the other on Luther's *Commentary on the Psalms.* Although they were separated chronologically by a thousand years, one theme kept cropping up in both seminars and it profoundly shocked me: the theme of anti-Judaism.[2] It recurred both in the patristic writings and in the work of the young Luther, although far less virulently than in the writings of his old age.[3] What was going on here? I wondered. Why this persistent animosity on the part of Christians—many of them canonized saints in my church—toward the people to whom they owed the origins of their faith?

About the same time, a friend and fellow graduate student handed me a book with the words, You *must* read this! The book was *Treblinka,* by Jean-François Steiner. It was my first real encounter with the *Shoah,* and I was profoundly shaken. I went on to read *Night* and Elie Wiesel's other books (there were only eight of them at the time). A door had opened that was never again to close. I had become haunted by the *Shoah,* and by the question: What has enabled this people to survive persecution for thousands of years, even the unparalleled catastrophe of this century?[4] For survive they did; and not only physically, as I also discovered during my years at Marquette. Through a close friendship with a Jewish couple who had recently moved from Reform to Orthodox Judaism, I was regularly invited to participate in the celebration of the Sabbath and of the High Holy Days. Jews now became for me, far more than my fellow Christians, the witnesses to God in the world. Thus, the *Shoah* was for me the gateway into Judaism. I began to pursue the study of Judaism wherever I could, beginning with Rabbi Dudley Weinberg's course at Marquette. Summer institutes for Catholics were being given at that time at Seton Hall University's Institute for Judaeo-Christian Studies and elsewhere, and I followed as many as possible.

As a teaching assistant, I had the opportunity to teach a course in the continuing education department at Marquette. I chose as the topic the relationship of Jews and Christians through the centuries. I focused on the first four centuries and the origin of the split and hostility between the two communities, which deepened my understanding of Christian anti-Judaism, a subject that has remained a lifelong central concern.

When it came time for the choice of a dissertation topic I knew it had to relate in some way to the *Shoah.* Through the kindness of Dudley Weinberg, I was able to meet Irving Greenberg, Michael Wyschogrod, Zalman Schachter, and Abraham Heschel. All were sympathetic to my search and gave generously of their time. A conversation with Rabbi Heschel made me realize that my original idea, to study the meaning of the *Shoah* for Christians, was a dead end. "My dear Eva," he said gently but emphatically, as we talked in his study at the Jewish Theological Seminary, "there is no meaning to be found in this event." This was part of an important learning process I underwent in those early years.

The subject I eventually chose was the impact of the *Shoah* on German

Christian theology, for which I did research in Germany in 1970. The real focus of my dissertation is indicated by the subtitle, "Christianity and Israel in Terms of Mission": What was the current attitude among Christian theologians toward the conversion of Jews? And what did this reveal about the church's self-understanding and its relationship to Judaism? My dissertation was later published as a book.[5]

My first opportunity to teach a course on the *Shoah* came in the spring of 1973.[6] I had joined the religion faculty at Montclair State College in New Jersey (it became Montclair State University in 1993) the previous fall, and the department encouraged us to teach courses we really wanted to teach. I knew that I wanted to teach the *Shoah,* despite some misgivings: How would such a course be received from an instructor who was a Roman Catholic? Would we be able to achieve in a classroom situation the climate of sensitivity and respect that I considered essential to any discussion of this subject? I did not want the course to become an investigation of the macabre, nor a history course, nor a collecting of numbers and statistics. My hope was to deal with the religious and moral issues raised by the *Shoah;* to awaken a certain sensitivity in the students that would make them more aware of injustice and oppression in our own time; to bring back the past for the sake of the present and future because, in the words of the Baal Shem Tov, "forgetfulness leads to exile, remembrance is the secret of redemption."

When the class met in early February, I found myself with a varied and disparate group of students, ranging from freshmen to graduating seniors, and including an Italian Jewish woman who had escaped death as a teenager by joining the underground and going into hiding. Only one student was a religion major. The Jewish students were easily identifiable by their deep involvement and personal comments. As to the rest, only gradually did the full complexity of the class become clear. In addition to the six Jewish students—one of whom was from Haiti, where her family had moved from Egypt—there was one Buddhist (a Kalmuk), one Moslem Arab Palestinian, one Roman Catholic nun from campus ministry; the rest were more or less Christian, or nothing in particular.

The level of knowledge about the *Shoah* in the class was very uneven. A student named Ben had been teaching eighth graders in Hebrew school and was frustrated and discouraged by the frequent parental opposition, at times outright hostility, he encountered. Others had read only Elie Wiesel's *Night* in an introductory course. I felt it necessary to establish a minimal common basis of knowledge as quickly as possible. During the first three weeks, while I gave some historical background, everyone was expected to read André Schwarz-Bart's *The Last of the Just,* Jean Francois Steiner's *Treblinka,* and Arthur Morse's *While Six Million Died,* a carefully documented account of the inner workings of the U.S. State Department in the years immediately preceding and during the catastrophe. At the end of the first week we saw the film *Night and Fog*. Five students had seen it already; all but one chose to see it again.

I had decided to use Raul Hilberg's *The Destruction of European Jews* as a basic text because of its excellent historical documentation. As the semester progressed, most of us, including myself, found ourselves reacting negatively to Hilberg's thesis that the Jews contributed to their own destruction through their passivity. Yet it was precisely this theory, and our anger, that led to some of our best class discussions, making us more aware of the complexity of the issue. Was it possible for any outsider, whether Jew or non-Jew, to know how she or he might react in a similar situation? If not, then who has the right to pass judgment? And what of the many forms of nonviolent resistance? I shall return to this subject below.

In the course of the semester, our discussions centered around certain key issues: apathy, the role of the churches, and Jewish "passivity." Apathy was symbolized most vividly for us by Wiesel's "Bystander" in *The Town Beyond the Wall* and its implications for us: Where does responsibility, the need for action, begin (and end)? Here are excerpts from two student papers:

Each time I witnessed the courtroom scenes in the movie (*Night and Fog*) I heard the "Who is responsible?" and the corresponding reply, denying guilt and complicity. Over and over again I experienced an awakening to the possibility of humanity—and me—repeating the same unimaginable crimes and denying all responsibility for our actions . . .

How would I act in a similar situation? Under the pressure of the terror of the camps, before the gas chambers, and the possibility of losing every semblance of my dignity, what would become of MY so-called humanity, much less my long struggled-for-faith in God and man (*sic*)?

The role of the churches became another much-argued issue and the topic for one research paper. After I had spoken on the subject in class one day, Ben asked if he could address a question to the Christians present: "How can you, in light of what happened, remain Christian?" Because the question was asked without hostility, we did not feel attacked or put on the defensive and were able to struggle for answers—answers different for each of us. One person tried to explain the difference between the church as institution and gospel teaching, pointing out that she confronted this problem in her everyday religious life. Another affirmed her faith in Christ, but felt that Christians had all too often betrayed his teachings. We recalled instances of individual heroism and martyrdom on the part of some Christians, though we admitted that these were woefully few when set against the background of apathy, collaboration, and murder. We spoke of the "muddy mixture" that the church is for many of us.

The question of Jewish passivity was discussed heatedly and from many angles. It had surfaced in our very first class, when another student, Hartson, exclaimed in anger, "I don't see how the Jews could have let this happen to them!"—a remark that instantly drew an equally angry retort from some other members of the class. As time went on and we studied the systematically planned dehumanization of the Jews by the Nazis, puzzlement gave way to growing understanding. Roger, our Moslem Palestinian, and Connie, also a non-Jew, both chose the topic of resistance for their papers. They discussed their papers for five hours one day, disagreeing strongly at times, and then were asked to present their conclusions to the class together. While Roger focused on armed resistance, Connie had become fascinated with the many forms of nonviolent resistance, with the sheer will to survive and keep one's humanity.

I believe that the students had confronted questions in our seminar that touched the very basis of human existence and were willing to live with these questions, willing to continue the search. Here are two excerpts from evaluations at the end of the semester:

One of the greatest gifts the seminar has given me is that I am now at peace with the reality that I may never have the answers to these deeply troubling questions. I live now, instead, in a profound realization that some persons did come through—in life or in death—miraculously—not less but greater and more beautiful than before. For me this is the cloud by day and the pillar of fire by night that leads the way . . . the hope that cuts through that dark despair that claims that we are simply prey to fate and can never master our own destiny.

The past was no longer merely the past, but had implications for the present and future:

The question that plagues me most is that of the bystander, What would I have done, if anything, if I had been there at the time? I also realize that even this question is in a way an attempt to stay away from a more general and, perhaps, more important question: what action, if any, should I take concerning such things as racism, Vietnam, and Wounded Knee?

The spring of 1973 was the time of the standoff at Wounded Knee. Early in the semester Hartson asked to be excused the rest of the week, because he felt he should drive to Wounded Knee and be present there.

The seminar was in many ways a painful experience for us all. For the Christian students, confronting the history of Christian antisemitism and the role of the churches during the *Shoah* was a heavy burden. For all of us, there were times when we felt overwhelmed by evil. We were able to support and learn from one another in our struggles, and to become a community in the course of those four months. Barriers were broken down and a level of trust was achieved that made it possible for us to challenge one another without threatening one another. We felt accepted as who we were, whether Moslem, Jew, or Christian. One of the Jewish students wrote that for the first time in his life he no longer felt ashamed to be a Jew.

For me, the seminar was an important stage in my teaching career, proof that the *Shoah* can be taught to college students of every background, and whether or not the teacher is a Jew is ultimately irrelevant. It deepened my belief in a newer generation, in its willingness to confront even the most painful issues. This belief has been confirmed for me as I have taught the *Shoah* repeatedly since 1973.

Before addressing the question, What has changed in my teaching and what has remained the same?, I shall speak of an event that bought me into Holocaust research at the national and international levels.

Shortly after arriving at Montclair State, I was invited to a meeting at the Episcopal cathedral of St. John the Divine in New York City to discuss the possibility of an international symposium on the Holocaust, to be hosted by the cathedral in the early summer of 1974. Under the dynamic leadership of Dean James Morton we formed a steering committee, and preparations for the symposium continued over the next eighteen months.

Held in June 1974, with the title "Auschwitz: Beginning of a New Era?" the symposium brought together scholars from the United States, Canada, and Israel. The papers presented defined Holocaust studies for some years to come. They dealt with theological reflections on the *Shoah,* Christian antisemitism, Christian mission toward Jews, the impact of the *Shoah* on Christian education, the State of Israel, the New Left and Israel (the meeting took place in the year following the Yom Kippur War), the new romanticism and biblical faith, blacks and Jews, art and culture after the *Shoah.* Daily coverage of the three-day symposium in the *New York Times* gave it wide publicity. It was my task to edit the twenty-seven papers and responses. The volume appeared in 1977. It is still in print, thanks to the remarkable Bernie Scharfstein of KTAV, and is used as a text in many colleges and seminaries.

Let me now return to the question, What has remained the same in my teaching and writing on the *Shoah,* and what has changed over the years?

The theme of *Christian antisemitism* remains central to my work. The last thirty years have witnessed a major turning in Christianity's attitude toward Jews, spearheaded by the 1965 declaration, *Nostra Aetate,* of Vatican II. Major official Church documents, a rethinking of Christian theology vis-à-vis Judaism, and Jewish-Christian dialogue at the grass roots as well as at sophisticated theological levels have revolutionized Christian teaching about Jews and Judaism. It has been accurately observed that more progress has been made in this area over the past thirty years than in the previous nineteen hundred years.[7] And yet, despite all this work and explicit teaching at the official level that Jews remain beloved and chosen by God, one still hears all too frequently sermons in which the Pharisees are portrayed as hypocrites and biblical history is presented as one long record of infidelity, in contrast to the "fidelity" of the Church. Historical criticism of the New

Testament is known only to a small minority. There persists widespread ignorance, among both Christian congregations and clergy, about the history of Christian antisemitism and the role it played in making the *Shoah* possible. This topic remains crucial to any teaching about the *Shoah,* particularly to Christian audiences, and will remain so, I believe, for years to come. A mentality that is centuries old is not changed overnight.

A word of caution, however, is necessary here. When Christians try to confront the shadow in their own history, they often begin to feel a deep sense of guilt. I have seen this happen in every one of my Holocaust courses. While such a reaction is natural and a sign of sensitivity, it also represents a danger point. At the St. John the Divine symposium Josef Yerushalmi (then of Harvard, today of Columbia) warned against the danger of a "collective mea culpa" on the part of Christians.[8] A sense of guilt can too easily become a new source of blaming the victims. This guilt will become fruitful only if it is turned into genuine repentance leading to a sense of responsibility for the here and now.

This area of guilt and responsibility may be the one in which I have made my best contribution to Holocaust studies. As a Catholic who, despite stringent criticism of her church still loves that church, I am able to speak of its sins and failures with a degree of credibility and conviction an outsider does not have. By saying *we* rather than *they* I am not pointing the finger, but am calling for repentance and a change of heart in my own faith community. This is important especially when speaking to Christians.

Another constant in my teaching is the subject of *resistance.* The question raised in my 1973 seminar with the remark, I don't see how the Jews could have let this happen to them!, continues to surface in every Holocaust course I teach. What it really is about is Jewish passivity, or, Why did they let themselves be led like sheep to the slaughter?—an unfortunate use of a beautiful text from Isaiah. Students need to have some knowledge of the infernal Nazi machinery of deception and dehumanization in order to understand how enormously difficult it was for Jews to fight back. It is also important to know that the Warsaw ghetto uprising in April 1943 was the first of its kind in all of occupied Europe. Given some basic historical knowledge, I find that most students come to agree with Elie Wiesel's conclusion: "The question is not, why did the Jews not resist, but rather, how is it that so many did resist?" It is also important to explore the many forms of unarmed resistance, such as the efforts to maintain a semblance of normalcy in the ghettos by running schools, and so forth.

Another recurring theme in my teaching is the attempt to break down, from the very beginning, the *we/they* category. When confronting such abysmal evil there is the danger of wanting to pin it on *the others* (Germans or Nazis), while *we* (the Allies) are good people. To think in these terms is to miss what I consider one of the most important lessons to be learned from the *Shoah:* that the event reveals not the evil inherent in one nation or people, but the evil of which all of us, as frail human beings, are capable, given certain circumstances; in other words, the abyss in the soul of every human being. In a world that in the same year has witnessed the slaughter in Rwanda and the former Yugoslavia this lesson appears more urgent and relevant than ever.

In saying this, I do not mean to downplay historical truth. A solid grounding in history—I usually spend the first two to three weeks of the semester on the historical background—is essential if we are to avoid the danger of making the *Shoah* into some sort of vague, evil "mystery."

While the *Shoah* does ultimately raise questions about human beings—and, for many, about God—which may be unanswerable, it was carried out by human beings, in a specific time and place. The origins and causes of the *Shoah* can and must be explained historically. To present the event as the work of some gigantic evil force is to absolve humans of all responsibility.

The question of *the relationship of Christianity to Judaism,* which formed the basis of my dissertation, continues to preoccupy me. If it is taken seriously (as in the works of Paul van Buren, Michael Kogan, and others) it may yet lead to a radical rethinking of their faith on the part of both communities.

I have thus far spoken of themes that have remained constant in my teaching. Let me now mention three themes that have emerged over the years. The first is the subject of *rescuers* or, as Jewish tradition calls them, of "the righteous among the nations": non-Jews who tried to save Jews during the *Shoah,* often at the risk of their own lives.

When I began my teaching in 1973, I was aware of only one book that dealt with rescuers: Philip Friedman's *Their Brothers' Keepers.*[9] The subject was neither discussed nor taught, but I was not troubled by this. For although I knew there had been rescuers, I was conscious of a certain reluctance in myself to approach this topic with my students. First, because the number of rescuers seemed so pitifully small compared to the millions, throughout Europe, who collaborated, murdered, or simply stood by. Second, because I was afraid that this subject, especially when taught to people who have little knowledge of the *Shoah,* could serve as a kind of escape valve. Instead of confronting the failure of their church, or their country, people might focus on the rescuers and conclude, "We were not so bad after all, look at the Christians who gave their lives for Jews!"

This danger is real. Nonetheless, I have now given the subject of rescue a solid place in every Holocaust course I teach. Two personal experiences, both of which occurred in 1979, brought about a major shift in my attitude.

The first was the publication of a book, Philip Hallie's *Lest Innocent Blood Be Shed,* in the spring of that year. It is the story of Le Chambon-sur-Lignon, a small mountain village in southern France which became a "city of refuge" during the war, saving some five thousand Jews. In his prelude to the book,

Hallie tells how he came to discover and write this story. As professor of philosophy at Wesleyan University he had for years been studying cruelty and at this time was studying the Nazis' experiments on children in the death camps. Hallie found that the only way he could continue was to become hardened to what he was studying. "My study of evil incarnate had become a prison whose bars were my bitterness toward the violent, and whose walls were my horrified indifference to slow murder."[10]

And then, one day, he came across a short article about a small village in southern France. The Vichy police had entered the village to round up the Jews they knew were hidden there. The pastor and villagers refused to give up the Jews they were hiding, even at the risk of their own deaths. Only one Jew was found. And as he sat in the otherwise empty bus, guarded by the police, waiting to be taken away, the villagers came up one by one, passing small gifts through the open window to the prisoner: a bar of chocolate, an orange, a role of toilet paper, and so forth—small treasures in wartime France. As Hallie recalled the scene that night he found himself weeping, and asked himself: Why do I run away from goodness? Why study only evil? Why not know joy? "Something had happened for years in that mountain village. Why should I be afraid of it?"[11] And so began the journey that one year later led him to Le Chambon, and to the writing of this book.

I was deeply moved by Hallie's account; I identified with him. For some time now I, too, had been aware of the heavy load of unrelieved evil I tried to confront with my students and of the danger of becoming hardened. Was I, too, afraid of goodness? I decided that Hallie's book would be part of my syllabus the next time I taught the *Shoah;* it has been there ever since.

A few months later, the National Christian-Jewish Workshop took place in Los Angeles; I was asked to lead a workshop on teaching the *Shoah.* At the end of the session, a man came up to me and introduced himself as Rabbi Harold Schulweis. He congratulated me on my presentation, then added: "But you must also speak of the rescuers. Our world, especially our young people, need heroes, models of courage and decency." I did not know Rabbi Schulweis at the time, did not know that his had been a voice crying in the wilderness for years, urging the world, and especially his fellow Jews, to make known the deeds and lives of the "Just Ones."[12] Because he was a Jew, I was able to listen, to hear. His words reinforced my decision to incorporate this—at that time almost unknown—chapter of Holocaust history into my teaching. The following spring, when I was invited as *Yom HaShoah* speaker to a large Reform synagogue outside Philadelphia, I decided, with some trepidation, to take the rescuers as my theme. My sermon was warmly received by the congregation and its rabbi, Dr. Bertram Korn. I was encouraged to continue my work in this area.

These encounters were eventually to open up a whole new field of research for me. In the spring of 1985, thanks to Yehuda Bauer of Hebrew University, I received a grant to study Catholic rescuers in France. Beginning at Yad Vashem in the archives of the Department of the Righteous, I went to France to interview any rescuers I could find.[13] I did not realize when I began this work how much it would come to mean. Through meeting women and men—often seemingly very ordinary people—who had risked their lives to save Jews simply because they recognized in them their persecuted sisters and brothers, I came into contact with authentic goodness. Rabbi Schulweis was right: We all need models of goodness if we are to believe in life.

There was a further benefit for me in this research. It brought me into contact with decency and courage in my own Catholic tradition. Yes, the record of the churches, including my own church, was one of dismal failure. But some individuals—among the clergy as well as the laity—had not betrayed the teaching of Jesus after all.

My entrance into this field coincided with a gradual awakening in the country at large. Ten years later we have a vast literature about rescuers, and it continues to grow.[14] I remain aware of the pitfalls in teaching this subject, and believe that careful attention should be paid to its place in the curriculum. It should be taught only after a consistent effort has been made to confront the evil that was the *Shoah*. But at some point, it must be taught.

More recently another new field is emerging in Holocaust studies: that of "the other victims." In 1987, a conference on this theme was organized in Washington, D.C., by Sr. Carol Rittner. This field of study ultimately touches on the question of the uniqueness of the *Shoah*. To what extent was it unprecedented? To what extent was the fate of Jews different from that of other victims of Hitler, such as Gypsies, Slavs, and homosexuals? The issue was hotly debated at the time of the building of the United States Holocaust Memorial Museum in Washington and continues to be debated.

I have long been aware of a danger that besets all of us who approach the world of the *Shoah:* The destruction of Jews, both in *what* was done to them and in *how* it was done, was so horrendous that it tends to overwhelm us, and can blind us to the sufferings of millions of others who were murdered by the Nazis. None of us who have worked in this field want to see the *Shoah* diminished. Indeed, we have fought against such attempts for years, and continue to do so. But how do we strike a balance? How do we speak of the uniqueness of the fate of the Jews—for to my mind it was unique—and at the same time give full weight to the suffering of millions of others? The debate surrounding this question is only in its beginning stages, but it is an important debate.

The third new field is that concerning the role and fate of women during the *Shoah*. It may seem strange to speak of this as "new," since the *Shoah* has been the object of intensive study for at least forty years. The fact is, however, that women were simply subsumed under "Jews." Neither their experiences as women in ghettos and camps, nor the circumstances of their murders or prospects for survival have been the object of serious study.

Given the Nazi resolve "to make this people disappear from the face of the earth" (the words are Himmler's), it should be evident that Jewish women, on whose child bearing the continuity of the people depended, were a prime target for destruction. Yet the easily ascertainable fact is that most of the best-known names in Holocaust literature, whether of survivors or scholars, belong to men. To test the truth of this statement, we need only see which names come most readily to mind!

Thanks in large measure to the groundbreaking work of Joan Ringelheim,[15] who in 1983 organized a conference on women and the Holocaust at Stern College in Manhattan—the first such conference ever held—this situation has begun to change. Evidence of this change, and a valuable teaching resource, is the volume *Different Voices: Women and the Holocaust.*[16]

In conclusion, I find that the "old" questions with which I began my work are with me still, because I believe they are basic. Some new questions have surfaced, however, and no doubt others will appear as more historical sources, particularly from Eastern Europe, become available and as our world continues to change. The world of the last decade of this millennium is not the world of 1970. In those days we hoped that we had learned the lessons of the *Shoah* and that we would never again witness such horrors. Today we are much less optimistic, as atrocities in the very heart of Europe fill our nightly news reports. The urgency to teach the lessons of the *Shoah* appears to be greater than ever.

Finally, what of the question that began to haunt me long ago: What has enabled the Jewish people to survive? It seems to me there is only one answer, although I am aware that many, including some Jewish friends, may disagree with me: the deep sense of Jewish identity, forged over thousands of years and still alive in even the most secular Jew—a sense of identity that I trace back to Sinai and the Covenant.

NOTES

1. Grailville, in Loveland, Ohio, is the U.S. center of the Grail, an international movement of women who are Catholic in origin.

2. This term refers to the centuries-old denigration by Christians of Jews and Jewish tradition. The more widely used term, antisemitism, originated in the nineteenth century and technically refers to prejudice against Jews as a "race"—a misnomer, since they do not constitute a race apart. In fact, anti-Judaism has so often and easily become antisemitism that the distinction between the terms is slight. I use them almost interchangeably in this chapter.

3. Most strikingly, *Against the Jews and Their Lies,* published in 1543, three years before Luther's death.

4. In speaking of the Holocaust as unparalleled, I am well aware that Jewish historians often rank it third (or fourth, if the 1492 expulsion from Spain is included) among major catastrophes in Jewish history: the first, the destruction of Jerusalem and the Temple and the Babylonian Exile, 586 B.C.E.; the second, the destruction in

the first war against Rome, 70 c.e.; and then the *Shoah.* My use of the word refers to modern times.

5. *The View of Judaism in German Christian Theology Since 1945: Christianity and Israel Considered in Terms of Mission* (Metuchen, N.J.: Scarecrow Press, 1975).

6. For a fuller account of this seminar, see my article, "Holocaust Seminar at Montclair State College, Spring 1973," *Journal of Ecumenical Studies* 11:2 (Spring 1974): 321–28.

7. The *Stimulus* series, *Studies in Judaism and Christianity*, published by Paulist Press, is a good indicator of the progress made and the issues being explored. The most recent volume in this series, *A House Divided: The Parting of the Ways Between Synagogue and Church* by Vincent Martin, 1995, is particularly helpful and breaks new ground.

8. See Eva Fleischner, ed., *Auschwitz: Beginning of a New Era?* (New York: KTAV, 1977), 106.

9. Philip Friedman, *Their Brothers' Keepers* (New York: Holocaust Library, 1978). First published by Crown Publishers in 1957—the early date is worth noting.

10. Philip Hallie, *Lest Innocent Blood Be Shed* (New York: Harper, 1979), 2. See also the beautiful documentary film by Pierre Sauvage made in 1987, *Weapons of the Spirit* (Los Angeles: Friends of Le Chambon and Pierre Sauvage, and New York: Anti-Defamation League).

11. Hallie, *Lest Innocent Blood Be Shed,* 3–4.

12. Harold Schulweis, rabbi of Valley Beth Shalom congregation, at Encino, California, has fought tirelessly for more than twenty-five years to gain recognition for the rescuers, and to encourage scholars to study them. As early as 1963, he began the Institute of Righteous Acts at the Judah Magnus Museum in Berkeley and encouraged scholars to interview rescuers. In 1986, together with the Anti-Defamation League, he founded the Jewish Foundation for Christian Rescuers, which is dedicated to finding rescuers, having them publicly honored, and supplying financial aid where necessary. It may be useful in this context to quote some recently published words from Franklin Littell: "Although the recognition of rescuers of Jews, *some* of whom were avowed Christians, is a noble gesture by Yad Vashem, the Anti-Defamation League's committee and others, quite another purpose is served when the Christian establishments pick up on this theme. The overtones and undertones ring false. We must always remember to ask: Who is talking? By what moral authority? For what purpose?" Franklin Littell, "Inventing the Holocaust: A Christian's Retrospect," *Holocaust and Genocide Studies* 9 (1995): 175.

13. This study was published under the title, "Can the Few Become the Many? Some Catholics in France Who Saved Jews During the Holocaust," in *Remembering for the Future,* Vol. 1 (Oxford: Pergamon Press, 1989), 233–47.

14. To list only a few titles from this growing body of literature: Carol Rittner and Sondra Myers, eds., *The Courage to Care: Rescuers of Jews during the Holocaust* (New York: New York University Press, 1986); Nechama Tec, *When Light Pierced the Darkness* (New York: Oxford University Press, 1986); Samuel P. Oliner and Pearl M. Oliner, *The Altruistic Personality: Rescuers of Jews in Nazi Europe* (New York: Free Press, 1988); Douglas Huneke, *The Moses of Rovno* (New York: Dodd, Mead, 1985); Mordecai Paldiel, *The Path of the Righteous* (Hoboken, N.J.: KTAV, 1993); Eva Fogelman, *Conscience and Courage. Rescuers of Jews During the Holocaust* (New York: Doubleday Anchor, 1994); David P. Gushee, *The Righteous Gentiles of the*

Holocaust. A Christian Interpretation (Minneapolis: Fortress Press, 1994). For a fuller bibliography consult Fogelman and Gushee.

15. Joan Ringelheim, "Thoughts about Women and the Holocaust," in *Thinking the Unthinkable: Meanings of the Holocaust,* ed. Roger S. Gottlieb (New York: Paulist Press, 1990); idem, "The Unethical and the Unspeakable: Women and the Holocaust," *Simon Wiesenthal Center Annual* 1 (1984); idem, "Women and the Holocaust: A Reconsideration of Research," in *Different Voices: Women and the Holocaust*, ed. Carol Rittner and John K. Roth (New York: Paragon House, 1993), 373–405.

16. Rittner and Roth, *Different Voices: Women and the Holocaust.*

3

In the Name of the Father

Harry James Cargas

I was twenty-eight years old before I ever heard the word *Holocaust.* I think
I can pinpoint the day, even the hour of my new awareness. It was about
1:30 P.M. on August 28, 1971. My wife and our two infant sons had gone
out of our New York apartment to run an errand and when they came back
they found me in our only chair that was not a part of the kitchen set,
weeping. I was not the kind of person who cried. Yet after reading a magazine excerpt from Elie Wiesel's *Night,* the memoir recording the death of
the author's father, I shed tears probably for the first time since my own
father's passing a decade earlier. I could not understand why I was so overwhelmed: not by the crimes of the Holocaust, but by a son's loss of his
father. When I was later able to reflect on my tears, I learned a great deal
about the *Shoah,* and also much about myself.

I think I must have been surprised almost as much as I was saddened on
that occasion. Big boys don't cry and that was part of my code. No real
emotion. The father of a family had to be a rock, a protector, one who hid
his own feelings, projected a kind of inscrutability. It was a mask, a pretense,
but I had enrolled myself in what I later identified as the John Wayne School
of Charm and that was that. Yet I feared otherwise: that *wasn't* that. Less
than secretly I realized I wasn't the toughest guy in New York. I could
protect my family only up to a (relatively small) point. But I could put up
a front, and I tried. Yet I knew it was a fraud.

My own background had not prepared me for a confrontation with the
Holocaust. My family was what I would call passively racist and passively
antisemitic. Nobody had to explain to me in our Detroit home that Negroes

were not welcome there; it was at our address that I learned what it meant to "jew someone down." We lived in a racially mixed neighborhood that was essentially trouble free (except for the fistfights that we boys regularly experienced) but that was because we all knew our places.

Dad was a bookie. An immigrant from Greece (who as a stowaway at age eleven got caught at Ellis Island, was sent back to Sparta, then sneaked back to the United States a year later), he had a chance to make it economically but a fire destroyed his bowling alley and an insurance company beat him out of what he should have collected. So he opened a poolroom that became a front for a small-time gambling operation. Visitors to our house, outside of a few relatives, were some of the regular bettors and the police my father had to bribe in order to stay in business—and there were plenty of those police. (All of this, as well as great acts of kindness to others by both my mother and my father, are part of another story.)

Fisticuffs were as natural as the air we breathed. My first battle in school came on the second day of kindergarten. In junior high school there was plenty of rough stuff and mini race riots were practically scheduled. In the summers we'd have softball games, blacks against whites, doubleheaders. The first game was for a case of soda, the second almost always ended in a brawl. A hard slide into second base might be enough to get the runner a ball in his face. A close call at first could trigger an argument, some name calling and wham, we were at it again.

After high school I began college but quit on four different occasions. I kicked around doing various jobs, even after I was married. My experiences included working in the Dodge Brothers factory (Detroit), at Anaconda Copper Smelter (Montana), as a short order cook (Indiana), a bouncer in a bar (Ann Arbor), a truck driver (Grand Rapids), an athletic director in a boys school (NYC), a wrestling coach (New Jersey), and various teaching positions as well as several editorial assignments.

But nothing had an impact on me like becoming a father. I was stunned by the responsibility and by an ability to feel love in a way that simply astonished me. It all "descended" on me with the birth of Martin de Porres, was then reinforced when Joachim James was born and somehow increased with the appearance of Siena Catherine, Manon Theresa, Jacinta Teilhard, and Sarita Jo. The feeling continues to last.

So when Martin was two and Joachim was in his first year, and I was still rather freshly reeling from being a new parent, I was able to pick up a magazine that I might ordinarily not have read except for personal circumstances. It was a Catholic periodical, *Jubilee*. The editor was Ed Rice, the former roommate and future biographer of Thomas Merton. His son was on a soccer team that I was coaching in New York where I taught at an exclusive boys' school. I was thus quite aware of the journal and its headquarters were just a couple of blocks from our apartment. So on that personally momentous Saturday afternoon I purchased a copy of the *Jubilee* with Wiesel's segment from *Night* and the direction of my life began to change.

What concerned me when I read of Wiesel's personal tragedy was not so much the overwhelming event of the Holocaust, but rather the relationship between father and son, the fifteen-year-old Elie and the older Shlomo. At a time when I was imprisoning myself in a cage constructed of steel rods that wouldn't allow me to show my sons (or my wife Millie) that I could be wrong, that I could be frightened, that I might not know the answers, and above all that I might not be the impenetrable shield of their safety else I would thus be a failure in their eyes—an incompetent father (what could be more disappointing than an incompetent John Wayne?)—I feared risking the loss of their trust, their love. And here I was reading about a child who continued to love *his* father, when even the man was helpless to prevent others doing harm to the son. In fact, Elie was assisting his father, finding him extra bits of food, teaching him how to march in time so as not to attract the attention of camp officials by his inability to step in rhythm with the other prisoners. I was shaken. Did this boy really love his father? Even when his father couldn't protect him? Did this have implications for me? Were Jewish families different from the kinds of families I knew? I had to find out.

So I began reading books about the Holocaust. First, of course, was *Night.* I had to learn the context. All the while, in these initial stages, my focus was not on the event, on the tragedy of the 5 million plus, but on father-child relations. What might I learn from this? So I read more and more as our family grew and perhaps I did too. And then one day I had another shocking, surprising illumination. While I was in a library reading another Holocaust memoir, came the crashing realization that probably every Jew killed in the Holocaust was murdered by a baptized Christian. There would be almost no exception, not necessarily a practicing Catholic or Lutheran or whatever, but one who had at least received the watery sacrament as a child. Questions abounded about the efficacy of baptism as well as those about the religious commitments of the machine gunners, the torturers, the gassers, those who buried victims alive, who bashed babies' skulls (we have to say these things) and the others, including those who knew and said nothing. (I had not yet learned that Adolf Hitler died while still on the tax rolls of the Roman Catholic Church, having never been excommunicated.) It was here that the seeds were planted for my "conversion" some years later, when I stopped calling myself a Roman Catholic and assumed the designation of a post-Auschwitz Catholic. That signifies that I have been more moved by what happened at the Nazi death camp (Auschwitz being a symbol for the entire *Shoah*) than by what did *not* happen in Rome during World War II. The silence of my church shouted out to me.

During some of the period I have been discussing, the trial of Adolf Eichmann was taking place in Jerusalem. He was the high-ranking Nazi officer, responsible for the deaths of countless Jews, who had escaped after the war but was finally tracked down by the Israeli secret police in Argentina where he was kidnapped and taken to Jerusalem. I was teaching in grade school then and the trial was big news. Jim Bishop, who wrote the bestsellers *The Day Christ Died* and *The Day Lincoln was Shot* broadcast daily television reports on the trial and it was all over the press. So I thought it might prove an exercise in creativity and thoughtfulness to stage a debate in class on whether Eichmann should be found guilty for crimes he, some had said, was ordered to commit. The participants in the debate were, of course, coached by their parents; I had given enough time for preparation but not for what I was about to hear. One of the main defense points was that "he did not kill five million Jews, he only killed three million." Perhaps it was then that I felt the call. Clearly, the all-too-obvious message of the Holocaust was not so obvious to some. Why not?

It may be too facile to blame the Christian churches for their role as accomplices in the centuries-long atmosphere of religious antisemitism, but some burden of guilt clearly exists. More recently some small statements of acknowledgment are promoted but they are in some ways ineffectual. True, they are a beginning, but after two thousand years of Jew-hatred or at least indifference to the significance of the Jewish message for Christians, it is an all-too-meager start. Jews, particularly after the Holocaust, can legitimately echo the cry of the Civil Rights movement in America, "Freedom now!"— "Obliterate antisemitism now!" Extraordinary tragedies require extraordinary responses.

Even when certain words are said, too often they are rendered practically in a vacuum. They come from the top: the World Council of Churches, the Vatican, certain presbyteries—but they stay there. The rank and file (the real Church—its members) receive relatively little of the inspiration. My own experience certainly confirms this. Since World War II there have been over twenty-six hundred Sundays, twenty-six hundred sermon opportunities for pastors to teach. As I have stated elsewhere, I have yet to hear a homily on the Christian relationship to Judaism. Nothing on the Holocaust. Where Hebrew prophets are mentioned they are only used in the sense of laying the groundwork for Jesus' message, not for value in themselves. I have heard homilies on why nuns who wear clothing other than their traditional habits are participating in a Communist plot; why it is a sin for me to wear Bermuda shorts; why Easter reminds us of the Easter bunny. I try to imagine the priest in his study thinking about what he will say on Easter Sunday. This is the day of highest attendance in the Catholic Church—women and men who attend Mass only once a year generally make this the day. Here is the one opportunity the priest may have to reach what are sometimes called "lax Catholics." So what does he choose to emphasize on the day that is used to observe the triumph of Jesus over death—the greatest miracle according to the Christian faith: the rabbit? "You're no bunny 'til some bunny loves you."

I need help in my search to strengthen my religious beliefs. My church is not doing much to help me when it serves up such trivia as nourishment for a questioning soul.

While in New York, I held several jobs for brief periods of time. One was as the editor of *Catholic Book Reporter* and another was as an editor of the *Catholic Youth Encyclopedia.* From there we moved to St. Louis where I became the editor of a Catholic youth magazine, *The Queens Work,* made famous by its (then deceased) founder, Daniel Lord, S.J. It was floundering financially, but the publisher forgot to tell me of his plan to close the operation down in less than a year.

From there it was on to Saint Louis University. My writings were being published in small publications with increasing frequency and I was asked to host a one-on-one type television program for the Central Education Network. It was a pleasure. I got to interview such personalities as Margaret Mead, Imogene Coca, Malcolm Boyd, and others. Then one day my producer phoned me to ask if I wanted to interview "some author" who was coming to town who had a new book out: Elie Wiesel. I almost screamed my acceptance of this opportunity. On two earlier occasions I had gone to hear Wiesel speak, determined to force my way into his presence after his talk in order to put certain questions to him. However, in each instance, when I was right up next to him, I realized that he was so exhausted (he always looks frail—he *is* frail) I could not disturb him so selfishly. Now here I was to have him to myself. I had by then read all of his books (*A Beggar in Jerusalem* was the latest) and was ready at a moment's notice.

Our encounter, as might be expected, was a memorable one for me. A number of things that Wiesel said during the program were particularly moving. In response to one of my questions he replied that Auschwitz represented a failure; it was a defeat for two thousand years of Christian civilization. I later asked if there was some way that it could be said that those who perished in the Holocaust triumphed and their executioners were defeated? He answered "No," and that the word *triumph* does not apply to anything relevant to the Holocaust. It was Man who was defeated there. He said that the Jew, because he is used to suffering and because of historic situations that he has known, came out, somehow, in a better way. "It happened that he was not the executioner, he was the victim. And in those times it was better to be victim than executioner. But no one triumphed. It was a triumph for nobody—for man or for God either." These words pierced my soul. I wanted to be a faithful Christian but there was the immovable question: How to remain one after Auschwitz?

When Wiesel arrived at the station where we were to do the taping of the program, the cameras were not ready. Thus we talked for about forty-five minutes before the shooting. I dislike having a conversation with a guest prior to the show because there is a tendency for the visitor to say some of his or her best things before air time, or say them in a more dynamic way than might be done later on camera. But this time it was a blessing. We had a certain encounter. Because of this I wrote to him the following week asking if he would consider doing a book together. He called me almost immediately and said that others had asked him but "in St. Looie we had a kind of 'communion' and I would like to try it with you." The meetings for the book, which took about a year to arrange (with preparation and schedule conflicts having to be resolved) lasted a weekend.

My first question, after plugging in my tape recorder, was "Why are you not mad?" Where did that question come from? I cannot explain it. Wiesel is not the kind of person you talk to about the New York Giants or traffic problems on Central Park West. "Why are you not mad?" He began his answer by distinguishing between clinical insanity and mystical madness. And we went from there. The resulting volume of wisdom, criticism, and autobiographical information became a treasure and was reprinted in 1992 with additional material as *Conversations with Elie Wiesel* (Justice Books, 1992).

Wiesel has been my personal rebbe ever since we met—and probably before that. He taught me much about the need to question. "Answers change, the questions alone are eternal." Through his books and through our personal relationship he has shown me what friendship can mean. He has exemplified what the sacred commitment of a writer can be: "the act of writing is for me nothing more than the secret or conscious desire to carve words on a tombstone. . . ." He has proven to the world that the writer *as writer* can be at least as valuable a mover as some more obviously revolutionary people try to be. His double exposé of silence in *The Jews of Silence* (1966) is a case in point. There he detailed the plight of Jews in the Soviet Union while also being critical of European and American Jews who ignored the problem. The volume has a resounding impact. Wiesel also showed how the writer could be an activist through his concerns for the suffering in Cambodia, South Africa, Argentina, of the Miskito Indians in Honduras, and in many other areas—a fact which the Nobel Committee recognized in awarding him its Peace Prize in 1986.

In part because of his impact on me, I initiated a course in Holocaust literature at Webster University; Wiesel suggested to me that this may have been the first such course in this country. I have written much on the subject (eleven of my thirty books are on the Holocaust), have lectured widely, and have learned to face my church with its failures, for its failures, trying to take a responsibility for now and for the future.

I began an interest in the Holocaust with my questioning of what it meant to be a father. I was concerned with myself as a biological father. But in learning of the horrors of which we are capable—and I certainly insist that I am a part of that "we"—I have broadened my concept of fatherhood to include my responsibility to all of the past, all of the present, and all of the future. I am moved in this way by Nikos Kazantzakis, who humbly recognized that he was the culmination of all that went before and a watershed for all that there is to come. I believe in Jung's collective unconscious and in Teilhard's noosphere, where no attitude or action is ever lost. We all contribute to each other. Einstein said that the past is a place. What can all of this mean for me?

I have grown (I hope) from a somewhat ruffian kind of character to perhaps a gentler person, one more alert to others and to what my relationship to them needs to be. Maybe. But as so many have taught us, the meaning is in the *striving*. Awareness of the Holocaust has made me at least want to strive.

There are, of course, issues at least tangentially connected to the Holocaust that are still before me, before all of us. One has to do with the State of Israel. Some think it is a result of the *Shoah*. Others object to the word *result* and substitute the term *response*. What does Israel itself mean? Is Zion a geographical location or a spiritual condition? Is it a question that has different implications for non-Jews than it has for Jews?

One can hardly think of a major contemporary topic that cannot be explored in the aftermath of the Holocaust. Jewish-Christian relations, of course, fatherhood (parenthood); family in general; pacifism; abortion; racial issues; women's rights specifically and human rights in general. There is also the very real question of art: Theodore Adorno cautioned that there can be no art after Auschwitz. Lawrence Langer and Alvin Rosenfeld have noted that there is no vocabulary available to writers to create objective correlatives (T. S. Eliot's term) for portraying the event. Yet there must be art after the Holocaust. Aesthetics (almost inappropriate in this discussion) provide a dimension of memory that will be ignored at our peril.

Memory, too, needs to continue to be explored. So do such huge topics as love, friendship, death, and the meaning of life. Theology in its various manifestations can never be what it was before World War II. The same is to be said regarding theories of history. How do the murders of a million Jewish children fit in with any concept of order or direction?

I was not yet a teenager during the Holocaust years. But it is a central event in my life. It should be so.

4

Being Catholic, Learning Jewish: Personal Reflections on the *Shoah*

Eugene J. Fisher

BEING CATHOLIC, LEARNING JEWISH

I grew up in a very Catholic environment (some would call it a "Catholic ghetto") in pre–Vatican II suburban Detroit. I should specify that my neighborhood was on the east side of the city, a fact the significance of which native Detroiters will instantly appreciate. At that time, Detroit was functionally two cities divided by Woodward Avenue, a major artery extending outward from downtown. The Jewish community of metropolitan Detroit, for reasons that had to do with both immigration patterns and patterns imposed by socioeconomic discrimination against immigrants, lived in certain areas of the west side, as, for similar reasons, the bulk of the Italian and Polish communities lived in certain areas of the east side. I don't recall having met any Jews while growing up, much less getting to know them well, although my father, an attorney, did have some Jewish colleagues, I now realize.

After attending public school for kindergarten, I went to Catholic grade school and Catholic high school. In the mid-1960s I attended Sacred Heart College Seminary and St. John's Provincial Seminary. At Sacred Heart, I became involved in civil rights. We organized, for example, a weekend for the seminarians in the homes of black families. Subsequently, virtually the entire student body and faculty, proudly bearing both the American and papal flags, marched as a unit with Martin Luther King, Jr., when he came to Detroit. It was in this period that I first met Hubert Locke, who was even then, along with Franklin Littell, pioneering the field of Holocaust studies at Wayne State University. I invited Hubert to speak at the seminary, not on the *Shoah* (a word I did not even know then), but on black history and slavery in American history. At St. John's I took extra Scripture courses and biblical Hebrew, a decision that I could only in retrospect realize had changed the course of my life.

In the summer between semesters at St. John's, I was invited to act as chaperone for a group of local Catholic high school kids on an exchange program in Ecuador. The class stratification among Spanish descendants, Indians, and blacks was stark and nearly absolute. The level of poverty of the majority of the population was something I had only read about in history books. The summer made achingly real for me essential realities of oppression and exploitation I had previously understood only intellectually.

Leaving St. John's, but wishing to pursue theology, especially Hebrew Scripture studies, I took a master's degree in Catholic theology at the University of Detroit. Though Jesuit, the University of Detroit had no doctoral program in theology or Scripture. Pursuing the latter, I thought it might be appropriate to study the Hebrew Bible with the people who wrote it. So after twenty-two years of Catholic education in the Midwest, on a warm day in early September 1968, I boarded a plane to enter the doctoral program in Hebrew Studies at New York University. Getting off the bus at Grand Central Station from the airport, a youngster picked up a bag I had set down. Mumbling something about carrying my luggage, he took off running with me straining after him carrying my other bag. Welcome to New York!

The changes and challenges in lifestyle, intellectual environment, and religious perspective I experienced in New York were dramatic. This was the period of massive antiwar demonstrations. I had been in the seminary just at the right time to go through the Second Vatican Council as it was happening, and had been fortunate to be quite actively involved in the Civil Rights movement in Detroit during the same period. The winds of social change promised a new and more equal American society, as the open windows of theological *aggiornamento* promised a reformed and more open Roman Catholic Church. For us, change represented hope, not something to be feared. One could acknowledge freely the shortcomings of the past, whether in society or the church, because both were actively engaged in rectifying what had gone wrong. Admitting American racism and Christian antisemitism, then, was not to risk becoming mired down in the guilt of the past (as it has continued to be for some time in some parts of Europe). It was simply to open oneself to hope for a better future.

Most, and sometimes all, of my classmates at NYU were Jewish. The tone, style, and content of the discussions were entirely Jewish. What people wrangled over were questions of what it means to be Jewish. The definitions of questions that framed the issues for debate were thus Jewish. I found this both refreshing and fascinating. If one is raised within a holistic worldview such as is provided by ancient traditions such as Rabbinic Judaism and Roman Catholicism, entire sets of interrelated frameworks make sense of and give coherency to reality, even to the often fractious internal debates that can divide a community against itself.

Fortunately, I was just at the right time of my life to be plunked down, intact (i.e., with a reasonably solid grounding in integral Catholicism), in the midst of an entirely different, but no less integral, worldview. Virtually everything I had ever learned, spiritually, culturally, philosophically, historically, or biblically, was viewed from a very different perspective. Of all the religious traditions that had flourished in the ancient Roman Empire, Judaism alone had been allowed to survive Christianity's triumph in Europe. Jewish communities often predated Christian communities in southern and western Europe and were founded alongside Christian communities in northern and eastern Europe. The Jewish memory of Christendom, therefore, is invaluable as the one non-Christian but still "insider" perspective on Western civilization over the past two millennia. These Jewish communities, I was to discover with a sense of infinite loss, were the communities, the memories, and the unique spiritual witness that Nazi genocide sought to end.

Before immersing myself in the New York Jewish experience, I had known nothing about being Jewish, save what I had learned in biblical studies under Catholic auspices. While academically sound, this perspective was only marginally useful for understanding how Jews today read their Scriptures, understand their history, and live their traditions. It was all new to me.

I did not at first encounter the Holocaust with great intensity at NYU. It was discussed as pertinent to a given topic of study. It did not dominate either the formal course work or the informal discussions of my classmates. Rather, it seemed to brood behind and beneath them, dwelling in the silence of the unspoken yet not unthought. This was in 1968, well before the NBC miniseries, "Holocaust," broke open the repressed memories and fears of so many in the Jewish community, survivors not least among them. What I encountered, rather, was the vibrancy of American Jewry, especially the New York variety. (The two are not coterminous, it turns out, but I thought so then—as, of course, did most of my classmates.)

I encountered both Jewish history and Jewish philosophy, the medieval *piyyutim* and the *Zohar, Tanach, Talmud* and *Torah* as a coherent, integral, and spiritually enriching way of life. It was profoundly different, yet not necessarily contradictory to my own faith life. As I learned to respect Judaism and its traditions, various facts and events occasionally intruded from that long past. I had known about the destruction of the Temple in 70 C.E. (another term then new to me, having grown up with A.D.). It was, after all, of great significance to the authors of the New Testament. I learned for the first time what happened to the Jews of the Rhineland during the first Crusade in 1096, about the expulsion of Jews from virtually all of western Europe over the succeeding centuries, culminating in the expulsion from Spain in 1492. If these and so many similar events had been taught in my Catholic education, they had hardly been highlighted. I had missed them. In effect, the words of Fr. Edward Flannery introducing his classic 1965 study (which I was not to read until later) were very apt for me: "The pages Jews have memorized have been torn from our histories of the Christian era."[1]

I did not deeply reflect on this then. It was a relatively minor theme of my major endeavor, learning about Jews and Judaism—a new world for me, a new reality that meant I had to reintegrate nearly everything I had ever learned, historically and theologically, into a new overall pattern that would be faithful to the integral vision in which I had been trained and which gave meaning to my life, and yet faithful to this other, compellingly different yet almost oddly familiar pattern. For with all the startling divergences in definition of ultimate issues and differing perspectives on shared issues, it was the same God, the same sacred history, after all, being studied, albeit so disparately from what I was used to. The tragic, suffering elements of that ancient, sacred history were there, to be sure. But they did not predominate for us at NYU in the late 1960s with civil rights and the peace movement capturing the lion's share of our nonacademic attention. I was involved in draft counseling; for example, at a Catholic Worker storefront originally called the Thomas Merton House, but which soon became the Merton/Buber house.

Two books given to me by the director of NYU's Institute for Hebrew Studies, David Rudavsky, of blessed memory, riveted my attention on the Holocaust: Elie Wiesel's *Night* and André Schwarz-Bart's *The Last of the Just*. These commanded a more personal response, as did a trip to Europe (my first) I took with my wife in the early 1970s. After some very pleasant days in Rome, Florence, and Venice, we took a train to Munich. I became uneasy when we went to a beer hall that night and realized that it was *the* Munich beer hall. The next day we went to Dachau, a short train ride to a near-in suburb. I had known it was real, intellectually, but the confrontation with reality was spiritually devastating. Although the Nazis never used the gas chambers they built there (state of the art as they were), they shot so many people so regularly that they had to dig a system of trenches to drain off the blood from the killing field.

I have visited a number of other death camps and Holocaust sites, including Auschwitz, since then. The sense of spiritual bereavement and bewilderment does not diminish. Nor can it be numbed. Each time, some new detail or perspective opens the wound again. All one can do, all I can do, is what Pope John Paul II promised to the remnant community of the Jews of Warsaw in 1987 and again to the survivors gathered at the Vatican for the Holocaust concert held there in 1994:[2] to join my voice to that of the Jewish people in permanent witness to what happened and never abandon the struggle to understand why, so that it can never be allowed to happen again.

STATUS QUESTIONIS: THE HOLOCAUST AND CHRISTIAN RESPONSIBILITY

I mention this by way of background to responding to the first questions posed by the editors of this volume. My early approach was not to the Holocaust as such, but to Jews and Judaism as very alive, contemporary entities with a fascinating past and an infinitely hope-filled future. So I did not start out with the approach of a problem to be solved, as did Jules Isaac, who in the midst of World War II wanted to know why Christian Europeans were attempting to murder his people.[3] When Isaac was writing, of course, neither the term *Holocaust* nor the term *genocide* was available in English or French. These terms were invented only later to describe what happened to the Jews in World War II.[4] Isaac found a potent forerunner of the racial antisemitism of twentieth-century Europe in the ancient Christian "teaching of contempt," as he so aptly called it, against Judaism. He traced this back to the fathers of the church in the earliest centuries of Christian history.

In 1974, Rosemary Radford Ruether took the step that Jules Isaac had not taken and Catholic scholar Gregory Baum had feared would be taken by someone reading Isaac.[5] *Faith and Fratricide* argued that one can find the direct precursor of modern, racial antisemitism in teachings essential to the New Testament itself.[6] While I have serious difficulties with Ruether's conclusion, there is no doubt that her challenge captured the attention of major Christian thinkers on both sides of the Atlantic in a way no previous work in the field had been able to do.

What I call Ruether's straight line method of arguing directly from the pages of the New Testament to Auschwitz, without pausing to consider what might have happened in the intermediate two millennia, precipitated quite a response from other Christian scholars who were by that time themselves deeply involved in the still nascent field of Jewish-Christian relations. In the fall of 1975, Msgr. John M. Oesterreicher, like Baum born a European Jew who found refuge in the Americas and a colleague of Baum's on the drafting committee advising Cardinal Bea on the text of the Second Vatican Council's declaration, *Nostra Aetate,* published a scathing critique of *Faith and Fratricide* under the title *Anatomy of Contempt.*[7]

While I did not read Oesterreicher's essay until later, I was deeply influenced by the papers, both Jewish and Christian, delivered at the international symposium on the Holocaust held at the Cathedral of St. John the Divine in New York in June 1974. Edited by Eva Fleischner with terse and telling introductions to each section,[8] the volume of papers from that symposium served both to consolidate the advances in the dialogue to that time and to define the terms and *Status Questionis* for the decades that would follow. Irving Greenberg's now classic, "Cloud of Smoke, Pillar of Fire: Judaism, Christianity, and Modernity after the Holocaust," reads as freshly and as challengingly now, for example, as it did then.

Another paper that redirected my thinking as a Christian was Harvard historian Yosef Hayim Yerushalmi's response to Rosemary Ruether's summary of her book. I think until that time I had just assumed in a general sort of way that since Christians had perpetrated genocide, traditional Christian teaching (although arguably not the Gospels themselves) must have supplied an underlying rationale for it. What Ruether's book had done was to sharpen that general sort of acknowledgment and make it very pointed. But after Yerushalmi's paper I had a new set of questions.

Here is how Eva Fleischner, I believe quite accurately, summarizes the Ruetherian thesis: "Anti-Semitism in the West is a direct outgrowth of Christian theological anti-Judaism. . . . Anti-Judaism [is] the claim that Jesus is the Christ. This claim *inevitably* pitted the Church against the synagogue. . . . This is the meaning of her statement that anti-Judaism is the left hand of Christology. In other words, anti-Judaism is *endemic* to Christianity, an *inevitable consequence* of the Christian kerygma" [italics added].⁹

This is an enticing definition of the question. If the problem is the Christian *kerygma* as such, one has only to change the *kerygma* to solve it. Two problems intrude on this comfortable solution, however, one theological and the other historical. Theologically, if Ruether is correct that "anti-Judaism" (and therefore antisemitism, which she sees as simply an extension of anti-Judaism) is "inevitable" and "endemic"; that is, as essential to the *kerygma* of the New Testament itself, then we Christians are stuck with the harsh choice between abandoning our Christian faith or simply learning to live with being endemically and inevitably antisemitic.

We will return to what I see as a false, forced choice. In the meantime, Yerushalmi asks the basic historical question that proponents of the straight line method from gospel to Auschwitz still have trouble with. If genocide is endemic to Christianity and its inevitable consequence, why did it take almost two millennia for the inevitable to manifest itself? As he puts it:

Is modern anti-Semitism *merely* a metamorphosed medieval Christian anti-Semitism? Through what conduits and channels did the transformation occur? . . . What happens along the way in the shift from religious to secular, theological to racial anti-Semitism? Here, it seems to me, Ruether's formulation explains little and glosses over much. The issue is physical extermination. Not reprobation, discrimination, or any variety of opprobrium, but—*genocide.* From Rosemary Ruether we gather that genocide against the Jews was an inexorable consequence of Christian theological teaching. I do not think that is quite the case. If it were, genocide should have come upon the Jews in the Middle Ages. . . . Even if we grant that Christian teaching was a necessary cause leading to the Holocaust, it was surely not a sufficient one.¹⁰

One need not agree with Yerushalmi's own historical conclusion that "the Holocaust was the work of a thoroughly modern, neo-pagan state" to realize the significance of his question for theories of Holocaust causality. "Necessary but not sufficient" may apply to more than one historical cause. Even a latter day proponent of Ruether's thesis such as Stephen R. Haynes writing recently in the *Journal of Ecumenical Studies* has to acknowledge the trenchancy of the question, even if he does not feel the need to assay a response to it:

A clear limitation of the rejectionist stance is one that afflicts each of the paradigms to varying degrees: The closer one gets to arguing that Antisemitism is a necessary concomitant of Christian belief, the more directly one must confront a historical paradox. For, if Jew-hatred is located at the heart of Christian theology, then one must explain why genocide never was resorted to in the centuries when the church possessed the power and influence to carry it out. To put the matter another way, if religious hatred was a sufficient condition for the Holocaust, why did it not occur until Christianity had lost its cultural hegemony?[11]

There it is again, the Yerushalmi distinction: "necessary but not sufficient." This is a formulation that by no means lets the church and its ancient teaching of contempt for Jews and Judaism off the hook. That teaching must be changed forever, and much of my professional life has been dedicated to bringing about and consolidating positive changes in Christian understandings of Jews and Judaism. But Yerushalmi's formulation does allow for a more nuanced and varied explanation of the widely varied and highly complex set of events that made up the Holocaust. Why did Italians, arguably among the Europeans most influenced by Roman Catholicism over the centuries, despite being first allied to Nazi Germany and then under Nazi occupation, risk themselves to save among the highest percentages of Jews (and virtually any other Jews who could get themselves into the hands of the Italian army) anywhere in Europe outside Denmark? Why were ardent French Catholics to be found among both the Vichyites and in the Resistance? Why the vast array of responses among Christians?

At the same time as it has the advantage of being able to accommodate the complexities of historical reality, the Yerushalmi formulation also enables the possibility of a theological resolution, which the Ruetherian view, in my opinion, logically precludes. Somehow we have to be able to remain Christian while still eschewing antisemitism. This is indeed the conclusion drawn by the twelve Christian, New Testament, and patristic scholars brought together by Alan Davies in 1979 to respond to Ruether's thesis in detail. Davies states in his introduction: "If a common motif in these essays can be described, it is the conviction that Christians need not choose between an ideological defense of their scriptures and the sad conclusion that the New Testament is so contaminated by anti-Jewish prejudice as to lose all moral authority. Instead, through careful study, Christians can isolate what genuine forms of anti-Judaism really color the major writings and, by examining their historic genesis, neutralize their potential for harm."[12]

This is an approach that has not proven easy, but it is the only one I know of that offers any real hope for a better future. In June 1995, I had the privilege of responding to a paper at the Catholic Theological Society of America (CTSA) delivered by Ronald Modras of Saint Louis University. The paper summarized the essence of Modras' study[13] of Polish Catholic literature on Jews and Judaism in the interwar period. His research has discovered that the bulk of antisemitic writings in Polish Catholic journals was driven, not by ancient theological canards such as deicide, but by post-Enlightenment, "secular" conspiracy theories (e.g., that the Jews use international banking, world communism, and Freemasonry to further their plots to take over the world). Modras asked me if I still held to the theory that specifically Christian anti-Judaism was a necessary but not sufficient cause to explain the racial antisemitism of Nazi genocide. Modras was beginning to doubt that there existed even this close a causal relationship.

From Leon Poliakov to Gavin Langmuir, the scholarship in the field that has most influenced my thinking has fallen within the flexible boundaries of the Yerushalmi paradigm. There exists continuity between ancient church teaching and modern antisemitism that cannot be denied if one is to understand what happened in the twentieth century. There also exists discontinuity and newness, from age to age and place to place, if one is to understand why it did not happen until the twentieth century and the widely different reactions among Christians to it.

In 1981, I published an article in *America* on "The Holocaust and Christian Responsibility," which has been widely reprinted.[14] This article relies on the Yerushalmi formulation. I confirmed to the CTSA members at the June conference that, indeed, I still believe this formulation to be the most adequate I have seen. It allows for the qualitative differences in Christian and secular attitudes toward Jews over the centuries and in different regions in a way that the "either/or" approach of Ruether cannot. It allows, in short, for the free rein of scholarly objectivity rather than forcing the issue ideologically, as in Ruether's famous phrase, "antisemitism is the left hand of Christology."

In 1993, in an epilogue to the collected volume of paired Jewish and Christian historical essays I edited based on the plenary presentations of the 1986 National Workshop on Christian-Jewish Relations in Baltimore, I cited as a very brief and superficial summary of these qualitative changes over the centuries, what I call the "Six Stages of Christian-Jewish Relations."[15] While I have undergone many shocks and revelations over the years, as I have encountered the Holocaust and its survivors from a myriad of differing perspectives, I believe the Yerushalmi paradigm is still eminently useful as a beginning point for discussion that is neither needlessly polemical toward Christians on the one hand, nor needlessly apologetic or defensive by Christians on the other.

HOLOCAUST EDUCATION AND LITURGY

Much of my work with regard to the Holocaust has involved developing materials and guidelines for the church's two "delivery systems," the classroom and the pulpit. During the summers between semesters at NYU, I returned to Detroit to teach summer courses at the University of Detroit. I taught Scripture and biblical archaeology, as well as several courses in aspects of Judaica, such as one on Martin Buber. In 1971, my wife and I returned to Detroit where I had a job as Director of Catechist Formation (teacher training) for the Office of Religious Education for the archdiocese, while also volunteering for the Ecumenical Commission in Catholic-Jewish relations. Here pieces began to come together.[16] From 1973 to 1976 I worked on developing training programs for religion teachers in the archdiocese. One, "Christian Value Analysis," centered a major portion of its focus on the Holocaust, not so much on the issue of Christian responsibility as discussed above but, as I put it in my preinclusive language days, *the* paradigm of "man's inhumanity to man," and, conversely, the equally difficult problem of goodness. Why had some become perpetrators, others saviors, and others frightened and cowed onlookers?[17] What are our potentials and moral challenges today? How do we as teachers instill in students the simple, basic values that the righteous exemplified?

With the Archdiocesan Ecumenical Commission, I drafted guidelines for Catholic-Jewish relations that were ultimately adopted as official guidelines in 1979. And since the Ecumenical Commission in Detroit was placed under the Department of Liturgy, the commission had the opportunity to recommend resources and approaches for homilists confronting the problematical passages of the New Testament and to develop, for example, prayers for the faithful for use during Mass on the Sunday closest to *Yom HaShoah*. These efforts were to provide a sound basis for future work I was to do with regard to similar documents for the National Conference of Catholic Bishops as staffperson for Catholic-Jewish relations.[18]

Working in a religious education office gave me access to all of the textbook series used by Catholics. So my dissertation analyzing them for their content on and portrait of Jews and Judaism was a natural. My first book, *Faith Without Prejudice,* is in essence an extended guide for teachers and preachers to reading the New Testament with a positive appreciation of Jews and Judaism rather than the apologetical or even polemic approaches of the past.[19] The book opens with an evocation of the scene on June 13, 1960, when Pope John XXIII received in audience the French Jewish historian, Jules Isaac.[20]

Over the years I have developed a large amount of material for Christian educators with regard to their treatment of Jews and Judaism, much of it necessarily directly related to the Holocaust and antisemitism. I am profoundly grateful to have had the opportunity to publish books with such distinguished Jewish colleagues as Leon Klenicki,[21] Annette Daum[22] of blessed memory, Daniel Polish,[23] A. James Rudin,[24] and Marc H. Tanenbaum, also of blessed memory. I have also attempted to assist Christian seminary educators deal with these topics.[25]

I have been greatly privileged while working for the Bishops' Conference to be able to serve on commissions and teams working on a variety of Holocaust-related projects. No life work could be more satisfying than this. Chief among these would be my involvement with the International Catholic-Jewish Liaison Committee.[26] I would also mention here the National Workshops on Christian-Jewish Relations, which I have chaired for some fifteen years; the National Catholic Center for Holocaust Education at Seton Hill College in Greenburg, Pennsylvania, which I helped to "midwife" and which has done extraordinarily important work in the past several years;[27] the Education and Church Relations Committees of the United States Holocaust Memorial Museum in Washington, D.C.; the Christian Scholars Study Group on Jews and Judaism (formerly the Israel Study Group); and the Annual Scholars' Conference on the Holocaust and the Churches.[28]

In the early 1980s, Rabbi Leon Klenicki and I developed a Christian-Jewish Holocaust liturgy that has now seen several forms and has been used widely both in the United States and overseas.[29] Its opening theme begins in silence and then moves through Genesis from the life-giving breath (wind, Spirit) of God, *rûah*, to the death-dealing devastation of the wind called *shoah*.[30] It acknowledges the deeds of the righteous gentiles, but as mute counterpart to the massive failure of the larger community. On a trip to Auschwitz taken with a group of Catholic and Jewish leaders, Leon and I prayed our liturgy together, as we had previously in cathedrals and synagogues in the United States.

THE HOLOCAUST AND CATHOLIC-JEWISH CRISES

The past decade has been marked by a series of crises between Catholics and Jews over issues related to the Holocaust. These have naturally formed a consuming portion of my professional and personal life. In 1988 I began to put together a chronicle of these events along with a commentary on their significance for Catholic teaching and theology. This chronicle dealt with the crises between Catholics and Jews that had been, ironically, bracketed by two of the most positive events in the history of the dialogue: the pope's visit to the Great Synagogue of Rome, April 13, 1986, and his meeting with four hundred leaders of the world's largest Jewish community in Miami on September 11, 1987. After the Hebrew *gematria* for life (*chai* = eighteen), I entitled the article "Eighteen Months in Catholic-Jewish Relations."[31] The crises that intervened between the first event in Rome to threaten the second event in the United States were Holocaust-related: the beatification of Edith Stein, the Auschwitz convent, and the meeting between the pope and Kurt Waldheim, then-president of Austria.

A case can be made that, viewed dispassionately, none of these events or even all three taken together should have raised anywhere near the level of emotion and controversy that spilled over into the public forum. Edith Stein was by no means the only Jewish convert to Christianity to be murdered by the Nazis for the crime of being Jewish. The convent, objectively, was not so placed as to be noticeable by visitors to Auschwitz-Birkenau. One could reasonably have presumed that its cloistered nuns would cause no more discomfort to visitors than had been caused by the presence of a similarly humbly placed Carmelite convent and chapel at Dachau over the previous decades. Mr. Waldheim, while having hidden his unsavory past, was by no means the most immoral or evil person with whom popes have met in pursuing state relations as head of the Roman Catholic Church.

What was at stake, I believe, was not so much the incidents themselves but what underlay the specifics of all three controversies. The real issue was (and is) *memory,* the memory of the victims, the memory of whether perpetrators and onlookers might, in history's eye, pass themselves off as victims. Rabbi A. James Rudin of the American Jewish Committee, for one, sensed this immediately concerning the Auschwitz convent. "You know, Gene," he told me during a phone conversation shortly after we had heard of the flap in far-off Belgium over a fund-raising campaign for the convent, "this molehill may well become a mountain to trip us all." That Rabbi Rudin was correct is an understatement.

In 1988, Rabbi Daniel Polish received an award from the Catholic Press Association for an article explaining to Catholics just what concerned the Jewish community reacting to such Catholic initiatives as the beatification of Edith Stein and the Auschwitz convent.[32] There were fears stemming from a history of forced conversions and a specific *Shoah*-related fear that the Catholic Church, whether consciously or not, was engaged in a series of actions that would, in effect, absorb the Holocaust into itself, making it a Catholic event, just as the church has made part of its own history the pre-New Testament history of Israel as recorded in the Hebrew Bible, redefining that history, including the Exodus and the prophets, as a promise fulfilled in Christianity. While I personally and professionally have sought to allay the Jewish concerns so ably articulated by Rabbi Polish, he puts them in a way that makes them comprehensible to Catholics.

We need today, as I have said on innumerable occasions, to work together through our memories of the past, not just of the Holocaust but over the centuries as well. Our memories of the past centuries will determine to a great extent how we remember and commemorate the *Shoah.* I believe that there is a danger in exclusively separate communal memories and commemorations. True, we will always encounter the *Shoah* from different historical experiences and spiritual needs. But these experiences and needs *can* be made comprehensible to one another. Only such a dialogical approach to the Holocaust in the long run, I firmly believe, will ensure a proper understanding of the event for future generations of Jews and Christians alike.

When Rabbi Steven Jacobs asked me for a contribution to a collection of essays on contemporary Jewish and Christian responses to the *Shoah,* I not only expanded the chronicle to include other and more recent Holocaust-related crises, but attempted a more systematic and theological approach to the whole. I entitled the result, "*Mysterium Tremendum:* Catholic Grapplings with the *Shoah* and its Theological Implications."[33] I will not repeat that paper here, but it may be of some interest to cite the section headings: Jews and Christians: *anamnesis* and *zikkaron,* Bitburg and the Theology of Forgiveness, Waldheim and the Theology of Repentance, Pope John Paul II and the Uniqueness of Jewish Witness to the *Shoah,* John Cardinal O'Connor and the Theology of Suffering, Edith Stein and the Theology of Love, The Auschwitz Convent and the Theology of Remembrance, The State of Israel and the Theology of Hope. In short, the Holocaust and the history that lies behind it, challenges a whole range of Christian theological assumptions. Again, the best and perhaps ultimately the only way to meet these challenges is in dialogue with Jewish thinkers as they respond to similar and other challenges.

The point, of course, is that these events did not "just happen." They reflect a very deep, unfinished agenda between our two communities, a clash of memory, symbol, and theology that is profound, but which is, I profoundly believe, ultimately reconcilable. That is to say the goal and vision of dialogue, for reconciliation between Jews and Christians, is possible and perhaps a historical imperative, certainly for Christians but perhaps also for Jews. It will necessitate profound repentance on the part of Catholics, such as the pope has called us to in the perspective of the coming of the third millennium of Jewish-Christian relations. And it will call, not for forgiveness on the part of Jews, but for an openness to dialogue that is painful because it will involve openness to trust in and risk for the future. But if the Holocaust has anything at all to teach us, it is that the course of the past two millennia between Jews and Christians needs correcting for the sake of our children and our children's children. To paraphrase the sages, it may not be given to us to finish the task, but we must begin.

NOTES

1. Edward H. Flannery, *The Anguish of the Jews: Twenty-three Centuries of Anti-Semitism* (New York: Macmillan, 1965), xi; (rev. 2d ed. New York: Paulist Press, 1985).

2. These texts and numerous others have been collected in Pope John Paul II, *Spiritual Pilgrimage: Texts on Jews and Judaism, 1979–1995,* ed. Eugene J. Fisher and Leon Klenicki (New York: Crossroad, 1995).

3. Jules Isaac, *Jesus and Israel* (New York: Holt, Rinehart and Winston, 1971). In his preface to the 1948 French edition, Isaac explained its origin: "Begun in 1943, in the course of a life already threatened and uprooted, soon to be ravaged and hunted; finished in 1946, in solitude and seclusion, this book has a history that explains it. . . . It was born of persecution. It is the cry of an outraged conscience, of a lacerated heart" (xxiii).

4. Indeed, as late at 1980, the word *Holocaust* as we know it, that is, used to describe what happened to Jews during World War II, was still considered an improper neologism by many French speakers. I can recall vividly in a meeting of the International Catholic-Jewish Liaison Committee arguing as an English-speaker with our French-speaking colleagues, both Jewish and Catholic, that the joint denunciation we had agreed to make of "Holocaust revisionism" had to use the term *Holocaust* to make sense. They argued just as strongly that that would be impossible, since "French has no word for 'Holocaust,' only the term 'genocide.' " Needless to say, the French prevailed.

5. Gregory Baum, who described himself at the time as "a Catholic born of a Jewish family" wrote his defense of the New Testament against the charge of anti-semitism, as he explains in his foreword, in response to Isaac's *Jesus and Israel,* with which he was largely in sympathy. See *The Jews and the Gospel* (Westminster: The Newman Press, 1961), 3–5.

6. Rosemary Radford Ruether, *Faith and Fratricide: The Theological Roots of Anti-Semitism* (New York: Seabury, 1974). Baum's introduction to Ruether's volume indicated that he had by that time come full circle to join Ruether in the view that "the Christian affirmation of Jesus as the Christ was accompanied by a refutation of the synagogal reading of the Scriptures. This accompanying refutation, which Rosemary Ruether calls 'the left hand of Christology,' is the source and origin of Christian anti-Semitism" (Baum in *Faith and Fratricide,* 12).

7. John M. Oesterreicher, *Anatomy of Contempt: A Critique of R. R. Ruether's* Faith and Fratricide (South Orange, N.J.: Seton Hall University, The Institute of Judaeo-Christian Studies, 1975).

8. Eva Fleischner, ed., *Auschwitz: Beginning of a New Era?* (New York: KTAV, 1977).

9. Ibid., 75.

10. Ibid., 102–3.

11. Stephen R. Haynes, "Changing Paradigms: Reformist, Radical, and Rejectionist Approaches to the Relationship between Christianity and Antisemitism," *Journal of Ecumenical Studies* 32 (Winter 1995): 81.

12. Alan T. Davies, ed., *Anti-Semitism and the Foundations of Christianity* (New York: Paulist Press, 1979), xv.

13. Ronald Modras, *The Catholic Church and Anti-Semitism: Poland 1933–1939* (Chur, Switzerland: Harwood Academic Publishers, 1994).

14. Eugene Fisher, "The Holocaust and Christian Responsibility," *America*, February 14, 1981, 118–21; also *Criterio* (Buenos Aires), September 24, 1981; *Christian-Jewish Relations* (London), September 1981, 21–27; and *Christians and the Holocaust* (New York: National Council of Churches of Christ, USA, 1993), 10–14.

15. Epilogue to *Interwoven Destinies: Jews and Christians Through the Ages,* ed. Eugene Fisher (New York: Paulist Press, 1993), 143–46. A more detailed survey of the scholarly literature, period by period, can be found in Eugene Fisher, "Anti-

Semitism and Christianity: Theories and Revisions of Theories," in *Persistent Prejudice: Perspectives on Anti-Semitism,* ed. Herbert Hirsch and Jack D. Spiro (Fairfax, Va.: George Mason University Press, 1988), 11–30.

16. The first three articles I published reflect something of the range of my interests at the time, having completed the coursework and taken the comprehensives for my doctorate but awaiting approval to begin a dissertation. They were: "The Radical Dilemma: Peace or Revolution," *Fellowship* (May 1969); "Gilgamesh and Genesis: The Flood Story in Context," *Catholic Biblical Quarterly* (July 1970); and "Typical Jewish Misunderstandings of Christianity," *Judaism Quarterly* (Spring 1973).

17. On this question, see my article, "Silence and Dialogue: Reflections on the Work of Elie Wiesel," in *Elie Wiesel: Between Memory and Hope,* ed. Carol Rittner (New York: New York University Press, 1990), 97–115.

18. See the appendix of my book, *Faith Without Prejudice,* 2d ed. (New York: Crossroad, 1993), 164–94 for the NCCB documents.

19. Ibid.

20. Ibid., 19.

21. See, for example, the many articles Rabbi Klenicki and I did together for *PACE* (Professional Approaches for Christian Educators), published now by *Our Sunday Visitor,* and the volume *In Our Time: The Flowering of Jewish-Catholic Dialogue* (New York: Paulist Press, 1990); *Anti-Semitism Is a Sin* (New York: Anti-Defamation League, 1989; 2d ed., 1994); and *Understanding the Jewish Experience: A Joint Educational Program* (New York: ADL, rev. ed., 1993).

22. See Annette Daum and Eugene Fisher, *The Challenge of Shalom for Jews and Christians: A Dialogical Discussion Guide to the Bishops' Pastoral on Peace and War* (New York: Union of American Hebrew Congregations, 1985).

23. Eugene J. Fisher and Daniel F. Polish, eds., *The Formation of Social Policy in the Catholic and Jewish Traditions* (Notre Dame, Ind.: University of Notre Dame Press, 1980) and idem, *Liturgical Foundations of Social Policy in the Catholic and Jewish Traditions* (Notre Dame, Ind.: University of Notre Dame Press, 1983).

24. E. Fisher, J. Rudin, and M. Tanenbaum, eds., *Twenty Years of Jewish-Catholic Relations* (New York: Paulist Press, 1986).

25. Eugene Fisher, *Seminary Education and Christian-Jewish Relations* (Washington, D.C.: National Catholic Education Association, 1983; 2d ed., 1988).

26. International Catholic-Jewish Liaison Committee (ILC), *Fifteen Years of Catholic-Jewish Dialogue 1970–1985* (Vatican City: Libreria Editrice Vaticana, and Rome: Libreria Editrice Lateranense, 1988) contains documents and papers from the ILC over the years.

27. See Eugene Fisher, "Why Teach the Holocaust?" in *Peace/Shalom after Atrocity,* ed. Gemma Del Duca and Mary Noel Kernan (Greensburg, Pa.: The National Catholic Center for Holocaust Education, 1991), 1–6; and E. Fisher, "In Our Time," in *At the Edge of the 21st Century: Second Scholars' Conference on the Teaching of the Holocaust,* ed. Gemma Del Duca and Mary Noel Kernan (Greensberg, Pa.: The National Catholic Center for Holocaust Education, 1993), 47–52.

28. See E. Fisher, "Memory and Triumphalism," in *Bearing Witness to the Holocaust 1939–1989,* ed. Alan L. Berger (Lewiston, N.Y.: Edwin Mellen Press, 1991), 333–40. Three institutes of Jewish-Christian studies not exclusively engaged in Holocaust work have likewise made major contributions. The first, of course, is the Institute

for Judaeo-Christian Studies founded in the 1950s at Seton Hall University by John Oesterreicher, the first such institute, to my knowledge, ever established in a major Catholic university. More recently, the Institute for Christian and Jewish Studies was established in Baltimore in the late 1980s as a follow-up to the National Workshop on Christian-Jewish Relations held there in 1986. A summary by Christopher Leighton of its efforts was included as an appendix to my *Visions of the Other: Jewish and Christian Theologians Assess the Dialogue* (New York: Paulist Press, 1994), 81–89, which contained major papers from the Baltimore Workshop. In the 1990s, Jack Bemporad founded The Center for Christian-Jewish Understanding at Sacred Heart University in Fairfield, Connecticut.

29. E. Fisher and L. Klenicki, *From Desolation to Hope: An Interreligious Memorial Service* (Archdiocese of Chicago: Liturgy Training Publications, 1983; rev. 1990). Spanish Edition: *De la Muerte a la Esperanza: Reflexiones Liturgicas sobre el Holocausto* (Bogota: Consejo Episcopal Latino-Americana, 1986).

30. This theme of Genesis, from *rûah* to *shoah,* was used by Elie Wiesel and Albert Friedlander as the organizing principle of their very moving book, *The Six Days of Destruction: Meditations Toward Hope* (New York: Paulist Press, 1988), which includes my liturgy with Rabbi Klenicki on pages 89–108.

31. Eugene Fisher, "Eighteen Months in Catholic-Jewish Relations (April 13, 1986– September 11, 1987)," in *Overcoming Fear between Jews and Christians,* ed. James H. Charlesworth (New York: Crossroad/The American Interfaith Institute, 1993), 139– 52.

32. I responded to that article in "A Painful Legacy: Response to Daniel Polish," *Ecumenical Trends* 17 (1988):60–64. The entire exchange is included in *The Unnecessary Problem of Edith Stein,* ed. Harry James Cargas (Lanham, Md.: University Press of America, 1994), 17–26.

33. E. Fisher, "*Mysterium Tremendum:* Catholic Grapplings with the *Shoah* and Its Theological Implications," in *Contemporary Christian Religious Responses to the Shoah,* ed. Steven L. Jacobs (Lanham, Md.: University Press of America, 1993), 59– 84. See also my most recent reflections on the subject in a two-part article for *The Priest* issued by Our Sunday Visitor Publications (Part I: August 1995, 11–15; Part II: September 1995, 34–38).

5

Post-Holocaust Jewish Reflections on German Theology

Susannah Heschel

As the daughter of a refugee from Hitler's Europe, I grew up in two worlds. Physically, we lived on the Upper West Side of New York City. Spiritually, my parents were living in Europe. My father was a professor of Jewish philosophy, my mother was a pianist, and our household was quiet and academic. Nearly all of my parents' friends were Jewish scholars who had escaped Europe, and they loved to tell stories about prewar Jewish life, or reminisce about professors, colleagues, and rabbis they had known in Europe. There was some sadness in that they were describing a world that no longer existed, but their stories had such vividness that they seemed to keep that world alive.

There is a popular myth that American Jews only began talking about the Holocaust during the late 1960s, after Israel's military victory in the Six Day War alleviated the anxiety of public discussions of Jewish powerlessness. That myth pertains only to a fragment of the Jewish community. For those in the refugee community, the Holocaust was omnipresent, constantly discussed, albeit not in the language of modern-day America. It was discussed by not using the word *Holocaust*. Instead, my parents and their friends and family talked allusively about "what happened," or simply left a blank in their sentences in the places where we today might use the word *Holocaust* or *Shoah*. "What happened" was so terrible, it could not be put into language, nor even expressed or described directly. A sigh or an "Achh" sufficed. Everyone knew what was meant.

Within my own family certain horrors stood out. The murder of family members was so terrible that it was discussed only rarely, perhaps once in five years, and then only in whispers. Mentioning even briefly what had happened to my grandmother, for example, caused a depression that hung over our household for days. More easily and frequently discussed, with a tone of outrage, was the involvement of German professors in the Nazi movement. The publication in 1946 of Max Weinreich's book *Hitler's Professors* was a profound shock to the Jewish refugee academic community who had trained in what they had viewed as the greatest academic centers of the universe, Germany's universities. Imagine the earthquake in their lives when they read Weinreich's details of the nazification of the universities and of the enthusiasm and collaboration of many of the most distinguished German scholars with Hitler's antisemitism, including their own teachers.

Part of the European ethos that was central to my growing up years was the notion that a professor was the noblest figure in any society. Scholarship was the greatest calling and intellectuals bore an aura of the elect. That they should so corrupt themselves was vile, and that antisemitism should infiltrate their work was the greatest pollution. Such were the attitudes I imbibed at home; they have determined, to a great extent, the agenda of my own research and the emotional reactions I have had to the discoveries I have made about antisemitism among German Protestant theologians.

A personal turning point came during my first year of college, when I took "Introduction to the New Testament." We were assigned to read Rudolf Bultmann's famous book, *Primitive Christianity in its Contemporary Setting,* which was originally published as *Das Urchristentum im Rahmen der antiken Religionen* in 1944.[1] The book was presented by our professor as a great classic of historical scholarship, describing the emergence of the Jesus movement into full-fledged Christianity. It seemed that I was the only one who reacted to the book's depiction of first-century Judaism's "legalism" as if I were reading an antisemitic tract.[2] The depiction of a degenerate "late" Judaism, in contrast to the religious revival allegedly brought about by Jesus and Paul, was accepted as historical fact by my fellow students and by our professor. According to Bultmann, the Jews' observance of the commandments "Meant making life an intolerable burden" (66); "The motive of ethics was obedience" (68); "The ritual commandments having lost their original meaning, man's relation to God was inevitably conceived in legalistic terms" (68); "For Judaism God has become remote" (79). By contrast, Jesus was "a tremendous protest against contemporary Jewish legalism" (72); in Jesus' teachings, God is concerned with "inner motive" (72); Jesus "brought God out of the false transcendence to which he had been relegated by Judaism and made him near at hand again" (77); Jesus taught that "God is near, and hears the petitions we address to him as a father listens to the requests of his children" (77–78). To me, each of Bultmann's derogatory statements about Judaism, its rabbis, God, and commandments, felt like a personal assault, as if my body and my life were being hacked up by his words.

While fascinated with the period of Second Temple Judaism, I turned away from graduate work in that field because the scholarship was so strongly dominated by figures such as Bultmann, Julius Wellhausen, Emil Schürer, Adolf von Harnack, Gerhard Kittel, and so many other German Lutherans whose biases against Judaism had stamped seemingly all aspects of their work. Instead, I turned to the history of modern scholarship, asking why it had taken shape as it had. One of the great, joyous moments of my graduate studies came when I discovered the writings of German Jewish theologians of the late nineteenth and early twentieth centuries, who had defended Judaism and attacked German Christian scholars for the untenable stereotypes of Judaism that had poisoned their work.

The first and strongest of those Jewish figures was Abraham Geiger, a household name when I was growing up because he was one of the founders of the Reform movement and a major figure in the *Wissenschaft des Judentums,* the scholarly study of Judaism that emerged in Germany during the nineteenth century. Geiger, I discovered, had closely monitored the writings of contemporary Christian theologians, criticizing their misrepresentations of Judaism and misreadings of Jewish sources. He noted that their unjustified identification of the Pharisees as hypocrites had led to all sorts of twisted readings of ancient texts, just as the failure of New Testament scholars to read rabbinic literature left them unable to place gospel passages within what he saw as their proper context.

Geiger's publications were widely read by German Christian theologians, who reviewed his books in their journals and argued with his conclusions in their books; indeed, Wellhausen devoted a series of lectures, later published as a book, to refuting Geiger's claims regarding the origins and nature of the Pharisees and Sadducees.[3] Clearly, Geiger's work was widely known to contemporary Christian theologians and made a strong impact, even if it evoked an angry response. The anger, it seemed to me, arose from the challenge posed by Geiger's arguments regarding Jesus' Jewishness to Christian claims of Jesus' uniqueness and originality. According to Geiger, Jesus was a Pharisee who preached the typical religious and moral teachings of the Pharisaic movement. If anything, Jesus was a somewhat conservative Pharisee, colored most likely by his background in the Galilee, a region characterized, according to Geiger, by its simple, lower-class, nationalistic, uneducated people. In a phrase that made Geiger notorious among Christian theologians, he wrote that Jesus "did not utter a new thought, nor did he break down the barriers of nationality. . . . He did not abolish any part of Judaism; he was a Pharisee who walked in the way of Hillel."[4]

The idea that Jesus might be identified with the Pharisees, those exemplars of hypocrisy, legalism, and religious degeneracy, was an outrage to Christian theologians, who minced no words in condemning Geiger. The difficulty, however, was refuting Geiger's evidence. The parallels he demonstrated between Jesus' words and those of the rabbis were striking and conclusive. Yet if Jesus said nothing new, what sort of Christian theological claims could be based on his ministry? Further, if liberal Protestants were true to their claim of looking for the faith *of* Jesus, rather than the faith *about* Jesus, what would it mean to discover that Jesus' faith was Pharisaic Judaism? From Geiger's perspective, Pharisaic Judaism was the liberal, progressive tradition that democratized the aristocratic tendencies of the priestly prerogatives. Only later, with the rise of Christian persecutions of Judaism, Geiger argued, did Pharisaic liberalism deteriorate into a rigid *halakhic* religion. The Reform Judaism that he helped to establish was, for Geiger, a revival and restoration of Pharisaic liberalism. Thus, if a Christian of the nineteenth century truly wanted to find the faith of Jesus, namely, Pharisaic Judaism, the best place to find it would be not among the Christian dogma constructed about Jesus, but among modern Reform Jews of Germany.

Geiger was not alone in claiming Jesus as a Jew, a rabbi, and even a Pharisee. Indeed, most modern Jewish theologians and rabbis have sought to emphasize Jesus' Jewishness as a way to smooth Jewish entry into Christian society; this was, after all, the era of Jewish emancipation and secularization. Yet the more Jewish they depicted Jesus, the more annoyed their Christian colleagues became. Yes, Jesus was a Jew, they acknowledged, but he was an exceptional Jew. Ernest Renan, author of the most widely read *Life of Jesus* published during the nineteenth century, cited Geiger's work on the Pharisees positively, agreeing that Jesus' life had to be placed within the context of its historical setting. Renan, however, then proceeded to describe the Pharisees negatively and define Jesus in contrast to them: "Jesus recognized only the religion of the heart, whilst that of the Pharisees consisted almost exclusively in observances."[5] Moreover, he wrote, "Jesus who was almost exempt from all the defects of his race, was led against his will into making use of the style used by all the polemics," and then continues, "One of the most prominent faults of the Jewish race is its bitterness in controversy, and the abusive tone which it always throws into it."[6] While Jesus began by trying to reform Judaism, he eventually gave up, Renan continued, and after visiting Jerusalem, "he appears no more as a Jewish reformer, but as a destroyer of Judaism . . . Jesus was no longer a Jew."[7]

Geiger criticized Renan in an *Open Letter* that he published as an appendix to one of his most popular books, a survey of Jewish history. Geiger wrote that Judaism functions in Renan's work, and that of other New Testament scholars, as a negative background to "let the picture of a rising Christianity stand out in more dazzling brilliancy," and as the brunt of blame for "whatever in Christianity did not please them."[8] Geiger identified the technique in the approach of most of the Christian New Testament scholars writing during the 1860s and 1870s, a period that inaugurated a revival of interest in describing the historical background of the New Testament.[9] Although New Testament scholars cited the research of Geiger and other Jewish historians, they consistently elevated Jesus as a superior religious figure whose message constituted not a reform within Judaism, but an utter rejection of it.

During the course of my research on Geiger and the reception of his work among Christian theologians of the nineteenth century, I happened to visit a library in Berlin belonging to the Center for Research on Antisemitism, part of the Technical University. While browsing in the library's collection, I came across several volumes of essays by prominent Protestant theologians published in Germany during the Second World War. Curious to see what they were writing during those difficult years, I began to read and discovered vicious antisemitic propaganda. The volumes, I noticed, had been published by the "Institute for the Study of Jewish Influence on German Religious Life," and edited by a professor of New Testament at the University of Jena, Walter Grundmann. I had never heard of that institute and began to look for information about it in the numerous and thorough histories of the churches during the Third Reich. I found only one or two small footnotes that mentioned the Institute, which was founded, I read, in 1939 by members of the German Christian movement.

Curious to know more, I read all the publications by Walter Grundmann that I could find in libraries in Germany and the United States. What I encountered was a theologian bent on creating a synthesis of National Socialism with Christianity, with a particular emphasis on "proving" the antisemitic pedigree of Christian theology. Jesus was no Jew, according to Grundmann; he was an Aryan whose mission was the destruction of Judaism, a violent and dangerous religion. Moreover, nothing Jewish had a right to exist within Christian auspices, and Grundmann and his colleagues not only rejected the Old Testament from the Christian canon, but issued a "de-Judaized" New Testament and hymnal, purged of all Jewish references and Hebrew words.[10]

After three summers at the Wiener Library at Tel Aviv University, a superb collection of German antisemitic materials, I was able to trace the development of such arguments within German Protestant theological circles long before Hitler came to power. The arguments went back and forth: whether the Old Testament had a place in the canon, and whether Jesus was a Jew or an Aryan. By the 1930s, of course, the debates became far more significant. The self-proclaimed *Deutsche Christen* ("German Christians") declared their solidarity with the Hitler regime and successfully worked to apply the Aryan Paragraph to the many regional churches they came to control. While most historians had claimed that these Aryan Christians lost influence and disintegrated as a group by the end of 1934, my discovery of the Institute, which had been founded in 1939, led me to question that claim.

During the summer of 1991 I was able to spend several weeks in Germany, examining archival materials at the Central Archives of the Protestant Church, located in the former West Berlin. Going through papers from the Nazi era, I found documents concerning the Institute, including discussions among high church officials about its establishment in the spring of 1939 and evidence that its funding had come from regional churches, funneled through church headquarters in Berlin. At a conference on the theological faculties during the Third Reich, I asked one of Germany's most distinguished church historians, who has written extensively on the Nazi era, if any of the Institute's own archives were extant. No, he told me, everything had been destroyed. Undaunted, I still hoped to find at least some traces that might indicate who had been involved in its work, and the extent of its activities, by visiting the church archives of the state of Thuringia, where the Institute's headquarters had been located. When I arrived at the archives in Eisenach in the summer of 1991, I was the first American and the first Jew the archivist had ever met. My area of interest was of interest to him as well, since he had studied theology during the postwar years with Walter Grundmann and other theologians from the Institute. He was reluctant, though, to show me materials. Eventually, he came up with a few folders containing letters and other miscellaneous documents by Grundmann and others. What I read confirmed the worst.

The Institute was founded at the initiative of a wide group of bishops, pastors, and professors, and functioned actively from 1939 to 1945, producing a de-Judaized hymnal and New Testament, a catechism and various other educational materials proclaiming Jesus' opposition to Judaism and status as an Aryan, and a host of pamphlets and books describing the horrors of Judaism. For example, in 1942, Grundmann published a book, *The Religious Face of Judaism,* in which he declared, "a healthy Volk must and will reject Judaism in every form. . . . If someone is upset about Germany's attitude toward Judaism, Germany has the historical justification and historical authorization for the fight against Judaism on its side! . . . So this work serves the great fateful fight of the German nation for its political and economic, spiritual and cultural and also its religious freedom."[11] In a series of pamphlets and articles designed to justify the war from a Christian perspective, Grundmann argued that Jews were violent and dangerous: "We know that Jewry wants the destruction [*Vernichtung*] of Germany."[12] "To this very day Jewry persecutes Jesus, and all who follow him, with unreconcilable hatred."[13]

Just holding those documents in my hands was a horror; when the archivist began justifying the work of the Institute, I began to tremble uncontrollably. Grundmann was no antisemite, he told me; he was simply describing Judaism objectively, as a scholar. Moreover, what the Germans had done to the Jews was not as bad as what the Americans had done to the Germans. What, precisely, was that, I asked him. "You wanted to drop the atom bomb on Berlin," he answered. "But we never did," I replied. "Yes, but just to have had the idea," he said to me, with a satisfied smile. What is there to say to someone like this? My body answered for me; the next morning I woke up covered with hives.

Over the course of subsequent years, I made quite a few trips to Eisenach, always discovering new material. The archives revealed that membership in the Institute included dozens and dozens of theology professors, drawn from nearly all the major universities of the Reich, from Kiel and Greifswald in the north, to Vienna in the south. By 1941, a branch of the Institute was opened in Rumania, apparently to offer a de-Judaized Christianity to ethnic Germans living there. The Institute sponsored numerous conferences at which distinguished professors delivered learned papers. Georg Bertram, professor at Giessen, contended that the goal of Jewish assimilation is to decompose a society and then take control over it, as seen in the Greco-Roman world as well as in modern Germany.[14] Johannes Leipoldt, professor of New Testament at the University of Leipzig, demonstrated the ways Jesus had fought against Jewish and Pharisaic ideas of his day.[15] Wolf Meyer-Erlach, professor of practical theology at the University of Jena, argued that Judaism had poisoned England through the Reformation, which is why England launched a war against Germany: "Today we know that through the so-called English Reformation . . . Christianity was not only 'englandized,' but that England's spirit and England's soul was deeply judaized. . . . England is the true Israel."[16]

Almost immediately upon being founded, the Institute's members got busy, organized into working groups. One of the most enthusiastic members was Johannes Hempel, professor of Old Testament at the University of Berlin and editor of the *Zeitschrift für alttestamentliche Wissenschaft*. Together with Karl Euler, instructor of Old Testament in Giessen, Hempel served as leader of the Institute's committee to investigate the alleged opposition between Aryan and Semitic religiosity. Two faculty members at Heidelberg, Rudi Paret,[17] professor of Islam, and Erwin Kiefer,[18] instructor in Hebrew, directed a committee to study hostility toward Jews and Judaism from the Greco-Roman world of late antiquity until the sixteenth century. Another group, composed of New Testament scholars, sought to develop a volkish-racist methodology for studying the early development of Christianity; the group included Gerhard Delling (NT, Leipzig),[19] Herbert Preisker (NT, Breslau),[20] Carl Schneider (NT, Königsberg),[21] Rudolf Meyer (NT, Leipzig),[22] Georg Bertram (NT, Giessen),[23] and Grundmann. Both pastors and professors worked together to produce one of the most notorious Institute publications, the de-Judaized version of the New Testament, which was published in 1940.[24] In it all references to Jesus' Jewishness were eradicated, including his descent from Old Testament figures, mention of Jerusalem and the Temple, and any positive references to Jews. For example, John 4: 22, "Salvation comes from the Jews," was changed to the famous antisemitic slogan, "The Jews are our misfortune." Bethlehem was shifted to Galilee, reflecting Grundmann's claim that Jesus could not have been a racial Jew because the Galilee was populated by Gentiles, including Aryans.[25]

That same year the Institute published a hymnal, purged of all Jewish references. Hebrew words such as *hallelujah, amen, hosanna,* and *zebaoth* were eliminated from all the hymns, as were references to Jerusalem and Zion.[26] Both the hymnal and New Testament sold all one hundred thousand copies of the first press run prior to publication; copies were purchased by churches in cities and villages throughout the Reich.[27] By 1943, two hundred thousand copies of the Institute's New Testament were in print.

The archives further revealed that the Institute's financial situation was never a problem. Its publications generated income and whenever it wrote to Berlin church headquarters requesting additional funds, its request was immediately granted. Records indicated that in 1943, in the midst of the wartime strains, the Institute actually enjoyed a surplus.[28]

The Institute continued to flourish through the war years. Grundmann, who served as academic director, was drafted into military service in 1943, and was replaced by Georg Bertram. Yet even as the war came to an end, both Bertram and Grundmann made efforts to keep the Institute open on the grounds that its work was scientific and scholarly, not propagandistic or political. Their requests for funding from the Church of Thuringia were denied, however. While Grundmann, after the war, lost his professorship at the University of Jena because of his early entry into the Nazi Party, no effort was made by the church or the universities to censure him or other members of the Institute on the basis of their antisemitic propaganda work in support of the regime. Indeed, Grundmann himself was replaced by another Institute member, Herbert Preisker, who had been professor of New Testament at the University of Breslau. Another former Institute member, Rudolf Meyer, was also appointed at Jena, and at other universities, Institute members retained their professorships or were unhindered in achieving new appointments. Bertram, for example, lost his professorship after American military authorities closed the University of Giessen from 1945 to 1954 because of its nazified faculty. But Bertram had no difficulty securing a position as instructor of Hebrew at the University of Frankfurt.

In his meetings with church authorities after the war, Grundmann was questioned about his involvement with the *Deutsche Christen* movement, but never about his antisemitism. The discussions focused instead on Grundmann's willingness to accept the theological terms of the Barmen Declaration, a 1934 statement by Confessing Church (a group founded to oppose the *Deutsche Christen*) pastors that proclaimed the supremacy of divine over temporal authority. He was retained for service in the Thuringian church, and after several years of serving as a rural pastor, was appointed rector of a teachers' seminary in Eisenach and as instructor at the theological seminary in Leipzig, both within the German Democratic Republic. He continued his work as a New Testament scholar, retained his membership in prestigious societies for biblical studies, and published extensively in the postwar years. Indeed, nearly every pastor and theology student I have met in Germany has at least one, if not several, of Grundmann's gospel commentaries, published in the 1960s, on his or her shelf; they are the standard works to consult in preparing a sermon. Naturally, Grundmann's postwar writings avoid certain terms, such as the word *Aryan,* but they continue to present Jesus' message in opposition to Judaism, depicting Judaism as a violent, dangerous religion.

In the typescript of an unpublished 1969 memoir that I found in the archives, Grundmann mentions in passing that he might have erred during the Third Reich: "We attempted to pose the questions raised by the period and not to avoid them. I admit that we in so doing made [big—this word is crossed out in the manuscript] mistakes." He claims in his memoir that he had stood in real danger of Nazi authorities as the result of his writings criticizing the Nazi theorist Alfred Rosenberg, a claim that is utterly unsubstantiated by the evidence. Although Grundmann had criticized Rosenberg's pro-pagan stance in the early 1930s, his comments were mild, never arousing antagonism that would hinder his career. If anything, the Nazi government ministries actively supported his advancement, including his appointment in 1938 to a professorship.

Perhaps most disturbing to me was discovering the nature of the "opposition" to the Institute from other theologians. While they opposed the Institute's radical changes of traditional Christianity, they did not object to its antisemitism. If anything, they evoked their own antisemitism in their very objections. For example, the distinguished New Testament professor at Marburg, Hans von Soden, who was active in the Confessing Church, wrote that the Institute's revisions of the hymnal and New Testament constituted a "spiritual Judaization" of the church; Jewishness, for von Soden, was a materialistic, antispiritual theology, precisely the sort of spirit that permeated the Institute. Even in rejecting the Institute's elimination of the Old Testament from the Christian canon, Confessing Church members appealed to anti-Judaism. They argued that the Old Testament should not be eliminated because it is not a Jewish book, it is an anti-Jewish book—look, for example, at the prophetic denunciations of Israel. Thus, both groups, the *Deutsche Christen* and the Confessing Church, could agree: anything Jewish has no place in Christianity; the question was determining whether the Old Testament was Jewish or anti-Jewish.

What do these statements of theologians have to do with the actual murder of Jews, I am sometimes asked. After all, Hitler's plans were conceived and carried out by soldiers, not ministers. The theology formulated by the Institute indicates, of course, the utter corruption of its members and of the hierarchy of the church, which not only failed to stop the propaganda, but actually supported it. Through the Institute, the church attempted to create a niche for itself within a Nazi regime that had little use for theologians. To become important, the theologians exploited one of their self-proclaimed strengths: their expertise as scholars of Judaism. Rather than confine that expertise to the academic realm, the Institute became a vehicle to disseminate propaganda in support of the persecution of the Jews. Certainly, an antisemitic sermon from a pastor, delivered each week from the chancel, carried a far greater impact on the moral vision of the public than the weekly newspaper, *Der Stürmer,* with its semipornographic offenses to bourgeois values.

On the other hand, the Institute should not be seen solely in terms of the politics of the Third Reich. Rather, its roots lie deep in a German tradition of Protestant New Testament scholarship that presented Jesus in opposition to the Judaism of his day, rather than as representative of it, as Jewish historians such as Geiger had suggested. Geiger's depiction of Jesus as a Jew was unacceptable, because of the terrible dilemma it created in undermining Christian claims to originality. Christian theological anti-Judaism, in other words, is not only the product of negative attitudes toward Jews and Judaism, but the result of unresolved dilemmas within Christian theology. Dissatisfied with the implications of a Jewish Jesus preaching the standard rabbinic teachings of his day, Judaism was projected as the supposed barrier to the kind of Christian theology liberal Protestants longed for. Judaism was fetishized as a degenerate, legalistic religion to distract from the failure of Christian theology to maintain a coherent claim to originality and uniqueness. So long as Christianity, particularly in its liberal Protestant manifestation, is unable to decide upon an original message, or accept the unoriginality of the teachings of Jesus, it will rely upon anti-Jewish maneuvers to constitute its theological significance. Ultimately, if the content of Jesus' teachings were unavoidably recognized as Jewish, then he might be "saved" for Christians by insisting that his racial identity was Aryan.

People often ask me how I can bear studying such ugly material. For the first few years, it was difficult, and I reacted psychosomatically, with trembling and headaches. Emotionally, it was a terrible strain; I was depressed and felt that filth was being poured over my soul when I read those documents. On the other hand, I've grown up wondering why I was born into this generation. A few years earlier, and I would have been killed along with the rest of my family. In exchange for the extraordinary gift of a late birth, should I not be willing to immerse myself in the filth of the documents and the history they represent?

But the gift of a late birth also means that I am aware that the story does not end in 1945. The postwar years in the German theological community have brought two trends, one that continues the antisemitism of the past, even the theological tendencies of the *Deutsche Christen,* and one that makes the overcoming of antisemitism its central preoccupation. Both tendencies coexist. One of the great shocks I experienced came when I began

reading the work of German feminist theologians. Not only did they perpetuate the same language of a Jewish "legalism" in contrast to a Jesus of
"love," but many blamed Judaism—especially the Hebrew Bible and the
Talmud—for patriarchy, war, violence, and sexual abuse of women. Worst
of all were statements drawing analogies between the Nazis' demands for
blind obedience to orders and the Jews' adherence to divine commandments; both, in the words of Christa Mulack, are ethics of "obedience to
authority" that typify patriarchy, of which Nazism is one manifestation.[29]

On the other hand, Germany today has some of the best Protestant theologians working on eradicating anti-Judaism from Christian theology and
creating a christology that also affirms Judaism. There is no one in the mul-
ticultural United States comparable to the great Friedrich Wilhelm Mar-
quardt, of Berlin's Free University, and the multivolume systematic
christology he has published. Nor are there as many New Testament scholars and students in the United States who make a positive relation between
Jesus and first-century Judaism so central to their work. It is remarkable
how many German students preparing to become ministers spend a year
or two studying in Israel, and how many of them declare that the central
issue of their lives is eradicating antisemitism.

Throughout my life I have fantasized about what my life might have been
like if "what happened" had not occurred. What if my father had remained
as a professor in Berlin, and I had been born and raised there? Would I
have studied at a German university, and would I have studied Second Temple Judaism or theology? Would the traditions of Wellhausen, Schürer, and
Harnack have changed if Hitler had not come to power? What if the *Deutsche Christen* and their Aryan Jesus had been laughed into oblivion? Would
today's Christian feminist theologians in Germany be speaking differently
had they grown up side by side with Jewish women engaged in parallel
feminist struggles?

All this is a daydream borne of a wish that history had proceded differently. Instead of growing up among people I knew as refugees, I would have
grown up among them in their own world. As enticing as that fantasy may
be, the more deeply involved I become in my research, the more I realize
the inevitability of what did happen. Ideas have consequences, and theological defamations are the ultimate victory for the forces of evil: once Jesus
was made to join the side of the antisemites, any moral qualms could be
lifted and the murder of Jews could become an act of *imitatio dei*.

NOTES

1. Rudolf Bultmann, *Primitive Christianity in its Contemporary Setting*, trans.
R. H. Fuller (New York: Meridian Books, 1956).

2. Peter von der Osten-Sacken, "Rückzug ins Wesen und aus der Geschichte,"
Wissenschaft und Praxis in Kirche und Gesellschaft 67 (1978), 106–22; Dieter

Georgi, "The Interest in Life of Jesus Theology as a Paradigm for the Social History of Biblical Criticism," *Harvard Theological Review* 85:1 (1992): 51–83.

3. Julius Wellhausen, *Die Pharisäer und die Sadducäer* (Greifswald: Bamberg, 1874).

4. Abraham Geiger, *Das Judentum und seine Geschichte* (Breslau: Skutsch, 1865), 117–18.

5. Ernest Renan, *Life of Jesus* (New York: Peter Eckler, 1925), 300.

6. Ibid., 325.

7. Ibid., 224–25.

8. Geiger, *Das Judentum,* 198.

9. Theodor Keim, *Geschichte Jesu von Nazara* (Zürich: Orell, Füßli & Co., 1867); Adolf Hausrath, *Neutestamentliche Zeitgeschichte. Erster Teil: Die Zeit Jesu* (Heidelberg, 1868); Emil Schürer, *Lehrbuch der neutestamentlichen Zeitgeschichte,* 1874; 2d ed., published as *Geschichte des jüdischen Volkes im Zeitalter Jesu Christi* (Leipzig: J.C. Hinrichs'sche Buchhandlung, 1886–87; 3d ed., 1898).

10. Grundmann joined the Nazi Party (NSDAP) on December 1, 1930; membership number 382544; Berlin Document Center (BDC), Grundmann materials. On April 1, 1934, he became a supporting member of the SS, with membership number 1032691; Thüringisches Hauptstaatsarchiv Weimar. *Personalakte* Walter Grundmann.

11. Walter Grundmann and Karl Friedrich Euler, *Das religiöse Gesicht des Judentums: Entstehung und Art* (Leipzig: G. Wigand, 1942), foreword.

12. "Das Heil Kommt von den Juden: Eine Schicksalsfrage an die Christen deutscher Nation," *Deutsche Frömmigkeit* 9 (September 1938), 1.

13. *Deutsche mit Gott: Ein deutsches Glaubensbuch* (Weimar: Verlag Deutsche Christen), 46.

14. Georg Bertram, "Philo und die judische Propaganda in der antiken Welt," *Christentum und Judentum; Studien zur Erforschung ihres gegenseitigen Verhältnisses.* Sitzungsberichte der ersten Arbeitstagung des Institutes zur Erforschung des jüdischen Einflusses auf das deutsche kirchliche Leben vom 1. bis 3. März 1940 in Wittenberg, hrsg. Walter Grundmann (Leipzig: G. Wigand, 1940), 79–106.

15. Johannes Leipoldt, "Jesus und das Judentum," *Christentum und Judentum,* 29–52.

16. Wolf Meyer-Erlach, *Der Einfluss der Juden auf das englische Christentum* (Weimar: Verlag Deutsche Christen, 1940), 4, 29.

17. Rudi Paret joined the NSDAP on July 20, 1934. BDC, Paret materials.

18. Erwin Kiefer joined the NSDAP on July 10, 1937; University of Heidelberg archive, Bestand PA-B3099: *Personalakten* Erwin Kiefer.

19. Gerhard Delling became professor of New Testament at the University of Greifswald in 1947.

20. Herbert Preisker succeeded Grundmann as professor of New Testament at the University of Jena in 1947.

21. Carl Schneider was director of the *Evangelische Akademie* in Enkenbach after the war.

22. Rudolf Meyer was appointed professor of Old Testament at the University of Jena in 1947.

23. Bertram joined the *NS Lehrerbund* on December 1, 1933; membership 227288. BDC, Bertram materials.

24. *Die Botschaft Gottes* (Weimar: Verlag Deutsche Christen, 1940).

25. Walter Grundmann, *Jesus der Galiläer und das Judentum* (Leipzig: Wigand, 1940).

26. *Grosser Gott Wir Loben Dich* (Weimar: Verlag Deutsche Christen, 1940).

27. Landeskirchen Archive (LKA) Eisenach, Akten betreffend *Grosser Gott Wir Loben Dich*.

28. LKA Eisenach, Akten betr. das Institut zur Erforschung und Beseitigung des jüdischen Einflusses auf das deutsche kirchliche Leben.

29. Christa Mulack, *Jesus: der Gesalbte der Frauen.* (Stuttgart: Kreuz Verlag, 1987), 155–56.

Part Two

ENCOUNTERS

6

How My Mind Has Changed

Alan L. Berger

Reb Nachman of Bratslav, the great-grandson of the Ba'al Shem Tov, founder of eighteenth-century Hasidism, reminds his listeners that, "No heart is as whole as a broken heart." As a mystic, Nachman embraced paradox, but not simply for appearance sake. Rather, he wished to point to the complexity of human existence and the imperative of acting against despair despite despair. His admonition, "Jews, do not despair!" was written on the shul of the Bratzlaver Hasidim in the Warsaw Ghetto. As a teacher of the Holocaust—how odd and impossible that phrase seems—I interpret Nachman's comment as a warrant for attempting to seek a *tikkun olam,* repair or mending of the world, in so far as this is possible. Following the enormous despair over God, humanity, and modernity unleashed by the *Shoah,* this repair can only be partial. Further, it can only be undertaken after the worst is known. Any call for hope or any "lessons" taught that either ignore the facts or are not based on knowledge of the doom of the Jewish people during the *Shoah* will, in turn, yield only false hope or what theologians term *cheap grace.* But this is to jump ahead in the discussion.

TEACHING THE HOLOCAUST: AN AUTOBIOGRAPHICAL NOTE

Why or, rather, how can I teach the Holocaust? Perhaps more appropriate still is the question, Can the Holocaust be taught? This question should be asked by all who undertake the task and it serves to underscore the crucial and transforming relationship between data and teacher. There are reasons both conscious and subconscious that impel the attempt to confront the kingdom of night. Autobiography is at least as important as intellectual concern. Or is it the other way around? My wife is the daughter of survivors, and our children are third-generation witnesses. Although I had read much of Elie Wiesel's work, it was only after my first trip to Israel—prior to my marriage—that I began systematic inquiry into the fate of the Jewish people, and the world, during the Holocaust. Over twenty-five years have passed since pilgrimages to Yad Vashem and Kibbutz Lohamei Haghetaot (Ghetto Fighters Kibbutz) helped clarify what had been an inchoate feeling about the relationship of the Holocaust to contemporary Jewish identity.

Much later, in Europe, my wife and I took our three young children to see Mathausen, one of the three camps where their grandfather had been imprisoned. On yet another journey, she and I traveled to Buchenwald, a second place of death that her father survived. These encounters shatter the soul. With trembling hands, I write my name and the date in Hebrew in the visitors' book—a feeble but overwhelmingly important gesture. A short time after, I go to the "Little Camp" (*Kine Kamp*). Set apart from the main portion of Buchenwald, this is the place where the Jewish inmates were confined. While there, I struggle to remove a portion of the cement post in which the ceramic housing was embedded through which electricity ran, thus ensuring that anyone who came into contact with the barbed wire would be electrocuted. Full of rage, I furiously work at my task. Writing about the experience afterward, I recall feeling both rage and a sense of holiness. Holy rage. Perhaps that is what best describes my feeling. Soon after, upon leaving Germany, the airport luggage inspectors ask about the strange objects appearing on the x-ray. Buchenwald, I tell them. They nod and smile, apparently relieved that their country is rid of an unwanted reminder.

Several years later, we are in Slovakia to visit my wife's natal city of Topolcony. Searching for the vanished Jewish section, we encounter a young Slovakian woman who confides that while she knows of Israel, she has never before seen Jews. An old man in the city square cannot remember that any Jews had lived in the town. Nor, it seems, can he remember Hitler. All that remains of the Jewish presence is a cemetery whose main entrance is guarded by a rusted and locked fence behind which is a growling dog and several scrawny chickens. Some weeks later, having returned to America, I take the members of my Jewish Studies Senior Seminar to the United States Holocaust Memorial Museum. There, in the list of destroyed Jewish communities, I see the name Topolcony.

My trips to the sites of labor and death camps deepened my own level of engagement with the *Shoah*. So, too, did our visit to the now *judenrein* Slovakian town where my wife was born. On the institutional level, I served two consecutive terms as chairperson of the Annual Scholars' Conference on the Holocaust and the Churches. Reading the various proposals, putting programs together, and editing the papers for publication convinced me that the story of the Holocaust had begun to penetrate at least certain strata of American culture. The issue is, however, complex. Its outline can be seen in two questions: How to teach about the *Shoah* without trivializing or distorting, and how Holocaust memory will be shaped by the generations yet to come.

QUESTIONS: THEN

From the beginning, a myriad of questions, which I subsequently began to address in my research and writing, arose. These issues concerned history, Jewish-Christian relations, pedagogy, and theology. In fact, the proximate intellectual impetus for my offering a course on the Holocaust, the first such credit course ever taught at Syracuse University, came from a symposium that I arranged under the auspices of the religion department. The participants, Emil Fackenheim and Franklin H. Littell, spoke about Jewish and Christian responses to the *Shoah* both during and after the event. Listening to the tapes in order to edit the proceedings, I returned repeatedly to the central issues raised by the two thinkers: the reactions of the victims during and after the catastrophe; the collapse of pre-Holocaust distinctions between sacred and profane behavior; and the "credibility crisis" of Christianity. I realized that the questions raised by the symposiasts, as well as my own queries, demanded to be heard, if not answered, by students. For many of them, this would likely be the first and last opportunity to confront what happens in a society whose citizens exercise skills independently of the harm they may cause, and what happens in a society in which allegiance to the leader is prized above commitment to compassion.

EARLY WRITINGS

My first writing on the *Shoah* was an article entitled "Academia and the Holocaust." In it I raised the question of the relationship between skills and values as this issue is illuminated by the assumptions of university teaching that stresses an objectivity too frequently not anchored in ethics. The issue for university professors is to keep alive the vision of the relationship between teaching and being human. The appalling moral failure of German academics during the Holocaust, most of whom were ardent supporters of Nazism or, perhaps worse, interested in doing anything to keep their jobs, stands as a warning. I believed then, and more so now, that teaching and learning need to be humanizing experiences. Professional competence is necessary, but not sufficient. Those who teach the Holocaust also need to recognize that being human requires at least as much competence. Nearly twenty years have passed since I wrote this article. My position remains the same. But American appropriation of the Holocaust has led me to extend my original pedagogical questions to include the issue of how to keep the *Shoah* from becoming normalized.

Teaching emotionally charged and theologically significant material requires a careful articulation of the relationship between unique and universal dimensions of the Holocaust. My Holocaust syllabus states that, "The red thread running throughout the course and linking its parts [pre-Holocaust and post-Holocaust world] is a twofold question: Why the Jews? Why does the Holocaust have universal implications?" Increasingly, my teaching and the questions I ask stress the relationship between the Jewish experience and the fate that may await any particular group. Or, in the words of Yehuda Bauer, "Who knows who the 'Jews' will be the next time?" Student responses to the course indicate that both Jews and Christians have been deeply touched. Some sample responses will serve to illustrate this contention. For example, one student wrote, "This course has made me confront my own values morally. At times I could not handle it, but I have learned that what I can do is . . . take responsibility." Another student wrote that, "Even though you and I were not personally involved with the Holocaust, we need to react in a personal way, on a one-to-one basis where possible."

One non-Jewish student appears to have traveled the farthest distance conceptually. Initially, she reported feeling resentful of her Jewish friends for making such a "big deal out of having distant relatives killed in the war." She, too, had lost an uncle who fought in the American army. By the end of the course, however, this same student wrote that she now "realized the difference between dying for your country because you have a cause and a choice, and being treated as an animal; humiliated, [deprived] of pride and [being the victim of a ferocious assault] on one's sense of self-integrity and control. I do not think there is any comparison."

A core question in my teaching and writing involves the relationship between the covenant and the Holocaust. Literature became the entry into the question of whether the covenant is still valid after Auschwitz. If so, what type of covenant? What of the role of the covenantal partners? Further, questions of theodicy led to reflections on the nature of evil and suffering. In my next article I turned to the fiction of Hugh Nissenson, a Jewish American author whose works wrestle with the continuing plausibility of the covenant after the *Shoah*. At this stage my questions were those asked by Nissenson's characters; these queries focused on the tension between faith and doubt and the permanence of evil. My students' reactions mirrored the covenantal conflict portrayed in Nissenson's various protagonists. For example, at the end of the course one student wrote, "How much more punishment can God's chosen people take?" Yet another student, however, found her faith affirmed by the *Shoah*. "The Holocaust," she wrote, "makes Judaism even more important, and it makes my belief in God more important. If something so horrible can occur on this earth, you have to put your faith somewhere, and you certainly cannot believe in man. God did not build Auschwitz."

My first book on the *Shoah, Crisis and Covenant: The Holocaust in American Jewish Fiction*, dealt with literary responses to the covenantal crisis engendered by the catastrophe. Literature reaches students at deep and primal levels. Covenantal issues such as faith and doubt, the role of God in history, and identity itself are raised—and re-raised by novelists. Moreover, these questions stimulate still more queries while revealing the variety of covenantal responses to Auschwitz. For example, I discerned three types of covenantal orientations among the novelists whose works I examined: religious, secular, and symbolic literary expressions. The first conducts a *din Torah* (trial of God) and is concerned with biblical, messianic, and mystical themes while asking about the relationship between evil and the sacred. Secular writers, for their part, speak of the covenant in ethical and ethnic terms, whereas those authors dealing with post-Auschwitz Jewish existence from a symbolic perspective tend to write of the *Shoah*'s psychological and sociological implications on contemporary Jewish expression in America. Uniting all of these works is the interface between literature and theological engagement in which the novelist emerges as theologian or, better, one who asks questions having great theological resonance.

My questions also include the attitude of culture toward the Holocaust. What American culture knows and accepts of the *Shoah* is reflected in various images of survivors in American Jewish fiction. Tracing the "literary career" of the survivor reveals a journey from viewing the Holocaust under the rubric of evil and suffering, to an appreciation of the uniqueness of the tragedy and the specific role that survivors may play as reality instructors. Early literary portrayal of survivors depicted them as psychically and physically damaged people who have nothing to teach Americans and are, in fact, in need of "rescue" themselves (Edward Lewis Wallant's Sol Nazerman). This view began changing when American culture itself became more familiar with the data of Holocaust research. Subsequently, Saul Bellow's Artur Sammler emerges as a teacher of morality and ethical behavior. Sammler is a "one-eyed seer" whose experiences in the *Shoah* made him a "judge and a priest." This literary evolution caused me to raise additional questions. For example, Was American culture on the path of becoming too comfortable with, that is, trivializing, the Holocaust? In response to this issue I wrote an article entitled "Domesticating the Holocaust," which explores American literary and pedagogical attempts to deal with the *Shoah*. The second question concerned the issue of how succeeding generations would shape Holocaust memory.

QUESTIONS: NOW

As a Jewish thinker, the *Shoah* for me stands as the eternal question mark of covenantal existence. This is the consistent focus in my thinking, writing, and teaching about the Holocaust. However, my explorations have expanded. Over a decade ago I became concerned with the second generation, daughters and sons of Holocaust survivors. Consequently, I published an article entitled "Holocaust Survivors and Children in *Anya* and *Mr. Sammler's Planet.*" This work is no less concerned with the covenant than its predecessors. But my focus is on the continuing psychosocial impact of the Holocaust on survivors and their families. How do the survivors, and their children, cope with post-Auschwitz life in America? One major factor in shaping my research interest was its natural evolution from my earlier work. However, another factor here is the changing audience. Increasingly it is the grandchildren, rather than the children, of survivors who are among my students. Further, there are more non-Jewish students in my classes. These students are interested, but have very little background in Judaism. Another development in the demographics of the classroom is the appearance of grandchildren of the perpetrators.

As the torch of remembrance is passed to a new generation, Holocaust memory begins to be shaped by those who were born after the event. Linked to survivor tales, the second generation nevertheless seeks its own memory in confronting the *Shoah*. For example, texts, including visual texts, written and made by the second generation speak about the difficulty of inheriting the Holocaust, but do so in their own idiom. For instance, this generation does not employ images of stacked bodies, mounds of human hair, and piles of shoes. Rather, it speaks about accidental death or disappearance of loved ones in attempting to come to grips with theodicy. Moreover, on the psychosocial level, these second-generation texts often portray difficult parent-child relationships, a lack of psychic boundaries, and a feeling that one's own problems do not matter. On the other hand, these works also reveal what may be termed a positive Holocaust legacy: strong family connections, a desire to learn more about the tradition, and a strong commitment to learning their parents' stories. The result is a confrontation with the Holocaust that is more controlled than that of the survivor generation.

This new direction in my Holocaust research and writing is also reflected in the type of video material I show to my classes. For example, Eva Fogelman's film *Breaking the Silence* is an eloquent testimony to the necessity of survivors and the second generation working through the Holocaust. So, too, is Moshe Waldok's film *Angst.* This film reveals the degree to which humor is a response to second-generation identity. I also show and discuss second-generation filmmakers' tributes to the helpers. Here it is important to mention Pierre Sauvage's *Weapons of the Spirit.* This film raises important questions of gender and religion in teaching about helpers and rescuers. Miriam Abramowicz's *As If It Were Yesterday* also speaks about these issues in relation to children hidden during the Holocaust.

My second book, *Children of Job: American Second-Generation Witnesses to the Holocaust* treats the continuing theological and pyschosocial impact of the *Shoah*. This work provided me the opportunity to refine my own theological position while dealing further with Elie Wiesel's notion of an additional covenant, Irving Greenberg's understanding of a voluntary covenant, and Richard Rubenstein's assertion of God after the "Death of God." Further, the message of the second generation participates in Fackenheim's call for a *tikkun olam*. Moreover, the appearance of a new generation of Jewish American writers and filmmakers, having a distinctive angle of vision on the Holocaust, Jewish identity, and covenantal perspective, enables the intertwining of literature and theology in such a manner that each is illuminated both by the Jewish experience of the Holocaust and by a distinctively American culture. For instance, this relationship is nowhere more graphically presented than in Art Spiegelman's *Maus,* which tells about the *Shoah,* its continuing impact on the lives of its survivors and their offspring, via the medium of the comic book. Indeed, Spiegelman confides to an interviewer that he understands comics as meaning the comixing of words and images. There is also a generational issue here. My work has focused first on the testimonial literature of witnessing authors, next on the Holocaust works of professional novelists, and now on analyzing the writings and films of the second generation.

The central questions for me—covenant, Jewish identity, and the role of ritual in post-Auschwitz Jewish life—have remained constant. What has changed is the gradual refining of these questions and their application to different populations affected by the *Shoah*. For example, turning to the children of the *Kindertransport,* I wrote about Jewish identity and Jewish destiny as they are reflected in the refugee writings of Lore Segal and Karen Gershon. Following the development of Elie Wiesel's own novels dealing with the role of the second-generation witness, I then wrote an article that detailed how—over the course of nearly two decades—the Nobel Prize winner has written four novels, each with an increasingly detailed portrait dealing with the role and function of the second-generation witness. Similarly, seeing the Americanization of the *Shoah,* I wrote a piece that spoke about the role of the second-generation witness in American culture. The presence of these witnesses serves to keep the story and the lessons of the Holocaust circulating in America. Furthermore, these witnesses act as a check against the tendency to trivialize the *Shoah*.

From the perspective of my own work, several things remain to be done. First and foremost, there is a need for a language that the children of victims and the offspring of perpetrators can use to speak to one another. Following on this, the need for honest dialogue remains only partially fulfilled. More efforts are needed at "working through" the Holocaust. This means first of all confronting what happened, and then seeking—much in the manner of Emil Fackenheim—a repair of the world. The exclamation that "too much attention" is paid the Holocaust is frequently yet another form of Holocaust denial. No one who fully comprehends the awfulness of the *Shoah* believes that the event should be consigned to the dustbin of history. Further, an effective strategy needs to be designed to deal with those morally deranged people, antisemites and others, who deny the Holocaust happened or argue that it was far less destructive than claimed.

At this point in my own thinking, teaching, and writing about the *Shoah* I see my work moving on four basic fronts. The phenomenon of hidden children needs far more attention. This generation is really the last to have actually experienced the Holocaust. What do they have to tell us about identity, covenantal Judaism, and Christian rescuers? On the other side of the continuum, there is the third-generation witness. Far less directly involved in the Holocaust, yet willing and eager to assume its legacy, the members of this generation will shape memory of the *Shoah* in a new idiom, even while continuing to tell tales of their grandparents' survival and experiences. This generation's relationship to the merging culture of Holocaust museums bears careful exploration. Third, the need for developing rituals that encourage tolerance may be the best contemporary expression of *tikkun olam*. Such rituals would enable participants to dialogue both with the past and with one another in order to help move the world away from the brink of further violence. Fourth, much greater emphasis needs to be placed on Jewish-Christian dialogue. While on one level great strides have been made in Jewish-Catholic relations since the Second Vatican Council and the promulgation of *Nostra Aetate,* the recent controversy over the Auschwitz convent shows that the agony continues. One wonders, for example, why the church has made no statement condemning Holocaust deniers.

CONCLUSION

Teachers do not just happen upon the *Shoah*. The material is too explosive; the questions raised by the catastrophe threaten to unhinge what is left of civilization; and the mirror it holds up to our faces is dark and unrelenting in the image it reflects. In short, the Holocaust can shatter those who are not ready to confront its reality. But, I wonder, is one ever ready for such a confrontation? The Mishnah (*Hagigah*) speaks of four who enter the forbidden kingdom (*PaRDeS*): one loses his faith, one loses his mind, one loses his life. Only Rabbi Akiva enters and leaves in peace. Both the *PaRDeS* and the *Shoah* share one thing in common. Once having touched the topic, one is, in turn, deeply touched by it. The difference between the two is, however, more striking. *PaRDeS* (paradise) is the acronym for various levels of understanding, beginning with the plain meaning (*Peshat*) and ending with the hidden, mystical, or secret meaning (*Sod*). Its illumination can convey redemption. The *Shoah*, for its part, eludes understanding. Or, rather, one masters more facts and data, keeps up with newly discovered or revealed documents, and immerses oneself in a new generation of interpretations and interpreters. Yet, the more that one masters the data, the less comprehensible is the great insanity of the Third Reich's compulsive obsession with murdering Jews and destroying Jewish culture. At the heart of the pedagogical enterprise there is the inescapable paradox that a perfectly rational system was established to achieve a perfectly irrational goal: the murder of the Jewish people for the "crime" of having been born. This is a dark illumination. Yet, above all and precisely because of this negative revelation, we must remember Reb Nachman's admonition against despair.

7

My Experience with the Holocaust

Franklin H. Littell

Encounter with the Holocaust is one of the most dramatic of personal events. Among those who can bear witness, the survivor and the rescuer, the liberator and the perpetrator are singled out by specialists—and accordingly their words are weighed for credibility. Not only the scientist, who must check evidence for professional reasons, is involved. Every person who is confronted by the story of the *Shoah* is challenged to prove and to test the testimony. The words of an eyewitness are most compelling and demand a response from both head and heart.

Among those of the generation that now studies in the School of Infinite Regret, there remains confusion as to who has permission to speak. The first survivors to speak were under severe psychological pressure. They spoke under moral compulsion, often unwillingly. They felt the guilt of surviving, when others just as worthy had perished. They felt the utter inadequacy of verbal reports. Sometimes they cried out in agony and poetic fury: they said that no one could understand who hadn't been there.

This saying, like most terrible truths, was a dual-edged sword. First, it cut through all pretense at purely objective, descriptive reporting. Second, the charge against the absentees chilled the heart and stopped the tongue of the outsider. Worse yet, it stopped the ear: taking refuge in a psychological cave, the rejected one shunted the Holocaust aside as "a Jewish affair." No Tree of Learning could grow in such darkness. No dialogue between participant and spectator could take place. When the last survivor had passed from the scene, the book would be closed; the event would be relegated to past history.

Survivor, rescuer, liberator, perpetrator—these are roles we can understand, with which we can identify. They are speakers whom we can hear.
But there was another key player on the scene: the spectator. The spectators
belong to an ambiguous genre, hard to put in place, their value even harder
to appraise. What of the large numbers who looked and then turned away—
their thoughts on paying the rent, feeding their families, keeping their heads
down, keeping out of trouble? There were spectators without number, now
passing from the scene, who peered from behind the window curtains as
other human beings were led away.

We do not trust those of privilege who, like Hitler's translator, Paul
Schmidt, later claim to have been only supernumeraries on the stage.[1] But
what of the common round of humanity, the chorus of those who at any
place and time live quietly, do not want anything to happen, go on living
and partly living?[2] We are instinctively driven perhaps to reject them as
"guilty spectators," at least to remove them from the neutral category of
the mundane and trivial. Perhaps we try to cast around them a large net of
collective guilt.

Then there are those spectators—and it is for their sake that we speak
and write—who hear the story after the event. They were not standing in
a circle among the players present—looking on, having other priorities,
holding a wet finger in the wind. They come later to hear about the event.

Will the story be communicated to them not only as fact but also as truth?
More and more those who speak to their children with integrity as survivors,
rescuers, liberators, or perpetrators are driven to attempt to answer this
mandate. Suppression and other forms of denial are destructive. On the
other hand, brute fact is without form and void until shaped by the word.
What is the story that strengthens the covenant of fathers and sons, the
voiced message that circumcises the heart and heals the soul?

Very soon the children will hear the story only from someone older, yet
someone who—like them—also was not physically present. Will the message be heard? What are the credentials of this messenger? How is he or
she accredited? Is his or her word good? Accreditation and credibility are
two qualities put in acute jeopardy by the Holocaust and its aftermath, especially in Christendom, its universities and churches.

TESTING THE CREDIBILITY OF THE MESSENGER

How is the credibility of the reporter to be established? The most important tests are two in number. One, does the reporter have integrity and
fairness in dealing with the materials at hand? Two, has the one who speaks
been personally changed by the encounter? Clearly, the kind of "scientific
objectivity" that is used as an excuse for moral and ethical impartiality, the
kind of "scientific objectivity" that rationalized the role of medics and other
scientists in "the Final Solution to the Jewish Problem," is different from

the fairness of the dialogue. The credibility of which we speak is established by respect for the data, fairness in the dialogue, and the *stigmata* of personal wrestling with the story.

"Fairness" is the goal rather than a spurious and self-destructing "objectivity." Fairness in the dialogue with the past and with those present includes all who are entitled to be a part of the discussion. History is a continuum, not a broken chain with separate links called "past" and "present" and "future." The rules of the dialogue apply equally well in historical research and in conversation with those around a table of common concern.[3] In confronting the Holocaust, neither *eiskalt* "objectivity," like that of the scientists who planned and supervised the program, nor denial by those who today cannot face the truth of the story has a place at the table.

Again, the parameters of personal participation in the dialogue about the Holocaust are set by two tests. One, who through personal experience or study of the event has a contribution to make that serves the common good? Two, who has been personally changed by the depth and intensity of his or her confrontation with the story? Never was there a high court where the unimpeachable credibility of the witness was of more measured consequence.

Soon, as the generations of those immediately affected pass on, the authenticity of the reports and the credibility of the witnesses will depend upon how well they pass these two tests.

THE CHRISTIAN SPECTATOR

What is the role of the Christian spectator then, realizing as he does that in a few short years all of the actual participants will be dead, the living voices of the witnesses will be gone?

His first responsibility is to speak with integrity: to know *who* he is, *where* he is, and *what* his place is in this history. In a very special sense he represents a unique possibility: that the Holocaust may be something more than a Jewish affair, that its lessons may serve the good of all humankind. If his concern and commitment of conscience cannot be integrated into the telling and interpretation of the story, then the Holocaust will take its esoteric place as merely an especially unfortunate episode in the life and death of the Jewish people—to be dwelt on from time to time by rabbis and Jewish narrators.

"To speak with integrity!" What could be worse than for the discussion of the Holocaust to be carried on with the same moral "objectivity" as the crime itself? The men and women who as specialists and technocrats ("technically trained barbarians") served the Nazi state so efficiently, and with such a high level of rationality, had been educated to be "objective." They were doctors, lawyers, political administrators, military officers, educational disciplinarians—all trained to keep their eye on long-range objectives and to avoid becoming emotionally involved with the objects of their attention.

The victims remember with incredulity, across decades of recollection, the cruelty and sadism of individual perpetrators. This memory, encountered so often in survivor literature, is misleading when we turn to the analysis of structures and powers. The central characteristic of the Holocaust is not to be found in such human emotions as cruelty, sadism, arrogance, and lust—present and wicked as they were in individual cases. The central motif of the Holocaust was its relentless rationality, the machinelike inexorability with which the final goal of rendering the world *judenrein* was pursued. The Holocaust was the bitter fruit of modern science, cut loose from the moral and religious moorings to which Christendom had for centuries tied its highest pursuits and keenest enterprises.

As Professor Max Born, one of the scientific giants of the twentieth century summed it up before he died at the age of eighty-seven in 1970, "I'd be happier if we had scientists with less brains and more wisdom."[4]

For the spectator in flight from himself and his history, there are escape mechanisms that parallel the "doubling" mechanism that relieves the perpetrator—for a time—of any sense of guilt. Jew or gentile, participant or spectator, the person who reduces the *caesura* of the Holocaust to one more misfortune in the history of an unfortunate people is psychologically removing himself from engagement with its unique story and its lessons. Gentile or Jew, the person who without stuttering brackets the Holocaust with African slavery, the plight of the Brazilian or American Indians, the status of women in patriarchal societies, or the practice of abortion is removing the special pain of particular awareness. The bracketing method, in whichever larger numbers of discrete particulars are encompassed in ever more inclusive generalizations, is central to the immense progress of hard science. The uneasy spectator uses the method to relieve himself of humanistic and humane *engagement* in any specific case that puts him personally to the question.

LEVELS OF RESPONSE: HUMANITARIAN, PATRIOTIC, RELIGIOUS

The Holocaust was mounted on the methodologies and inventions of the modern university. It was driven by a manic hatred of the Jews, which could be unleashed by the German *Führer* during the exigencies of a modern war.

Well-meaning civic and church agencies have long condemned antisemitism,[5] which is usually presented as a particularly nasty form of "racism." This was my first encounter with the problem, as it was defined sixty-five years ago in social science courses on campus and in study units for the Epworth League (the congregational unit of youth work in the Methodist Episcopal Church). Ten years later, when I first did volunteer work with the

Detroit Roundtable of the National Conference of Christians and Jews (NCCJ), the humanitarian perspective had changed little. Everett Clinchey, the great-hearted genius who founded and led the NCCJ through its formative years, was soundly convinced that bigotry and intolerance were immoral and destructive. Christians and Jews should work together to combat them and to "educate for tolerance."

In the free societies, World War II brought a new urgency and a new dimension to the Christian-Jewish problematic. Very few churchmen then perceived that modern antisemitism,[6] epitomized in the Nazi ideology and killing program, was a fundamental issue for Christians as well as Jews. James Parkes[7] in Britain and Reinhold Niebuhr[8] in the United States were almost alone in their perception that Nazi antisemitism was an assault on Christianity as well as the Jews, a religious as well as a political challenge. Nevertheless, in rallying the British and the Americans to fight Nazi power, the British Council of Christians and Jews (founded 1941) and the NCCJ in the United States (founded 1928) had a signal significance far beyond their actual circles of power and direct influence.

During World War II, two important political decisions were reached in the United States that were initially dictated by a high patriotism and later were seen to have basic religious significance as well. One was the recognition of conscientious objection to military service as a legitimate individual stance. Even in this most imperative war of democracy against dictatorship, Congress passed considerably more enlightened legislation to protect civil liberties than prevailed during "the war to defend democracy" (World War I). This practical respect for the integrity of a person's conscience has profound theological as well as immediate political import in undermining any tendency toward deification of the state. (After the war we encouraged the new German Federal Republic to recognize the validity of the exceptional case: "conscientious objection" [*Kriegsdienstverweigerung*]. The Federal Republic provided for this exception for the first time in German history.[9])

The second action was dictated in the immediate sense by patriotism, but in the long-term carried theological significance: the development of a military chaplaincy with significant equality and close cooperation between ministers, rabbis, and priests. The chaplaincy gave content to the slogan "Cooperation Without Compromise": in general services and in last rites a chaplain of any of the accredited religious communities was authorized to execute the pastoral office. The place of the military chaplaincy in gaining general public acceptance, as well as juridical assent to interfaith cooperation, has yet to be properly researched and appraised.

SERVICE IN GERMANY

My father, who was a professor and intended that I should be one too, started me at home in learning the tools of the historical method. German became my favorite foreign language. Reinhold Niebuhr, who later became my chief mentor, kept us seminarians aware of the crisis for Christians and for the Jewish people that was rapidly reaching its climax in the Nazi Third Reich. He splendidly combined biblical teaching and preaching with political activism.

More than any other Christian leader or theologian in North America, Niebuhr declared the fatal nature of the attack of Nazism on the Jewish people and upon those of the baptized gentiles who did not betray their Christian calling.[10] He wrote a large number of editorials and articles about the church struggle, about the importance to Christians of the genocidal assault on the Jews; he questioned traditional Hebrew Christian missions as early as 1928; in 1943 he was the first Christian leader to champion the creation of a Jewish state in *Eretz Israel.* After 1948 he was a constant friend of the new nation, in contrast with many church leaders who—even after the Holocaust—could not unlearn the endemic theological and *Kultur-antisemitismus* with which their conventional educations had indelibly stained them.

Due to Reinhold Niebuhr, I met Dietrich Bonhoeffer—later a martyr of the German Church Struggle (*Kirchenkampf*), when he was at Union Theological Seminary for a few weeks in the late spring of 1939. I was one of the students who talked with him and had a chance to debate with others the significance of what he felt free to tell us.[11] I spent the summer of 1939 in Europe, trying to learn firsthand about the confrontation of Christian faith with the ideology and practice of National Socialism. On a trip through Germany, traveling as a delegate to the First World Christian Youth Conference at Amsterdam, I heard from our German Methodist bishop that "Hitler was God's man for Germany!" I was not convinced. But everything that I saw convinced me that war was imminent, and I said so to friends and fellow activists when we were back home.

Nevertheless, for a young man who grew up in the congregation and on the campus as a liberal pacifist in the Midwest, the transition to political realism was not easy. My daily association with anti-Nazi activists "downtown" in Manhattan, and my access to reports out of Hitler's *Grossdeutsch-land* and *Festung Europa* combined to dislodge me from the religious optimism and political isolationism with which I had arrived at Union in the fall of 1937.

But it was very painful to contemplate estrangement from the senior ministers who had encouraged me to enter the ministry, and from friends of many years of activism in the Methodist youth movement—several of whom went to prison as nonregistrants and several dozen of whom were enlisted in alternative service. I did not feel free publicly to break from liberal pacifism until the war officially ended.[12]

In the meantime, with a wife and children, I continued in the civilian work of the ministry in an America at war with an evil far greater than anything for which our church had prepared us. While doing religious work I did my Ph.D. with the other two teachers—Roland H. Bainton and Kenneth Scott Latourette—who (after my father and Niebuhr) most profoundly influenced my thought and vocation. I did my dissertation on the sixteenth-century origins of the peace churches, noting especially their pioneer witness for religious liberty.[13]

I was haunted by the question put by Bonhoeffer's martyrdom: Why did so few Christians stand up against the wickedness of the ideology and violence of the Third Reich, while the vast majority of the baptized in European Christendom floated with the current like dead fish belly-up? How could it be that most of the leaders of Nazi-dominated Christendom—with the Lutheran Archbishop of Denmark and the Orthodox Patriarch of Bulgaria the only conspicuous exceptions—either supported the dictatorship with its murderous programs or quietly accommodated to it? With all honor to those who resisted the Nazi manipulation of the churches, how had most Christians failed so badly to oppose the wickedness of the dictatorship itself and to intervene for the targeted and victimized groups over whose bodies the triumphant engine of the *Führerstaat* was rolling?

When I was approached as a specialist in German religious history to join in the democratic reconstruction of Germany, I accepted as soon as I could manage my release from a contract with the University of Michigan. For most of the next decade I served under different auspices in the American occupation, doing fraternal work especially with the faculties of theology, the student Christian groups (*Evangelische Studentengemeinde*), the church conference centers (*Evangelische Akademien*), and the great laymen's movement, *Deutscher Evangelischer Kirchentag.*

While in Germany I was able to facilitate conferences at which church leaders and academics discussed one of the most neglected questions in Christian doctrine: At what point is the committed Christian compelled to become a conscientious objector—a resister against immoral acts by a legitimate government, or a confrontational opponent and perhaps martyr against an illegitimate government?[14] I found allies and made friends among Germans, French, British, and Dutch churchmen who were agonizing over the same questions that were driving me.

We saw that the Christian churches have across the centuries produced a vast library on the virtue of obedience, submission to the "higher powers," but only a scant shelf on the time, place, and methods of open resistance to gross wickedness in high places. As an American, it was clear to me that in view of the centuries of explicit admonition against disobedience and rebellion, reinforced during the Nazi rule by both Roman Catholic and Protestant establishments, there could be no surprise that there were few rescuers of the hunted Jews. There were few resisters, except when the churches' own political and economic interests were threatened. Neither at Barmen (1934) nor at Stuttgart (1945), where the most signal statements were issued on the Christians' responsibility in confrontation with Nazism, was there any mention of the Jews.

By August 1949 the basis of my concern was beginning to shift from the tragedy of widespread betrayal of the faith in Christendom to the tragedy of the physical assault on the Jewish people. A newsletter that I was circulating among friends at home referred to "the Holocaust."[15] It had become clear to me that the murder of *circa* 6 million Jews in the heart of Christendom—a program carried out by baptized Roman Catholic, Protestant, and Orthodox communicants—presented a breakdown far more fundamental than a simple break from the humanitarian and democratic virtues that had emerged with the Enlightenment. Antisemitism was much more serious than simple "racism"; this spiritual cancer in Christianity was both endemic and systemic, and might be fatal.

Where was one to begin in treating a fundamental malaise that corrupted the interpretation of the Christian Bible, the lesson units taught in the Sunday school, the sermon outlines for preaching in the pulpit, the training of each generation of clergy?

STATESIDE

These were the questions that I brought back with me, beginning my graduate seminar on the Church Struggle and the Holocaust at Emory University. My little mimeographed newsletter, which I had started in Germany to report to friends back home, began to carry book reviews, seminar and consultation reports and the like on antisemitism, Bonhoeffer studies, and course offerings on the German Church Struggle and the Holocaust.

I was also designated Consultant on Religion and Higher Education to the staff of the National Conference of Christians and Jews; from 1958 to 1983 I traveled to regional offices and university campuses under NCCJ auspices to further the Christian-Jewish dialogue. In 1959, a group of us set up a national professional association, ACURA (Association of Coordinators for University Religious Affairs), for furthering interfaith cooperation among campus ministers in the Hillel, Newman, Wesley, Westminster, and other programs with students.

Initially responsible in the American occupation of Germany as a specialist in religious liberty, ecumenical cooperation, and Christian-Jewish relations, I was also privileged to work with German and international leaders who believed in the possibility of a unified and democratic Germany in a united Europe. Writing in 1995, I can look back with some satisfaction to the fact that—to the degree that such human efforts can be successful—those objectives have been achieved.

Basic to that recovery have been many factors, among them the spiritual and intellectual impact of President Heuss' 1949 launching of the German Societies for Christian/Jewish Cooperation (*Gesellschaften für Christlich-*

Jüdische Zusammenarbeit) and the political and economic thrust of Chancellor Adenauer's 1952 understanding with David Ben-Gurion on partial compensation (*Wiedergutmachung*) to the Jewish people for the genocidal assault of the German Third Reich on the Jewish people.

Since returning stateside I have gone back to Germany at least once a year, and seven times in the year of reunification (1989). Since 1970 my commitment to the survival of the Jewish people has been strengthened by collegial and personal friendships with Israelis as well, and as of this date I have made more than thirty trips to Jerusalem.

The Holocaust remained a loadstone to my thinking, but it was profoundly unhealthy for the event to be the center of Jewish self-definition and Christian interpretation. (Among other things, it confirmed the worst aspects of Christian triumphalist theology.) By 1970 the network was strong enough to make possible the launching of three organizations expressing an affirmative Christian commitment to the survival of the Jewish people.

JEWISH SURVIVAL: THREE PRACTICAL AFFIRMATIONS

Both cultural and political antisemites opposed Holocaust education and defamed Israel. The invidious thread connecting the two themes was the speaker's attitude to Jewish survival.

First, in 1970 I wrote 754 personal letters (before PCs!), and 233 friends and colleagues responded affirmatively to the founding of Christians Concerned for Israel (CCI). A. Roy Eckardt, professor at Lehigh University and a leading writer on Christian-Jewish relations and Israeli affairs, agreed to be vice chairman of this working party. I edited an occasional newsletter—*CCI Notebook,* which gained a readership of several hundred pastors, priests, and lay people. In 1978, CCI merged with some two dozen other Christian organizations concerned for Israel's survival and well-being, creating the National Christian Leadership Conference for Israel (NCLCI). Consisting of liberal and conservative Protestants and Roman Catholics, the board of NCLCI has had to fight anti-Israel propaganda—both Communist and pro-Arab League—in the churches. On the affirmative, it has—especially under eight years of inspired leadership by Sister Rose Thering as executive director— helped several dozen study groups to travel to Israel, stood up for Israel's well-being in the public forum in America, and tried to influence churches to purge their endemic antisemitism and take official positions friendly to Israel and the Jewish people.

The second effort begun in 1970 was a program to reach the churches' intellectuals. With the assistance of Sister Ann Patrick Ware, at that time seconded to membership in the ecumenical staff of the National Council of Churches, I called together and chaired for several years the Israel Study Group. Now called the Christian Study Group on Israel and the Jewish People, the optimal group was composed of ten Roman Catholic and ten Protestant theologians.

The study group was founded in the realization that basic changes had to be made in the preaching and teaching of the Christian churches, sometimes involving doctrines and dogmas that go back to the family quarrel between the followers of Jesus and the followers of other Jewish teachers in the first centuries of the Christian movement. There were two specific purposes. First was to provide intellectual guidance and spiritual support to confessors of the faith engaged in a difficult—even dangerous—task. Second was to ensure that the testimonies of those who in past generations had died in the faith would be a live part of the dialogue, testimonies neither to be slavishly parroted nor to be frivolously tossed aside. Meeting two or three times a year, members of the study group have read papers to one another, shared problems both professional and personal, and during a quarter of a century have published dozens of articles and books to provoke the thinking of churches about the mystery of Jewish survival and value of Jewish well-being.

The third movement had a decade of informal antecedents before it took relatively firm form in 1970 as the International Scholars' Conference on the German Struggle and the Holocaust.[16] Professor Hubert Locke, who participated in founding the campus interfaith professional association in 1959, was host chairman of the founding conference at Wayne State University. That was the first conference at which the themes of the Church Struggle (*Kirchenkampf*) and Holocaust (*Shoah*) were joined. It was also the scene of a famous exchange between Elie Wiesel and Richard Rubenstein, the report often reprinted, which showed the depths of the Jewish crisis of faith after Auschwitz—a crisis that had its parallel among thinking Christians like those of the study group.

PHILADELPHIA

In 1969 I moved to Temple University, a state university that was developing a new Department of Religion. The plan was adventuresome: to bring together professors and graduate students who were adherents of the major religions to practice interreligious dialogue as well as to study different religions.

At Temple I was strengthened especially by three colleagues who shared my concern for reworking Christian preaching and teaching in the shadow of Auschwitz. Leonard Swidler had founded the *Journal of Ecumenical Studies* at Duquesne University in 1963, bringing it with him to Temple. Under his editorship it has been for more than three decades the strongest journal of interreligious discussion circulating in academic and religious circles. The author of several books on dialogue between the world's religions, he published an excellent article, "Dialogue Decalogue: Ground Rules for

Interreligious Dialogue," in 1983[17] that has been copied and circulated by the thousands. Gerard Sloyan, a leader in Roman Catholic liturgical reform and in biblical studies, deepened the discussion with such books as *Jesus on Trial* (1973) and *Is Christ the End of the Law?* (1978). Paul van Buren, whose theological critique of the culture of Christendom—especially in *The Secular Meaning of the Gospel* (1963)—had in the eyes of the media landed him in the "Death of God" camp, published in 1976 *The Burden of Freedom: Americans and the God of Israel.* During the 1980s he confirmed his eminence as a world-ranking, systematic theologian through his four-volume work, *A Theology of the Jewish-Christian Reality.* My book *The Crucifixion of the Jews* (1975) was developed in the privileged setting of collegiality with such minds and spirits.

In 1975 I founded a seminar in Holocaust studies. My first Ph.D. in the field, Mordecai Paldiel, moved upon graduation to his post as director of the division on the Righteous of the Nations at Yad Vashem in Jerusalem. His writing on rescuers is widely studied.[18]

In 1975 we also started a series of annual Philadelphia conferences on Holocaust pedagogy, which ran for eight years. Also in 1975, we launched the second Holocaust education center founded in the United States, now known as the Philadelphia Center on the Holocaust, Genocide and Human Rights. In 1978 President Carter invited me to join a group, of which Elie Wiesel was the center, to encourage *Yom HaShoah* observances nationwide and to found a national museum on the Holocaust. I served until the museum opened in 1993.

In 1975 I cochaired, with Claire Huchet-Bishop, the first conference on the Holocaust and the Church Struggle on German soil—held June 5–7 at Haus Rissen, Hamburg. The next major German conference came nearly twenty years later, when, in 1993, we brought together over five hundred participants to Humboldt University in Berlin for papers and discussions on Western civilization after Auschwitz. Our Philadelphia Center provided the American base of operations, cooperating with Dr. Elisabeth Maxwell of London, who had been the prime mover of the first "Remembering for the Future" conference in Oxford and London in 1988. The German chairman was Professor Dr. Erich Geldbach of Bensheim/Marburg, and the international coordinator was Sharon Gutman—vice president of the Philadelphia Center. Dean Jan Colijn of The Richard Stockton College of New Jersey was chairman of the American committee, with Dr. Marcia S. Littell in charge of the office on this side of the Atlantic.

This combination of research and activism is still criticized in some academic circles for lack of "objectivity." In my judgment, the fault of the German academics was precisely that they failed to note the early warning signs[19] on the corruption of their profession and to take remedial measures. I worked with the leaders of the Evangelical Academies as they conducted dozens of seminars and conferences on professional and vocational ethics

(*Berufsethik*) with different specialized groups. The purpose was to reconstruct the shattered value systems and morale of specialists, many of them university alumni, who had helped organize and sustain the structures of the Nazi Third Reich.[20] One of the basic lessons of the Holocaust is certainly this: that developing an early warning system on impending disaster is imperative. An intimately related lesson is the importance of maintaining the internal discipline of professional associations, closing ranks against infiltration by expounders of the language of assault and proponents of terrorism and violent politics.

The present writer, who has been asked to discuss what he has learned during years of intellectual and spiritual confrontation with the Holocaust, was blessed with teachers who were not balcony-sitters. My father and college major professor, Clair Francis Littell, was both a severe academic taskmaster and a politically courageous moralist. Under his guidance I developed a permanent fascination with constitutional law, with the responsibility of religious communities for democratic education in the political commonwealth, and especially with the implications for state and church of the principle of religious liberty. Enriching these concerns, my seminary mentor Reinhold Niebuhr—also a scholar and an activist—opened me to awareness of the magnitude of social sin, and the evil of governments abusive of human liberty and dignity.

I strongly believe that Holocaust research and activism belong together, just as I believe that adequate Holocaust education must be interfaith, international, and interdisciplinary.

UNFINISHED BUSINESS

There remains the credibility crisis of Christianity, with most of the church establishments still engaged in subtle forms of denial. Nevertheless, a school of Christian churchmen and theologians has emerged who are convinced that the Holocaust was not only a tragic event in the history of the Jewish people. In a different but no less earnest measure, the Holocaust was a geological faultline in the history of Christianity. The record of church leaders and baptized gentiles during the Holocaust has created the most serious credibility crisis in the history of the Christian faith.

The first serious problem confronting this company of earnest reformers was the deafness of the church establishments, the unwillingness of church officials to consider changing conventional preaching and teaching about Jewish death or survival, the determination of the baptized gentiles to dismiss the Holocaust as—ethically—another instance of "man's inhumanity to man" and—politically—"a Jewish affair." That the Holocaust was a theological issue, even at the level of salvation itself, was far from their thoughts; they had not yet even begun to master the implications of the struggle within the German churches (*Kirchenkampf*), the message of the martyrdoms of men like Bonhoeffer and Alfred Delp, S.J.

Nevertheless, the number of serious theologians who have come to think of the frontier between the Christian and the Jewish people as the front line of doctrinal reconstruction and interreligious cooperation has grown steadily in America and in Europe. In seminars and conferences, as well as in articles and books, the new reformers have chipped away at the walls of the ancient fortress of Christian antisemitism.

At this time they suddenly have found themselves engaged on a second front: there are Jewish spokesmen, some of them very vocal, who deny the Christians and their questions any place in the dialogue. *Yom HaShoah* observances, in which Christians and other gentiles had participated from the beginning, have steadily shifted out of the public and interreligious arenas into the synagogues and Jewish community centers. When courses are begun on campus, they are usually listed in "Jewish Studies." When, because of community or student body demand, a Holocaust course has to be initiated, it is often taught by an ethnic Jew—whether he or she is academically qualified to teach such a subject or not.

In America, where certain gentile academics—including Christian clergymen—pioneered in Holocaust education a full decade before any of the Jewish "defense agencies" became interested, as official histories began to be published, non-Jews were airbrushed out of the picture. Jewish revisionism, although hardly as politically dangerous as Holocaust revisionism, has its own long-range counterproductive potential.

In jeopardizing a common future for Jews and Christians, subtle Christian denial and subtle Jewish sectarianism are unwitting allies.

Activation of the membership of the synagogues and the churches to study of the other, and to sponsorship of joint programs, is not only possible in America, it is imperative if another way is to be found from that which fatefully controlled Christian-Jewish relations for 1,500 years in European Christendom. Religious liberty is not only a negative against intolerance and persecution: its vigor and health require active and imaginative interfaith dialogue and cooperation.

The well-being of the republic requires an affirmative and participative citizenry. Our liberties cannot be secured purely by litigation and other negatives. Again the encounter with Nazism is illuminating. As the fateful issues took on more clearly defined boundaries, certain points became clear. One was that the best of the resisters, like the Protestant theologian Dietrich Bonhoeffer and the Jesuit Alfred Delp, lacked the doctrinal heavy arms needed to fight a demonic regime. For centuries the Christian churches had taught the virtue of obedience to authority; there were but slender, occasional tracts by individual thinkers suggesting when and under what circumstances the Christian might resist the actions of government. In the end, Bonhoeffer had to anchor his stand in his convictions as a citizen of moral integrity and his instincts as a decent human being. In the end, Delp's op-position to Nazism was sustained by a devotional life of unsurpassed purity.

The plight of both Bonhoeffer and Delp revealed the failure of churches across the centuries—now unconscionable with the disappearance of "the divine right of kings"—to develop an adequate doctrine of political respon-sibility for free citizens.

Before the modern period no one assumed that the laity—ordinary in-dividual Christians—could be allowed to exercise the responsibility of per-sonal conscientious choice. The ruling professionals, in their appointed places as theologians or church officials, were expected by those in power to be loyal enforcers of obedience to the rulers. When "subjects" became "citizens" with "liberties," along with responsibilities as participants in pop-ular sovereignty, most Christians in Christendom were put in a situation for which they had received no guidance from the churches. In fact, except for the radical Reformers of the sixteenth century, the radical Puritans of the seventeenth century, and the radical Pietists of the eighteenth century, the Christian establishments have resisted—and in large sectors still continue to resist—the whole idea of democracy, in the general society and even more emphatically in the churches.

A totalitarian religious structure is dysfunctional in a democracy or a re-public. The citizen must learn voluntarism and democratic participation at the primary social level of family and church or synagogue. We may look for a day when "laity abuse" will be noted as critically as "child abuse" or "spouse abuse." The Holocaust and subsequent genocides have been mounted on the capabilities of persons who were trained to obey orders, not to raise questions, not to engage in lively dialogue with all those entitled to be heard.

Understanding and declaring the religious and political meanings of early warning make study of the Holocaust an affirmative action for the common good, not a mere pathological exercise for elites.

NOTES

1. Schmidt titled his autobiography, published after the demise of the Third Reich, *Statist auf diplomatischen Bühne.*

2. Adapted from the second recitative of the Chorus in T. S. Eliot's *Murder in the Cathedral* (1935).

3. See Leonard Swidler's "The Dialogue Decalogue"; reprint from *Journal of Ecumenical Studies* 20 (Winter 1983): 1.

4. Cited in *The Bulletin of the P & I Office of the [German] Federal Republic* 17 (January 20, 1970) 1:3.

5. The correct translation of Wilhelm Marr's invention, *Antisemitismus*, is "anti-semitism," without the capital and without the hyphen. "Semitism," like "Aryanism," may conceivably have a place in seminars in anthropology, but neither "Semitism" nor "Anti-Semitism" is a fit rubric for the public forum.

6. Antisemitism developed in three layers during centuries of Christendom: theological, cultural, and modern. At the lowest level there is a closed system of official Christian triumph over Judaism and the Jewish people. At the secondary level the language and the cultural artifacts reveal, often unconsciously, the contempt for the Jews that the baptized imbibe with their mothers' milk. The third level was reached with two parallel developments: Marr's invention of the word and use of the language of assault as an ideological weapon, and the tsarist use of the *pogrom* as a political tool. See my book, *The Crucifixion of the Jews* (Macon, Ga.: Mercer University Press, 1986), passim.

7. The University of Southampton, where Parkes' library and papers are given special facilities, held an international conference on the centenary of his birth, September 10–12, 1996.

8. See my "Reinhold Niebuhr's Christian Leadership in a Time of Testing," in *Burning Memory: Times of Testing and Reckoning,* ed. Alice L. Eckardt (New York: Pergamon Press, 1993), 95–107.

9. My office gave logistical support to the conference that wrote the first draft of the law recognizing conscientious objection, bringing together representatives of the American Peace Churches (Mennonites, Brethren, Quakers) and key personnel from the German parliament (*Bundestag*) and the Ministries of Interior, Defense, and Economics at Arnoldshain Evangelical Academy.

10. See my essay on "Reinhold Niebuhr and the Jewish People," *Holocaust and Genocide Studies* 6 (1991): 45–61.

11. Although we didn't know it, Bonhoeffer had been followed since 1934 as a dangerous enemy of the Reich. A measure of our naivete as American students was how little we realized that in a neutral America where Nazi agents and native German-American Bundists moved about freely, DB put himself in jeopardy even to talk with us.

12. In "The Inadequacy of Modern Pacifism," *Christianity and Society* 11 (1946): 18–23, I distinguished modern liberal pacifism from the peace testimony of the historic peace churches.

13. *The Anabaptist View of the Church* (Chicago: American Society of Church History, 1952), several times republished.

14. A representative conference report was published after a conference at Tutzing Evangelical Academy, edited by Bernhard Pfister and Gerhard Hildmann, *Widerstandsrecht und Grenzen der Staatsgewalt* (Berlin: Duncker & Humblot, 1956). I discussed the problematic in a conference called and report edited by Carl J. Friedrich, "The Protestant Churches and Totalitarianism (Germany, 1933–1945)," in *Totalitarianism* (Cambridge: Harvard University Press, 1954), 108–19. See also "From Barmen (1934) to Stuttgart (1945): The Path of the Confessing Church in Germany," *A Journal of Church and State* 3 (1961): 41–52.

15. On my use of the term and the *theological* importance of the watershed event (*Shoah, Churban,* Holocaust . . .), see my article "Inventing the Holocaust: A Christian's Retrospect," *Holocaust and Genocide Studies* 9 (1995): 173–91.

16. Sponsored for a decade by the NCCJ, the Scholars' Conference—presently called the Annual Scholars' Conference on the Holocaust and the Churches—now moves to a different campus each year to make attendance possible for more younger scholars and graduate students. The host committee has a major influence on the program and the working title each year. Continuity is provided by the office

of the executive director, Dr. Marcia S. Littell, P.O. Box 172, Merion Station, PA 19066. Annual conference volumes with selected papers are published each year, and more recently entire proceedings are available on CD-ROM.

17. Leonard Swidler, "The Dialogue Decalogue," *Journal of Ecumenical Studies* 20 (1983).

18. Mordecai Paldiel, *The Path of the Righteous: Gentile Rescuers of Jews During the Holocaust* (Hoboken, N.J.: KTAV Publishing, 1993).

19. On the development of an early warning system on potentially genocidal movements, such as the NSDAP in 1923, for example, see my "Early Warning: An Essay," *Holocaust and Genocide Studies* 3 (1988): 483–90.

20. The story has been well told by the leading figure in the Academies movement; see Eberhard Mueller's *Die Bekehrung der Strukturen* (Zürich: Theologischer Verlag, 1973). See also his little masterpiece on the dialogue method of decision making: *Die Kunst der Gesprächsführung* (Hamburg: Furche-Verlag, 1954).

8

Penetrating Barriers: A Holocaust Retrospective

John T. Pawlikowski

The Holocaust cut off human options, moral and otherwise, to an unprecedented degree. The Nazis forced upon their victims a range of "choiceless choices," as Holocaust commentator Lawrence Langer has termed them. Those of us who served on the original Exhibit Design Committee for the United States Holocaust Memorial Museum approved early on in our discussion the idea of setting up a permanent barrier in the pathway visitors normally take as a way of having them experience the limitations faced by the Nazis' victims at every turn.

Barriers of another kind have also frequently affected our understanding of the Holocaust. I speak here of attitudinal barriers. Two in particular concern me. The first is the "excessive guilt" approach that one finds among well-intentioned Christians; the second is an undue emphasis on the "irrationality" of the Holocaust, something one finds among both Jewish and Christian commentators.

As a Christian scholar living fifty years after the Holocaust, I clearly feel a need to see my faith community engage in public repentance for its failures in responsibility during the Nazi era. Pope John Paul II's recent general call for repentance for the "acquiescence given, especially in certain centuries, to intolerance and even the use of violence in the service of truth"[1] as part of the Catholic Church's preparation for the millennial celebration of Christianity must certainly be applied to the period of the Holocaust. I likewise have no hesitancy in asserting that I feel a deep sense of responsibility for the failures of Christianity during the Holocaust that obligates me to teach about the history of the Christian antisemitism that provided an indispensable seedbed for support of the Nazi program, active or tacit, within the churches. And without question there remains an ultimate impenetrability to the Holocaust experience.

But recognition of the necessity for Christian repentance, as well as acknowledgment of the Holocaust's impenetrability, should not become barriers to continued human probing into the event. From the very outset of my own involvement in study of the Holocaust and participation in Holocaust commemoration, which dates back to the late sixties, I have been convinced that we do not fully honor the memory of the victims if we stop at expressions of repentance and proclamations of the Holocaust's irrationality. Both my commitment to Jewish-Christian understanding and my professional training as a social ethicist have convinced me that we need to delve ever further into the reality of the Holocaust in order to better appreciate the continuing threats to human survival in our day. Unless we move to this second phase we have not fully honored the memory and the sacrifice of the victims.

My initial involvement in Christian-Jewish dialogue began while I was still a seminary student with the Servite Fathers in Lake Bluff, Illinois. One of my teachers at that time was the Scripture scholar of some contemporary notoriety, John Dominic Crossan. At the close of the Second Vatican Council, Professor Crossan delivered a major address at Chicago's Loyola University on the New Testament's antisemitism. That talk had a lasting impact on the direction of my life and work. While a graduate student at the University of Chicago, Professors J. Coert Rylaarsdam and Martin Marty further stimulated my interest in Christian-Jewish relations in their historical and contemporary dimensions. This growing academic interest eventually led to involvement in ongoing dialogue programming with the Catholic Adult Education Center in Chicago where I began working with Sister Rose Thering, O.P., who did the initial Catholic study on religion textbooks and prejudice against religious, racial, and ethnic outgroups (especially Jews), and Hans Adler of the Chicago office of the Anti-Defamation League.

In this early phase of my involvement in the Christian-Jewish dialogue, the Holocaust was not a central issue. In fact, it was hardly an agenda item at all. Neither the Christian nor the Jewish side saw fit to raise it. It was only after several years that my general involvement in Christian-Jewish relations began to incorporate the Holocaust as a major concern. My contact with the pioneering scholar and activist on Holocaust issues, Professor Franklin Littell, certainly was an important factor in raising my consciousness in this regard. While I did not take part in the International Scholars' Conference on the German Church Struggle and the Holocaust held at Detroit's Wayne State University in 1970, I was asked to review the volume of papers from the groundbreaking event when it appeared in 1974.[2] Doing this review began the process of firmly rooting the Holocaust into my basic understanding of the Christian-Jewish relationship. This in turn was shortly followed by my first invitation to speak on the topic during a Holocaust commemorative service organized by the Hyde Park Council of Churches and Synagogues at which I gave the principal address.

The directions I took in that presentation at the Lutheran School of Theology in Chicago have basically remained in place. Two in particular stand out. The first is that while we may say that there is a dimension to the evil of the Holocaust that will remain forever impenetrable, we cannot dismiss the Holocaust as an "irrational" event. On the contrary, it was a highly planned undertaking created and executed by people many regarded as among the best and the brightest of the age. Second, while there remain real connections between the long history of Christian anti-Judaism and antisemitism, and while this history provided an indispensable seedbed for the participation/acquiescence of so many members of the Christian community in the Nazi endeavor, the Holocaust must ultimately be seen as primarily the result of distinctly modern forces that had been percolating in Western consciousness for nearly a century before the Nazis arrived on the scene. In the end, though the Nazis selected the Jews as their primary targets (the disabled were the first victims chronologically) and though this selection was rooted in the centuries-old degradation of Jews and Judaism in the churches and Christian societies, it is clear that the Nazis remained in principle as opposed to Christianity as to Judaism in terms of the "advanced" form of society they were planning to create.

In the almost quarter century since the Holocaust first became a dimension of my approach to Christian-Jewish relations, these two aspects have remained consistent components of my basic understanding of the Holocaust. My thinking, of course, has undergone considerable development as well. In fact, the situation that prevailed during the initial phase of my involvement in Christian-Jewish dialogue, namely, little or no mention of the Holocaust, has been quite dramatically reversed. Over the years the Holocaust has become increasingly central not only to my perspective on the Christian-Jewish relationship but also to my approach to theology and ethics generally. I have come to accept it as what Holocaust commentator Irving Greenberg has called an "orienting event" for contemporary society. As I see it, the Holocaust has had a decisive impact on how we today understand God, Christ, and ethics.

The scholarly research on the Holocaust that has been a major part of my academic career began with a focus on the Holocaust's significance for the question of God in our time. From there I moved on to reflections on its meaning for public ethics. More recently, I have tried to pick up on an issue that I raised some years ago but never pursued in earnest, namely, What does the Holocaust have to say to our understanding of Christology today? I have also begun to pursue the question of the victimization of non-Jews by the Nazis with a special interest in the Nazi attack on the Polish nation. I am becoming more and more convinced that, while Nazi fury against the Jews both in terms of intensity and comprehensiveness was altogether special, Jewish victimization in general must be seen as an integral part of a greater Nazi scheme for human "purification" and "advancement" that included the Gypsies, the disabled, the Poles, homosexuals, and others. In opting for this "integral" perspective I obviously part company with other respected Holocaust scholars, Jewish and non-Jewish, including Steven T. Katz, who is in the process of producing the magnum opus on the uniqueness of Jewish victimization.[3]

If I were asked to identify the most important issues I have raised in Holocaust studies I would cite the following: (1) highlighting the fundamental ethical questions provoked by the challenge of Nazism; (2) probing how our understanding of the Holocaust experience affects contemporary Christology; and (3) how an enhanced understanding of non-Jewish victimization under the Nazis deepens and expands the significance of the Holocaust. I would like briefly to expand on each of these areas.

From my study and reflection on the Holocaust I have come to understand that there are two overriding ethical concerns facing us in the late twentieth century. The first is our basic perception of the relationship between God and human persons and communities. The Holocaust shattered equally exaggerated notions of human and divine sovereignty. Yet such notions served as the foundations of both traditional and liberal ethics in the modern world. No one can truly be called a "Holocaust theologian" in my judgment unless they begin their theologizing with this fundamental premise. Many well-intentioned Christian theologians have turned their attention to the uprooting of antisemitism from Christian theology as a response to the Holocaust. Certainly this is a basic requirement. But as significant as it remains, the removal of all vestiges of antisemitism from Christian theology does not represent a fully adequate response to the challenge of the Holocaust.

In the final analysis the Holocaust represents the beginning of a new era in human self-awareness and human possibility over which hangs the specter of either unprecedented destruction or unparalleled hope. With the rise of Nazism the mass extermination of human life in a guiltless fashion became thinkable and technologically feasible. The door was now ajar for an era when dispassionate torture and the murder of millions could become not merely the act of a crazed despot, not just a desire for national security, not merely an irrational outbreak of xenophobic fear, but a calculated effort to reshape history supported by intellectual argumentation from the best and the brightest minds in a society. It was an attempt, Emil Fackenheim has said, to wipe out the "divine image" in history. "The murder camp," Fackenheim writes, "was not an accidental by-product of the Nazi empire. It was its essence."[4]

The fundamental challenge of the Holocaust lies in our altered perception of the relationship between God and humanity and its implications for the basis of moral behavior. What emerges as a central reality from the study of the Holocaust is the Nazi effort to create the "superperson," to develop a truly liberated humanity, to be shared only by a select group, namely, the Aryan race. This new humanity would be released from the moral restraints previously imposed by religious beliefs and would be capable of exerting virtually unlimited power in the shaping of the world and its inhabitants. In a somewhat indirect, though still powerful, way the Nazis had proclaimed the death of God as a guiding force in the governance of the universe.

In pursuit of their objective, the Nazis became convinced that all the "dregs of humanity" had to be eliminated or at least their influence on culture and human development significantly curtailed. The Jews fell into this "dregs" category first and foremost. They were classified as "vermin." The Nazis could not imagine even a minimally useful role for Jews in the new society to which they hoped to give birth. The Polish and Romani peoples as well as gay persons and those suffering mental or physical disabilities were also looked upon as polluters of the new level of humanity envisioned by the Nazis. Proper distinctions between these victims and the Jewish people need to be maintained because, with the possible exception of the Rom community (or "Gypsies"), none were definitely slated for the same kind of wholesale extermination that was to be the ultimate fate of the Jews, although they too were considered obstacles to the advancement of human consciousness to new levels of insight, power, and self-control.[5] Their destiny under the rubric of humankind's purification assumes a theological significance intimately related to the Jewish question.

The principle theological problem raised by the Holocaust is this: How does humankind properly appropriate the genuine sense of human liberation that lay at the heart of Nazi ideology without surrendering its soul to massive evil? However horrendous their legacy, the Nazis were correct in at least one respect. They rightly perceived that some basic changes were underway in human consciousness. The impact of the new science and technology, with its underlying assumption of freedom, was beginning to provide the human community on a mass scale with a Promethean-type experience of escape from prior moral chains. People were beginning to perceive, however dimly, an enhanced sense of dignity and autonomy far more extensive than that which most of Christian theology had previously conceded. Traditional theological concepts that had shaped much of the Christian moral perspective, notions such as divine punishment, hell, divine wrath, and providence were losing some of the hold they had exercised over moral decision making since biblical times. Christian theology had tended to accentuate the omnipotence of God, which in turn intensified the impotence of the human person and the rather inconsequential role played by the human community in maintaining the sustainability of the earth. The Nazis totally rejected this previous relationship. In fact, they literally tried to turn it upside down.

The challenge facing theology in light of the Holocaust is to discover a way whereby the new sense of human freedom that is continuing to dawn might be affirmed but channeled into constructive rather than humanly destructive purposes. The understanding of the relationship between God and human persons must be significantly altered in light of the Holocaust. The intensified sense of power and human enhancement that the Nazis championed as a *novum* of our age needs to be acknowledged as a crucial and inescapable element in the ongoing process of humanity's salvation. There is simply no way of reversing the consciousness of a profound readjustment in the nature of the divine-human relationship. That is why the mere repetition of biblical images and precepts, even those that develop a positive covenantal linkage between Jews and Christians, is insufficient by itself as a response to the Holocaust.

The question at hand is whether post-Holocaust theology can develop an expression of God and religion that will help prevent the newly recognized creative power of humanity from being transformed into the destructive force unveiled in all its ugliness during the Nazi era. Put another way, can post-Holocaust humanity discover a relationship with God that will provide warrants for the vast power to shape itself and the creation it has inherited? This fundamental issue has been basically ignored by most Christian theologians up until now.

Let me add here that the development of a meaningful post-Holocaust notion of God will need to be related to the experience of liturgy and worship. Historian George Mosse[6] and others have written of the profound significance of the so-called "public liturgies" of the Nazis to their overall effort. Again, despite their barbarity, the Nazis were obviously attuned to the continuing impact of the symbolic in human life. And I remain convinced that the realm of the symbolic, experienced in worship and liturgy, is critical for the challenge facing post-Holocaust humanity. The Holocaust has destroyed any simplistic notions of a "commanding God." But it has likewise revealed our desperate need to restore a relationship with a "compelling God," compelling because we have experienced through symbolic encounter with this God a healing, strengthening, and affirming that buries any need to assert our humanity through the destructive, even deadly, use of human power. This sense of a compelling Parent God who has gifted humanity, who shares in our vulnerability through the cross, is the foundation for any adequate moral ethos in the contemporary world.[7]

In terms of foundational morality in light of the Holocaust I have recently also been drawn to the question of particularistic/universalistic identity as a vital question over and above the issues I have just outlined. Two books in particular have raised for me the central role of nationalism (especially for non-German collaborators with the Nazis). They are *Judaism and Christianity under the Impact of National Socialism 1919–1945* edited by Otto Dov Kulka and Paul R. Mendes-Flohr[8] and *The Catholic Church and Anti-*

semitism: Poland, 1933–1939 by Ronald Modras.[9] In differing ways both suggest that nationalism may have been a stronger force in garnering non-German support for the Nazis than classical antisemitism. But European nationalism's definition of the Jew as the preeminent "outsider" may in some ways be linked to more traditional antisemitic stereotypes. This needs to be probed further, as does the question of nationalism's legitimacy in light of its role during the Holocaust.

Turning to the second major issue that has occupied my attention over the years, namely Christology in light of the Holocaust, I am always prodded on this question by the remark made years ago by Franklin Littell that if Jesus and his disciples had been alive during the Nazi era they would have certainly been headed for the extermination camps while most other Christians might have escaped. But as challenging as such a remark may continue to be in linking Jesus to the Holocaust, it is insufficient as a theological response. Hence, along with a few other Christian colleagues such as Johannes Metz, Rebecca Chopp, James Moore, Jürgen Moltmann, and Franklin Sherman, I began to explore how our statement of Christology might be affected by the reconsideration of the meaning of divine presence in light of the Holocaust. It has rather mystified me that many of the Christian theologians who have probed the God question have never moved on to examine Christology, despite the intimate connection between them.

Initially in a contribution to a volume of the *Concilium* series,[10] and more recently in presentations at the Remembering for the Future II Conference at Humboldt University in Berlin, Germany, and in a 1994 address to the Catholic Theological Society of America,[11] I have attempted to put forth the outlines of a Christology rooted in a post-Holocaust vision of the God-humanity relationship. Originally, in the *Concilium* essay, I placed great significance on the development of an incarnational Christology anchored in part in appreciation of Jesus' links with the Pharisaic revolution of his day. The ultimate significance of a Christology so understood lies in its revelation of the grandeur of the human as a necessary corrective to the demeaning paternalism that often characterized the sense of the divine-human relationship in the past. In this sense all authentic Christology is ultimately theological anthropology. In my view this fear and paternalism, associated in the past with the statement of the divine-human relationship, bear at least partial responsibility for the attempt by the Nazis to produce what the late Uriel Tal termed a total reversal of human meaning.

With a proper understanding of the Christ event, men and women can be healed, finally overcoming the primal sin of pride, the desire to supplant the Creator in power and in status, that lay at the heart of Nazi ideology in my judgment. Critical to this awareness is the sense of God's self-imposed limitation manifested in the cross. This is where Jürgen Moltmann's theology of the cross, insufficiently appreciated in the dialogue, can make a significant contribution. His notion of the "divine vulnerability" revealed through the cross can be a powerful Christological myth used to remind us that one need not exercise power, control, and dominance to the "godly." But let me say that if the notion of "divine vulnerability" is to serve in the above way, it must be disassociated from the direct linkages to Jewish suffering during the Holocaust found in the writings of certain Christian theologians in the dialogue. This sense of "divine vulnerability" manifested in the cross of Jesus will also aid development of that sense of humility that Stanley Hauerwas has rightly seen as critical in light of the Holocaust.[12]

In my more recent essays I have come to recognize that my initial approach to Christology after the Holocaust, while still valid, stands in need of some expansion. Here is where the inchoative reflections of Christian scholars such as David Tracy and Rebecca Chopp, who have stressed the need for a post-Holocaust Christology that directly relates to the victims of current history, and the argument of James Moore for a post-Holocaust Christology of discipleship that includes resistance, appear to me very much on target. Christology must become more than a theoretical affirmation of human dignity. It must also provide the impetus for a concrete manifestation of that belief through identification with, and support of, the victims of oppression through personal and political means. This will enhance the dignity not only of the victim, but also of the person who reaches out. Only through this kind of bonding can the instinctive patriarchal impulse, rooted in relationships based on power rather than mutuality, be overcome and a central force for the continued misuse of technological capacity be neutralized. Only in this way can we guarantee that killing will never again become a force for supposed human healing, as Robert Jay Lifton has put it.

The third, and most recent, major question that I have explored is the victimization of non-Jews under the Nazis and its relationship to the victimization of the Jews. My views on this issue are still developing. But I have now done sufficient research to argue certain general premises. In general, I am now convinced of the need for a basic paradigm shift in Holocaust interpretation that moves our understanding of the event from a mere repetition of classical antisemitism to a distinctly modern phenomenon whose central intent went beyond making Europe (or even the world) *judenrein*. In that context, while the annihilation of the Jews became all consuming as an initial Nazi goal (and classical antisemitism undoubtedly influenced the designation of the Jews as the primary victims), there is now sufficient evidence to suggest that the Nazis intended to do much more.

The first victims chronologically were in fact the physically and mentally disabled. While the attack on them was suspended as a result of considerable public outcry, including protests from religious leaders, it is probable the Nazis would have tried to complete the elimination of all disabled people once they had eliminated the Jews. And more and more evidence is emerging from both Jewish and non-Jewish scholars to suggest that the annihilation of the European Gypsy community was taking place simultaneously with that of the Jews even though it received far less publicity. And the Nazi attack on the Polish nation, which included an effort to wipe out all vestiges of Polish culture, was evidently much more than a mere effort to subdue militarily a neighboring state. But even when the Nazis had accomplished that task in a relatively short time despite determined Polish opposition, they committed military power and human resources to the Polish front in the drive to reduce the population of Poland to subhuman status. And evidence has now surfaced in the form of remarks of Himmler and Hitler that give credence to the view that the Nazis might well have attempted the total annihilation of the Poles (and perhaps other Slavic peoples) if they had been allowed to pursue their plans. Clearly the Nazis regarded these attacks on the disabled, the Gypsies, gays, and Poles as crucial to their overall plan for the emergence of a new humanity. And obviously these attacks were not motivated by antisemitism.

This emerging evidence relative to non-Jewish victims reveals the need for new language to describe the relationship between Jewish and non-Jewish victims of the Nazis. Some of the more popular formulations such as "Jews were killed for who they were; others were killed for what they did" simply no longer meet the test of the available data.

My basic assertion that the Jewish victims can no longer be regarded as totally unique in their victimization does not mean I eschew all important differences between them and the others who suffered because of Nazi ideology. There are indeed differences and these should not be lost in the process of reworking our more fundamental descriptive categories. First of all, to repeat what has been emphasized earlier, European Jewry nearly disappeared as a result of the Nazi attack. While this may have been the ultimate goal of the Nazis for some of the other groups, it was never realized to the same degree. This is a difference we can never forget.

Second, there was both a "sacral" and a historical dimension to the Nazi hatred of the Jews. Antisemitism had not only been around for centuries, it had also become an integral part of the Christian religious tradition. This clearly added a distinctive dimension to the victimization of the Jews, as Richard Rubenstein has emphasized of late. Ian Hancock and others have shown the existence of a continuing pattern of discrimination against Gypsies for most of the second millennium of European society. While this discriminatory pattern somewhat parallels that which developed in relation to the Jews, it lacks any corresponding "sacral" dimension. This "sacral" dimension clearly rendered Jewish victimization distinctive. It accounts for the selection of the Jews as the primary victims, always receiving the harshest treatment in the camps. It likewise accounts for the considerable popular support, or at least indifference, that the Nazi attack on the Jews generated among the masses, even among other victim groups. This religious antisemitism combined with political nationalism during the period between the two world wars to produce an intense religio-political nationalism that came to regard Jews as the preeminent "outsiders" constituting a grave threat to authentic political and cultural sovereignty. Feelings along these lines were sometimes directed against Gypsies, but without quite the same intensity because the religious compulsion was missing.

In short, then, the need obviously remains to maintain a clear measure of distinctiveness relative to the attack on the Jewish people. But no longer can we regard Jewish victimization as wholly unique. We must begin to acknowledge, far more than we have thus far, that the elimination of Jews, Gypsies, Poles, and the disabled (and perhaps homosexuals) fell under the same umbrella effort to purify humanity and raise human consciousness to a new, supposedly higher level of maturity. The best paradigm for doing this in my judgment remains the proposal first put forth by Bohdan Wytwycky, and subsequently endorsed by Michael Berenbaum, which depicts the Nazi victims in terms of concentric rings extending out from the center of a hell occupied by Jews. It is a paradigm drawn from Dante's *Inferno*.[13]

In short, then, the Holocaust continues to serve for me as a watershed event in terms of understanding contemporary society and the theology and morality that are required to shape it if we are to avoid a repetition of the uncontrolled evil unleashed by the Nazis. There is no possibility of a simple return to a pre-Holocaust era either morally or theologically. In that sense we do live in a brave new world with unprecedented power and responsibility, but also with dangerous uncertainty regarding this power and responsibility.

NOTES

1. Pope John Paul II, Apostolic Letter, "As the Third Millennium Draws Near," *Origins* 24:24 (November 24, 1994): 411.

2. Franklin H. Littell and Hubert Locke, eds., *The German Church Struggle and the Holocaust* (Detroit: Wayne State University Press, 1974).

3. Cf. Steven T. Katz, *The Holocaust in Historical Context: The Holocaust and Mass Death before the Modern Age* (New York: Oxford University Press, 1994).

4. Cf. Emil Fackenheim, *The Jewish Return into History* (New York: Schocken Books, 1978), 246.

5. Some questions have now arisen regarding the Poles. A few discovered statements from Hitler and Himmler seem to indicate that these two Nazi leaders at least gave some thought to the eventual total extermination of Poles. But this was never acted upon, and it is conjecture as to whether it would have occurred if the Nazis had managed to continue on their course.

6. Cf. George Mosse, *The Nationalization of the Masses: Political Symbolism and Mass Movements in Germany from the Napoleonic Wars through the Third Reich* (New York: New American Library, 1977).

7. I deal with this issue in my essay, "Worship After the Holocaust: An Ethician's Reflections," in *Living No Longer for Ourselves*, ed. Kathleen Hughes, R.S.C.J. and Mark R. Francis, C.V.S. (Collegeville, Minn.: The Liturgical Press, 1991), 52–67.

8. Cf. Otto Dov Kulka and Paul R. Mendes-Flohr, eds., *Judaism and Christianity under the Impact of National Socialism 1919–1945* (Jerusalem: The Historical Society of Israel, 1982).

9. Cf. Ronald Modras, *The Catholic Church and Antisemitism: Poland, 1933–1939* (Chur, Switzerland: Harwood Academic Publishers, 1994).

10. Cf. John T. Pawlikowski, "The Holocaust and Contemporary Christology," in *The Holocaust as Interruption,* ed. Elisabeth Schüssler Fiorenza and David Tracy (Edinburgh: T. & T. Clark, 1984).

11. Cf. John T. Pawlikowski, "Christology in Light of the Jewish-Christian Dialogue," in *Proceedings of the Forty-Ninth Annual Convention,* Catholic Theological Society of America, 1994, 120–34.

12. Cf. Stanley Hauerwas, "Jews and Christians Among the Nations," *Cross Currents* 31 (Spring 1981): 34. While I agree with Hauerwas on the need for humility after the Holocaust, he fails, in my judgment, to combine this sense of humility with an equally necessary sense of enhanced human cocreational responsibility.

13. Cf. Michael Berenbaum, "The Uniqueness and Universality of the Holocaust," in *Holocaust: Religious and Philosophical Implications,* ed. John K. Roth and Michael Berenbaum (New York: Paragon House, 1989), 95–96. Also Cf. Bohdan Wytwycky, *The Other Holocaust: Many Circles of Hell* (Washington, D.C.: The Novak Report on the New Ethnicity, 1980).

9

Once and Not Future Partisan: A Plea for History

A. Roy Eckardt

When you write you are the last writer and the first. That means every word should be the first word you have ever written and the last. You take upon yourself all the books that were written before you, whether you have read them or not. They become part of your book, except you go one step forward.

—Elie Wiesel

RETROSPECTIVE

Amidst a persistent and odd serendipity that this poor lad out of Brooklyn, New York, will never fathom, I have been granted a place among "pioneers" of a world-historical revolution (of grace, sheer grace, yes that is what it is) within an ages-long *Auseinandersetzung,* whereby the Jew and the Jewish people are no longer unaccepted alien objects but most welcome subjects (my sister/my brother/my mother/my father).

I am somehow able to boast as my own spiritual contemporaries and colleagues Americans Franklin H. Littell, Reinhold Niebuhr, Carl Hermann Voss; Britishers Peter Schneider, W. W. Simpson; Dutchman Cornelius A. Rijk; French women Marie-Thérèse de Sion, Elisabeth Meynard Maxwell; Germans Gertrud Luckner, Rudolf Pfisterer, Rolf Rendtorff, Carola and Klaus Scholder; Guernseyman James Parkes and his wife Dorothy; Italian Angelo Giuseppi Roncalli; Scotsman Malcolm Hay; Swede Raoul Wallenberg; yet, no less, on the Jewish and/or Israeli side Yehuda Bauer, Yaffa Eliach, Emil Fackenheim, Blu Greenberg, Irving Greenberg, Israel Gutman, Jules Isaac, Abba Kovner, José Patterson, David Patterson, Livia Rothkirchen, Marcel Simon, Uri Tal, Marion Wiesel, Elie Wiesel. None of this—the list is unforgivably truncated (though it *is* restricted to older persons)—is to covet equality of attainment with any of these heroines/heroes of mine; it is only to celebrate their willingness to receive me as a fellow laborer in one and the same revolutionist vineyard. (I must write as well for the sake and the memory of my own lost [separated] family of Germany.)

TWO CAVEATS

In a magisterial study, *To Mend the World,* Emil Fackenheim attests that "one cannot be a modern Jewish thinker without also being a philosophical one." I am persuaded that this judgment applies as well to a modern Christian thinker. In these late days I should have to say: a postmodern Christian thinker—but only because the world in which one must live, work, and die is the dispensation after and beyond Christendom. For with the end of Christendom came too the end of modernity. It is fifty years since the *Shoah* yet the appellations "Christian theology" and "Christian theologian" continue to exude the stench of murder. Yet this is no way insinuates any contrasting purity for "philosophy" or the "philosopher."[1]

In *Jews and Christians* I refer to a moral prescription that has always penetrated my vocational effort: It is wrong to use a Christian vantage place to argue the insufficiency or invalidity of Jewish existence; it is wrong to use a Jewish vantage place to argue the insufficiency of Christian existence. The essay before you marks out selected experiential variations within that ongoing (though debatable) norm.

ANTISEMITISM IS THE HEART[2]

My initial publication appeared in 1946.[3] The short piece declaimed against "the religion of Nazism" as a "pagan absolutism of blood, nation, and soil," and hence as perforce annihilative of the Jewish people and Judaism, whose God and ethos transcend and fight all such sacrilege. My first book, grounded in a doctoral dissertation in the Department of Philosophy, Columbia University (1947), began: "Before a British military court at Luneburg, Germany, on October 1, 1945, a Rumanian Jew testified that eighty thousand Jews, the entire population of the ghetto of Lodz, Poland, had been killed and burned in a single night" at the Oswiecim death camp.[4]

Do such historical declarations and like materials within these and subsequent writings of mine serve to label me a "philosopher of the Holocaust"? That phrasing is not happy. Any Christian thinker who desires to be identified via such language is met by a massive obstacle, at once analytic and substantive: The *Shoah* is unable to comprise the ultimately decisive event, prompting, or concern upon the Christian side of the relation—simply because, for all its salience and horror and fatefully determinist power, the *Shoah* is no more than/no less than the logical, moral (immoral) climax of some nineteen hundred years of Christian antisemitism. It is assuredly a fact—long a truism—that the Holocaust is unqualifiedly "unprecedented" (Emil Fackenheim) as a world-historical and world-decisive concatenation of events. Accordingly, we are impelled to classify the *Shoah*—I speak with full scientific objectivity—as a uniquely unique event. That is to say, its inner, unparalleled, and wholly originative *meaning/purpose* was in no way something "mystical" or "mystifying"! That *meaning/purpose* was and remains the final (*endlich:* cf. *Endlösung) excising* ("excision: *Surg.* the removal of a foreign body") of every Jew, every Jewish sperm, every Jewish ovum from planet Earth.

Nevertheless, Christian *Judenfeindschaft,* objectively construed, cannot be assimilated to the Holocaust; the Holocaust has to be assimilated to Christian antisemitism. We are forbidden to appeal the sentence that history has passed upon us. Robert A. Everett reminds us how James Parkes *did not* need the *Shoah* in order to wage his lifelong war against Christian antisemitism. Parkes' battles well *preceded* Nazism. So too, the single and singular motivation of my own poor endeavors inside the Christian-Jewish *Begegnung* was always and remains now the struggle against antisemitism. At once sociopathological, theological-pathological, and psychopathological, the historic (and history-making) world Christian campaign against the Jewish people is in its terrifying depth, so I have long held, a campaign against the Jew Jesus Christ and the moral/spiritual demands he is held to make. Since the gentile/pagan soul no longer has any way to destroy Jesus the Jew vis-à-vis, it must direct its wrath against the people of Jesus: the Jews. The people of God are the Jewish people; the chosen people of the Devil are the antisemites.[5] Antisemitism is the all-determining laudation of the Devil as Death, implementational of a world-cosmic death wish. (How does God talk back to Godself as Devil? Via the State of Israel [*haim*].)[6]

That the Christian drive against the Jews abides is proved, that is, tested, in the truth that while in Christian circles the *Shoah* has been long since loudly and universally condemned (yet of course years and years too late), theological antisemitism still moves secretly, though sometimes even overtly, among us. Thus, no less than a half century after the Holocaust, Raymond E. Brown must continue to *belabor* (his recent book is—Good God!—an unbelievable 1608 pages in length) the responsibility of Jewish leaders for Jesus' death[7]—in Brown's semiotic legerdemain, they were "responsible" though not "guilty"!—all this, centuries beyond Jesus' crucifixion (at the hands of, in scientific/historical truth, the Roman authorities).[8] Perhaps some kind of misfire has beset Brown's brain, inspiring him, in effect, to freeze himself into medieval/Reformation diabolism, when the actual time in which he lives will soon be the quite unfrozen year 2000.

A half century back
Nippon lived "in infamy" (F.D.R.)
Now are the bygones
All gone:

>   Sony
>   Toshiba
>   Nissan
>   Nikon
>   Toyota.

Nineteen centuries
Are too short for
Other bygones to go.
"Responsible" stay "the Jews"
For wasting Jesus—so
Perpetuates Raymond Brown
(*The Death of the Messiah*)
Over sixteen hundred and eight pages.
>   If Jews
>   Could
>   Just be
>   Nippon. . . . [9]

More simply put: "We are only following orders: Keep the pot boiling!"

One *Shoah* is finished; preparedness for sequels is in the workshop. The international neo-Nazis (skinheads, American "militiamen," many others[10]) need not despair: Help is ever on the way. What Robert A. Everett describes as the distinctive Christian ideology of Jewish victimization remains alive and not unwell.

THE RESURRECTION

In the matter of developments in my thinking and other recent experiences of mine, several universes of discourse may be introduced.

Beginning in 1986 I reaffirmed the Resurrection of Jesus Christ, having previously raised serious questions respecting that pillar of Christian faith— moral questions that must continue to haunt the Christian community. The Resurrection is of weighty and direct bearing upon any Christian moral/ philosophic stance respecting the *Shoah*. But there is neither space nor need to expatiate here upon that crucial consideration.[11]

My reaffirmation of the Resurrection has been widely and repeatedly published, this over quite a period of time. A full decade ago, in *Jews and Christians,* while continuing to reject any ideology of the Resurrection that victimizes human beings, I expressed the conviction that a nontriumphalist teaching of that event can continue to find an integral place in Christian faith and teaching.[12] I reproduce another early instance of this reaffirmation (1987).

What would be a better joke on those reactionary Sadducees than for God to raise her own Pharisee-liberal Son from the dead! She would be having a go at one of her dearest truths, and would also be giving at least a few of her people a foretaste of the things that are to come. Maybe best of all, she would be reminding the Sadducees exactly what she thought of them, meanwhile assuring her good friends the Pharisees that she was on their side.[13]

A much fuller exposition of and attestation to Jesus' Resurrection by me appeared as far back as 1990 in an essay entitled "Why Do You Search Among the Dead?" elsewhere called "The *Shoah* and the Affirmation of Jesus' Resurrection" (a public address before the Nineteenth Annual Scholars' Conference on the Holocaust and the Churches, Philadelphia, March 5–7, 1989).[14]

It might have struck you that Raymond Brown is not the only belaborer among us. Do read on.

THE INVASION OF HOLOCAUST SCHOLARSHIP BY SLOVENLINESS AND MISREPRESENTATION

Slovenliness

It is a truism of responsible scholarship that whenever we report upon the views of a colleague we must provide the most up-to-date available description of our subject's viewpoint—unless, of course, we qualify our reporting by identifying a given representation as an earlier and perhaps superseded one.

Several reputed scholars of the Holocaust—all males, I am relieved to say—are guilty and hence responsible (or, if you like, responsible and hence guilty) for falsifying my long-held and continuing position upon the Resurrection of Jesus Christ.

No less than eight years after my published repudiation of a negativist rendering of that eventuality, Stephen R. Haynes incorrectly makes that very rendering still operative for me. He falls into the same error in another essay published as late as 1994.[15] In point of truth, rejections of my earlier position, made in 1986, 1987, and most especially 1990 and 1991 (cf. also 1993, 1994, and 1995),[16] appeared in more than adequate time for Haynes to have used these in his analyses. Unfortunately for him, his error enters at the all-deciding juncture of scholarship-ethics-theology; because of his falsification of fact, his entire assessment of my overall theological/moral position falls on its face.

Haynes' fault is repeated in Darrell J. Fasching and in Donald J. Dietrich,[17] both of whose writings appeared, along with Haynes', well after my published changes in position on the Resurrection. The irony is that all three of these men are normally responsible and careful scholars. In my case, however, they seem to be honoring the one watchword: "Report what Eckardt once believed and said but do it in a way that forces him still to believe it; under no circumstances report the diametrically opposite position that he has been arguing for some ten years."[18]

Together these people exemplify Jacob Neusner's devastating finding, in another context: Some scholars inexcusably fail "to do routine bibliographical homework."[19] Incidentally, or perhaps not incidentally, after I read the foregoing, concerted falsifications of my work, I found it refreshing to contemplate Michael S. Kogan's line (despite the personal trouble I have with it), "we Jews can no longer dismiss the Easter faith out of hand."[20] Kogan's words somehow reminded me that I have not read any Jewish scholars campaigning, in effect, to forbid me to change my mind: There is comfort in this.

Distortion

The note of partisanship contained in the title to this piece is about to be compounded: Self-defense is joined by spouse-defense.

In the initial volume of *The Holocaust in Historical Context,* Steven T. Katz accuses Alice and Roy Eckardt of disseminating a form of mystification respecting the nature and meaning of *Shoah.* In point of truth, and together with every one of our joint writings on the subject, the programmatic essay that bears the brunt of Katz's calumniation[21] explicitly condemns any and all mystification of the Holocaust—this, in behalf of an entirely contrary historical, empiricist, even historicist understanding. It is explicitly avowed by us that to characterize the *Shoah* as inexplicable or incredible is to assault the dignity of the victims. Against Katz's unconscionable accusation to the opposite effect, we will have no part in any such moral travesty. Katz's exposition is an irresponsible, indeed total, misrepresentation of our unchanged and unchanging viewpoint.[22]

In order that the present exercise proceed along other, less unpleasant lines (although such moral chastening does have its perversely hedonic side), readers are simply referred to the now-current number of *Shofar* for full documentation of the present point.[23] Steven T. Katz makes an enjoyable target, but he cannot compare to God. Please read on.

OBEDIENCE/DISOBEDIENCE TO THE ABUSING GOD

In *New Theology Review,* editor (and friend) John T. Pawlikowski writes tellingly: "The Holocaust has shattered all simplistic notions of a 'commanding' God. Such a 'commanding' God can no longer be the touchstone of ethical behavior."[24]

The contemporary crisis of Jewish, Christian, and (why not?) Muslim theological ethics centers in the moral issue of whether God any longer deserves (or ever deserved?) to be obeyed.

A fine virtue of David R. Blumenthal's study *Facing the Abusing God: A Theology of Protest* is his enlarging of "survivor" from survivors of the Holocaust as such to survivors of child abuse and of woman battering, though without muting the distinctive voices of the three sorts of victims. Philosophically/historically, the *Shoah* is incapable of staying self-contained: The vast imperium of abuse engaged in by God is too big for it. Diane, survivor of child abuse, attests: God's commandment told me to "honor the father who raped me and the mother who watched and did nothing."[25] My one moral/analytic problem with Blumenthal's expansion is (Are you listening, Steven T. Katz?): Why stop there? Why stop anywhere? What about *this* young mother of a colleague at Lehigh University whose body became stuffed with cancer and, on the precise day I write these words, was forced to abandon in death her two young children and husband? Pray for Ann Wright and her family. Yet, Emil Fackenheim is always, and rightly, warning us against oneupmanship regarding radical evil. The Devil's crimes seem to meander from nonchalance to randomness to indiscriminateness: He is in that one sense somewhat unbiased—rather like God. And as, with typical wisdom, Jeffrey Burton Russell has it: *Historically,* the Devil is "a part of the deity. *Sine diabolo nullus Deus.*"[26] So let's keep the blame where the blame belongs: The abuser is God—here, David R. Blumenthal never once flinches. When God behaves abusively, we are the wholly *innocent* victims, and abusive behavior is *never* excusable.[27] Nor does Blumenthal fall even a bit into what we might label the Zoroastrian dualist temptation, much less into the Augustinian sleight of mind, whereby, monistically (and with comparable diabolism) evil is transmogrified into very nice negation. Richard Pryor, whose repetitiveness of offensive words drives me up a wall of monotonousness, but whom I nevertheless adore, meets our own linguistic and spiritual need: "Let's stop the shit!"[28]

What am I to say now? What am I to do now? I am far from sure, far from assurance.

Once more: The pronouncements and findings of history are as remorseless as they are morally determinative. Nothing less than the history of history is our burden. Can it also be our opportunity? We have been catapulted into an era that castigates obedience as ethical motivation. "We were only following orders" has been hanged at, of all places, Auschwitz. But yet, the question, the eventuality does not depart from us: In a postobedient time, could it be that even in its death throes, the voice of obedience may yet be able to whisper something to us?—You shall obey no commandments unless and until God gives penitential evidence of obeying them as well. Your role model here, your historic warrant, is none other than Abraham, from a long time ago. (I must not say "patriarch Abraham" because that has become a no-no; how about "Abraham, nobody-just-like-the-rest-of-us"?): "Shall not the Judge of all the earth do what is just?" (Genesis 18:25). For once, let us be good fundamentalists: "Listen to the Word of God."

Postobedient affirmation has the quality of a comedy (incongruity; cf. final heading below), a protest, a means of living with ourselves, a weapon wielded by human integrity. It is also a way to rise above the divine unrighteousness for the sake of a righteousness that, in the very act of judging God, may uncover, even incarnate, another, "wholly other" dimension of divinity. Thus, if it is so that for all God's abusiveness, God is yet *praying that the divine mercy overcome the divine anger*—such is the Babylonian Talmud's discovery of the content of the prayer of God[29]—then is the human responding gestalt of postobedient obedience enabled at last to become an authentic *imitatio dei*.

But how is the love of God ever going to obliterate the abuse of God? Does our necessary moral rebellion against God, does our struggle for individual and social justice, have its home in God (the *imitatio dei*) or does it explode only from within ourselves? There is no way to tell: We have been thrown into existence, and the Face of God stays hidden. Any moment-faith (Irving Greenberg) that we may manage to eke out has to be directed into hope, and only the future will tell whether the hope has any truth to it.

I conclude this item by filling out the citation from John T. Pawlikowski, with whom I clearly agree: "The Holocaust has also exposed humanity's desperate need to restore a relationship with a 'compelling' [contra 'commanding'] God, *compelling* because we have experienced through symbolic encounter with this God, a healing, a strengthening, an affirming. . . . The sense of a compelling Parent God who has gifted humanity, whose own vulnerability has been shown on the Cross, is the [a?] meaningful foundation for any adequate moral ethos after the Holocaust."[30]

A final item may afford me, as perhaps you, a little further help and/or hope.

THE SHADE OF THE *SHOAH*: TOWARD A DIVINE COMEDY

In 1989 I packed up my gear and moved over into the philosophy of comedy, a dimension of life that has always captivated me, been practiced by me, and is subliminal to much of my ongoing work. Most of my recent endeavor while in residence at the Centre for Hebrew and Jewish Studies of the University of Oxford has focused upon that subject. The study and the life of comedy are vast, penetrating the humanities and social sciences, as well as such other sciences as psychology and biology (cf., in both these latter cases, the physiology of laughter).

I have by no means surrendered the concerns for which I am ordinarily

known, as exemplified thus far in this essay. In order to forge immediately
a connection for you, I might simply commend the important and liberating
study of Steve Lipman, *Laughter in Hell: The Use of Humor during the
Holocaust,* particularly his initial chapter, "Humor, Faith, and the Holocaust."[31]

Construing comedy as *incongruity*—specially manifest at boundary
lengths and depths of life—I esteem the queendom of comedy for its entire
coherence with, and indeed its highly sensible culmination of, the intellec-
tual/spiritual pursuit of the Holocaust and the Christian-Jewish encounter.
(A competing and, sometimes I think, no less sensible response to the
Shoah is despair and self-destruction, as within recent suicides of Holocaust
survivors. Death is a final comedy [incongruity] of life,[32] yet so too is Resurrection.)

I have already done a large trilogy in this blessed area.[33] I am now completing one other volume, entitled *The Comic and the Ethicist: A Kind of
Team,* which comprises the *dénouement* of my thinking in the lengthening
shade of the *Shoah*. It will be my final academic book. I seek therein to
conjoin three components: a last reflection upon comedy/humor/laughter
under the aspect of depth-incongruity; the ironies, indeed the terrors, of
doing philosophic (also theologic?) ethics in a postmodern universe of un-
knowing/chaos/accountability/anguish/anxiety; and a twofold, heuristic en-
visionment of comedy as breaking out into morality, and morality as
breaking out into comedy—the whole in thanksgiving for such a grand lady
as Gilda Radner, of blessed memory and whom I loved. For Gilda, "humor
is just truth—only faster."

It remains to coax a creative comedy of incongruity into our overall rubric.
I shall do this via the eschatological salvation of God—not *by* God, *of* God.

Human beings need salvation because of the evils they *responsibly* commit. God needs salvation because God is *culpable* for allowing radical evil
in a world where the creatures of God have no say whatsoever in being
born. The *thrownness* of human beings into life is the novel and central
focus behind all my most recent writings. H. Richard Niebuhr, my teacher,
attests: "Here we are, 'thrown into existence,' fated to be. . . . [We] did not
elect ourselves into being. . . . [This] self which lives in this body and this
mind did not choose itself."[34] It would be delicious (cf. Kierkegaard: All I
ask for is plain ordinary honesty) to witness through the fabricated window
of a Nazi crematorium the burning alive of one Adolf Hitler as of other Nazis
of today. But such enjoyment has a problem: No human being, not even
the worst human being—who *is* that?—ever had the prevenient power to
create its own existence.

Matching the Niebuhrian observation is Wylie Sypher: Tragedy is birth-
struggle-death; comedy is birth-struggle-death-resurrection.[35]

In *The Trial of God (as it was held on February 25, 1649 in Shamgorod),*
Elie Wiesel uncovers for us that the only figure in the entire crude court-

room who will volunteer to defend God for the divine crimes is—the Devil.[36] (Thus takes place the funeral of all theodicy.) The "trial of God" emerged relatively early in my thinking, but for some time it remained inchoate. It was Jewish spokespersons and friends alone who brought me to assert this truth unreservedly.)

The moral question of today's existential cosmos/chaos is: Who, if anyone, is left to speak for God? (It is here that comedy stumbles outright into our presence, but of necessity in the figure of a Barnum and Bailey clown: *God* is supposed to forgive *humans,* stupid. [No, not you, my bright and gentle reader.] What's this crazy talk about submicroscopic humans forgiving God?—that One who has stayed in hiding there: over Sinai, behind the Cross.)

Who will stand, if only in silence, with the God who has individually decreed (performed?) many capital crimes but who is alone now, who is forlorn, who is friendless, who must pass endless days and endless nights (days and nights that once were the very sovereign workplace of God) consigned to death row?

Perhaps nobody. Or perhaps one single soul or even two (in simple iteration of their [infinitely innocent] archetype Jesus). In standing with God, this one/these two plunge inside a *mysterium tremendum* that exceeds, for intensity and terror, though also in opportunity (Revelations 21:5: "See, I make everything new"), one or another *mysterium tremendum* of the past, of the present, of the future. For this one/these two take upon themselves an accountability that is utterly gratuitous, terrifyingly "wrong" (it accepts the unacceptable).

Yet, were the *Devil,* Evil of Evil, to rise to defend God, while the people of God were at that very moment failing, refusing to do so, would there not come into being the worst, the saddest irony of all? But will a defense of God by the people of God only shipwreck them upon the lost island of the Devil? Of course, the Devil's defense of God only shrieks out a diabolic unfaithfulness. The Devil's proposal to defend God is a consummate joke: It is on Purim that he makes his offer! When the people of God (this one/ these two) speak for God it is not that they are "defending someone." It is not that they are falling into an apologia. Rather do they merely speak the truth—and fast!—the truth that holiness is proved by righteousness (Isaiah 5:16). The power of love, of *agape,* enters the scene. It is possible—indeed, is it not morally determinate (*grace-full*)?—that the child will speak out for the parent who lies tied up and forsaken at the final hour, bone of the child's bone, flesh of the child's flesh, blood of the child's blood: "You made me without my consent, yet you are my Mother, you are my Father."

This standing in solidarity with the finally guilty One may comprise, in truth, all that is left of faith and for faith amidst the ashes, amidst the "secrets of European responsibility" (Derrida), amidst the unforgiving aftermath of Europe's fall. From out of the abyss a kind of consolation may be aborning, a kind of spirituality beyond spirituality, the start of a condition in which God and humankind, having been made as one in their crimes, may now become one as forgiving and forgiven lovers: a comedy that is divine.

NOTES

1. Consult A. Roy Eckardt, "Is There A Way Out of the Christian Crime? The Philosophic Question of the Holocaust," *Holocaust and Genocide Studies* 1:1 (1986): 121–26.

2. Cf. A. Roy Eckardt, "Antisemitism is the Heart," *Theology Today* 41 (1984): 301–8; also published in *Christian-Jewish Relations* (London) 17 (1984): 43–51.

3. A. Roy Eckardt, "A Theology for the Jewish Question," *Christianity and Society* 11 (Spring 1946): 24–27.

4. (Later published as) A. Roy Eckardt, *Christianity and the Children of Israel* (New York: King's Crown Press, Columbia University, 1948), 1.

5. Consult A. Roy Eckardt, "The Devil and Yom Kippur," *Midstream* 20:7 (1974): 67–75; idem, *Your People, My People: The Meeting of Jews and Christians* (New York: Quadrangle/New York Times Book Co., 1974), chap. 7, "Enter the Devil."

6. Cf. Eckardt, "Is There A Way Out of the Christian Crime?" 126.

7. Raymond E. Brown, *The Death of the Messiah* (Garden City, N.Y.: Doubleday, 1994).

8. Consult A. Roy Eckardt, *Reclaiming the Jesus of History* (Minneapolis: Fortress Press, 1992), 71ff. and see index under "Death of Jesus." This rather large study in contemporary Christology has gained little attention but the position therein upon Roman culpability for the death of Jesus as seditionist is preponderantly taken in Second Testament scholarship.

9. A. Roy Eckardt, "Could History Just Repeat" (unpublished).

10. It is a waste of all-too-fleeting time and energy to attempt rational and scholarly refutations of so-called historical revisionists, who cannot in fact believe that there was no German Nazi slaughter of the Jews. We may of course denounce them as the antisemites and devils they are, but we can have no illusions that this will do any good. They *must* kill the Jews a second time—and to eternity.

11. To such an end, consult Alice L. Eckardt and A. Roy Eckardt, *Long Night's Journey into Day: A Revised Retrospective on the Holocaust* (Detroit: Wayne State University Press; Oxford: Pergamon Press, 1988), 136–43 and passim.

12. A. Roy Eckardt, *Jews and Christians: The Contemporary Meeting* (Bloomington: Indiana University Press, 1986), 85ff., 155–56.

13. A. Roy Eckardt, *For Righteousness' Sake: Contemporary Moral Philosophies* (Bloomington: Indiana University Press, 1987), 310.

14. A. Roy Eckardt, "Why Do You Search Among the Dead?" *Encounter* 51:1 (1990): 1–17. In substance, the public address was published in *Bearing Witness to the Holocaust 1939–1989,* ed. Alan L. Berger (Lewiston, N.Y.: Edwin Mellen Press, 1991) under the title "The *Shoah* and the Affirmation of the Resurrection of Jesus: A Revisionist Marginal Note," 313–31.

15. Stephen R. Haynes, "Christian Holocaust Theology: A Critical Reassessment," *Journal of the American Academy of Religion* 62 (1994): 553–85; "Changing Para-

digms: Reformist, Radical, and Rejectionist Approaches to the Relationship between Christianity and Antisemitism," *Journal of Ecumenical Studies* 32 (1995): 81–82. In the first piece Haynes also misreads the Eckardts' *Long Night's Journey into Day.* He tries to make us assert *"no* conflict between Jesus and the Jews of his day" ("Changing Paradigms," 86). It is incomprehensible to me that Haynes could know nothing of the serious and ongoing controversy between Sadducees and Pharisees, with Jesus clearly ranged on the latter side.

16. Eckardt, *Jews and Christians* (1986); *For Righteousness' Sake* (1987); "Why Do You Search Among the Dead?" (1990); and "The *Shoah,"* in *Bearing Witness,* ed. Berger (1991). See also Eckardt, *Collecting Myself: A Writer's Retrospective,* ed. Alice L. Eckardt (Atlanta: Scholars Press, 1993); *No Longer Aliens, No Longer Strangers: Christian Faith and Ethics for Today* (Atlanta: Scholars Press, 1994); *How to Tell God from the Devil: On the Way to Comedy* (New Brunswick, N.J., and London: Transaction Publishers, Rutgers University, 1995); and *On the Way to Death: Essays Toward a Comic Vision* (New Brunswick, N.J., and London: Transaction Publishers, Rutgers University, 1996).

17. See Darrell J. Fasching, *Narrative Theology After Auschwitz* (Minneapolis: Fortress Press, 1992), 26–27; Donald J. Dietrich, *God and Humanity in Auschwitz* (New Brunswick, N.J., and London: Transaction Publishers, Rutgers University, 1995), 185. In another place Dietrich writes history backwards. He says: "In Eckardt's early work, the position taken seems to be almost identical to the view adumbrated by the German Protestant Church of the Rhineland" in 1980. Were he to be true to sequential history, Dietrich would say that the Rhineland statement is almost identical to the position taken many years earlier by Eckardt.

18. It is true that James F. Moore's analysis "Back to Eckardt" in his recent book does not go beyond the Eckardt(s) of 1982 (*Christian Theology After the Shoah* [Lanham, Md.: University Press of America, 1993], 130ff. and passim). But the carefully crafted dialectical character of Moore's rendering of my/our work, as of his own position, helps keep him clear of the faults delineated above.

19. Jacob Neusner, "The Academic Study of Judaism, the Religion," *Journal of the American Academy of Religion* 62 (1994): 1066n.

20. Michael S. Kogan, "Toward a Jewish Theology of Christianity," *Journal of Ecumenical Studies* 32:1 (1995): 105.

21. Steven T. Katz, *The Holocaust in Historical Context,* Vol. 1 (New York: Oxford University Press, 1994), 13, 16, 24, and throughout; Alice L. Eckardt and A. Roy Eckardt, "The Holocaust and the Enigma of Uniqueness: A Philosophic Effort at Practical Clarification," *The Annals of the American Academy of Political and Social Science* 450 (1980): 165–78. Through the years, the Eckardts have striven to avoid believing that a little demon is out there working away scrambling their surname, a perverse incarnation of printer's devil. But when in reading Katz's book they beheld "Eckardt" and "Eckhardt" *barely two words apart and on one and the very same line,* their struggle against superstition received a sizable jolt. How can such excruciating proximity bespeak anything but painstaking artistry? And now, in the presence of repeated pronouncements that the male Eckardt could not possibly believe in the Resurrection of Jesus, his ordinarily quasi-rationalist sentiments against any conspiracy theory of history, or at least of scholars, is being sorely tested.

22. Our most extensive study of the Holocaust is *Long Night's Journey into Day,*

as completely revised by Alice Eckardt for the 1988 edition (replacing the 1982 edition).

23. Alice and A. Roy Eckardt, "Steven T. Katz and the Eckardts: Response to a Misrepresentation," *Shofar* 13:4 (1995): 73–78.

24. John T. Pawlikowski, "Reclaiming a Compelling God" (editorial), *Theology Review* 8:3 (1995): 3.

25. David R. Blumenthal, *Facing the Abusing God: A Theology of Protest* (Louisville: Westminster/John Knox Press, 1993), 200. In *The Comic and the Ethicist* (forthcoming) I provide a full exposition and critique of Blumenthal's work.

26. Jeffrey Burton Russell, *The Devil: Perceptions of Evil from Antiquity to Primitive Christianity* (Ithaca, N.Y., and London: Cornell University Press, 1987), 31–32.

27. Blumenthal, *Facing the Abusing God,* 248.

28. Richard Pryor, with Todd Gold, *Pryor Convictions and Other Life Sentences* (New York: Pantheon Books, 1995).

29. Babylonian Talmud *Berakot* 7A, XLIX, as cited in Jacob Neusner, *Telling Tales* (Louisville: Westminster/John Knox Press, 1993), 134–35.

30. Pawlikowski, "Reclaiming," 3–4.

31. Steve Lipman, *Laughter in Hell: The Use of Humor during the Holocaust* (Northvale, N.J., and London: Jason Aronson, 1991).

32. Cf. Ernest Becker, *The Denial of Death* (New York: Free Press, 1973): also Jacques Derrida, *The Gift of Death,* trans. David Wills (Chicago and London: University of Chicago Press, 1995).

33. A. Roy Eckardt, *Sitting in the Earth and Laughing: A Handbook of Humor* (New Brunswick, N.J., and London: Transaction Publishers, Rutgers University, 1992); *How to Tell God from the Devil* and *On the Way to Death.*

34. H. Richard Niebuhr, *Faith on Earth,* ed. Richard R. Niebuhr (New Haven and London: Yale University Press, 1989), 65.

35. Wylie Sypher, as cited without a source in Norman N. Holland, *Laughing: A Psychology of Humor* (Ithaca, N.Y., and London: Cornell University Press, 1982).

36. Elie Wiesel, *The Trial of God (as it was held on February 25, 1649 in Shamgorod),* a play in three acts, trans. Marion Wiesel (New York: Random House, 1979).

10

From Ignorance to Insight

Carol Rittner

Indifference to evil is evil.

—Elie Wiesel

One month after I entered the convent in September 1962, Pope John XXIII opened the first session of the Second Vatican Council (1962–65) in Rome's St. Peter's Basilica. John died before the council completed its work, but thanks in large part to the pastoral tone he set, the Roman Catholic Church underwent an enormous transformation. Among the many changes initiated by the council, two seem particularly important to me. First, the Roman Catholic Church came to a new appreciation of Judaism and has since tried to free its teaching from inherited anti-Jewish rhetoric. And second, the Roman Catholic Church discovered a new sense of solidarity with other religious communities and with the whole human family.

After completing my bachelor's degree, as well as the religious formation program of the Sisters of Mercy, I graduated from College Misericordia in 1967. That September, I was sent to teach English in a Catholic high school in a small community near Scranton, Pennsylvania. I spent three years there before being assigned, in 1970, to a large Catholic high school in rural western Pennsylvania. A year later, I accepted a fellowship at the University of Maryland to begin full-time study for a master's degree. Just as I was making the transition from teaching in high school to studying in graduate school, someone gave me a copy of Viktor Frankl's Auschwitz memoir, *Man's Search for Meaning*.[1] I had never heard of Viktor Frankl, a Viennese psychiatrist whose entire family, except for his sister, perished in Nazi Germany's death camps, but I did know about Anne Frank, a young Jewish girl who died during World War II.

Until my encounter with Frankl, I had a romanticized understanding of Anne Frank's diary, and when I read Alvin Rosenfeld's essay about *The Diary of Anne Frank* a few years ago, I realized how accurately he captured my own response to Anne and her diary. Many people, myself included, heard in her voice a buoyant message:

They saw Anne Frank as a young, innocent, vivacious girl, full of life and blessed with an optimistic spirit that enabled her never to lose hope in humanity, even as its worst representatives were intent on hunting her down and murdering her. They understood her story as deeply sorrowful but perhaps not as ultimately tragic, for they also found in it strains of tenderness and intimacy, courage and compassion, wit and humor, sincere religious feeling and an aspiring romantic idealism, all of which undercut the sense of historical catastrophe that Jan Romein [a Professor of Dutch history] stressed. Indeed, whereas he read it primarily as a revealing historical document, most others preferred to see the diary as a moving personal testimony, a wartime story, to be sure, but also a work of bright adolescent spirit, one that portrayed a life shadowed by daily tension and lingering threat but also inspired by nascent love and humane intelligence.[2]

Yes, that was the Anne I knew and about whom I taught my high school sophomores: bright, funny, sassy, independent-minded, a lover of life, but basically dehistoricized. I thought of Anne as a child, but not as a child of World War II and the Holocaust. I knew Jews had suffered during the war— so had non-Jews—but, about the Holocaust, Hitler's planned systematic attempt to annihilate every Jew on the face of this earth, I still had much to learn. Consequently, I did not raise questions about antisemitism, about collaboration, or about resistance against the Nazis in Holland, nor did I examine the brooding sense of mass death that pervaded the Secret Annex, as the Frank family's hiding place has been called. My ignorance of the Holocaust disabled me. I was not able to probe beneath the surface of the words Anne had written during those two years she lived in the shadow of death in that cramped attic on the top floor of the narrow building on the Prinsengracht Canal in Amsterdam. I read—and taught—*The Diary of Anne Frank* as a story about the "triumph of the human spirit," not as a primary document revealing a historical catastrophe.

But what I missed when I read *The Diary of Anne Frank,* I could not avoid when I read *Man's Search for Meaning.* Perhaps I was more mature, freer, emotionally and intellectually, when I read Frankl's book. I cannot say now, but I do know that when I finished reading it, I was shattered. How could a place like Auschwitz have existed within the very heart of Christian Europe? How could human beings, in the form of Nazi Germany, turn their most ferocious powers on themselves? How could they separate Jews from the human species, force them into concentration camps, demean and starve them, then funnel them into gas chambers and burn them in ovens? Where were the churches? Where were Christians? Why didn't they help the Jews? Today these seem naive questions, but thirty years ago I did not yet know that Hitler and the Nazis had built their deadly ideology on the twin foundations of racist antisemitism and anti-Judaism in Christian theology.

If I were beginning my graduate studies now, I would concentrate on the Holocaust, but in 1971 I followed a more conventional path, taking the required M.A. courses for a degree in English: Chaucer, Shakespeare, British and American literature, the novels of Charles Dickens and William Faulkner, the poetry of Gerard Manley Hopkins, T. S. Eliot, and Marianne Moore. My professors did not seem interested in the questions confounding me, so I kept them to myself and followed my own course of study about the Holocaust, eventually coming upon the work of the French scholar Jules Isaac, a historian by profession, a humanist by vocation, and a Jew by origin. He had been Inspector General of Education for France before World War II, but after France surrendered to Nazi Germany in 1940, the collaborationist Vichy government deprived Isaac of his position, not because he was incompetent, but because he was a Jew. While the soldiers of Nazi Germany occupied France, Jews were forced to flee from town to town to escape the fate that Hitler and the Nazis had decreed for them. The Isaacs moved to a temporary home at Riom, but on a day Jules Isaac happened to be away, the Gestapo caught his wife, daughter, and other members of his family. They were interned, deported, and murdered at Auschwitz.

Isaac fled into hiding. He was unable to understand why the Nazis and their collaborators were killing people simply because they were Jews. From where did this murderous antisemitism spring? What was its origin? Why was the Christian world so silent and apathetic concerning the fate of the Jews? Why didn't the pope in Rome speak out and condemn the Nazis? These were some of the questions Isaac asked himself as he moved from hiding place to hiding place across France, always just a step ahead of the soldiers of Nazi Germany.

When the war ended, Isaac immersed himself in research on the history and origins of antisemitism. His book, *Jesus et Israel*[3], appeared in France in 1948. This book, which he began on a small table in a hotel room in 1943, sent shock waves through the postwar French Christian communities, Catholic and Protestant alike. Translated and published in English a few years later, Isaac's book is "a moving account of the love Jesus had for his people, the Jews, and of the contempt that Christians later harbored for them."[4] It is a compendium of questions, meditations, research, wrath, and persuasive and sometimes harsh polemics about what Isaac called centuries of Christian "teaching of contempt" for Jews and Judaism. Although never intended as a technical or scholarly volume, it is, nonetheless, carefully constructed and beautifully written. Before her death a few years ago, Claire Huchet-Bishop told me she considered it a "literary masterpiece."[5]

In *Jesus et Israel,* Isaac compared texts from the New Testament (Christian Scriptures) with various Catholic and Protestant commentaries on those texts. He showed how many Gospel commentaries presented a completely distorted picture of Jesus' attitude toward Israel and of Israel's attitude toward Jesus. He argued that these commentaries—which for centuries had influenced Christian teaching, preaching, and liturgy—were inaccurate, although widely used by priests, ministers, seminarians, teachers, catechists, and students as the basis for their own teaching and preaching. According to Isaac and, as I later discovered, other scholars as well, for centuries Christians had negated Jewish existence, legitimating their demonization of the Jews and Judaism by citing Scripture, especially the Gospel of John, certain passages from the Gospel of Matthew, and other sections of the New Testament, and then using material from inaccurate commentaries to support their interpretation. Such demonization contributed to pogroms and to what became genocidal hatred of the Jews by Christians, who often were unaware of their own compulsive hatred. Monarchs and secular rulers incarnated Jewish negation into their laws and social structures, and not even the Enlightenment, or the spirit of emancipation fostered by the French Revolution, completely freed Jews from this demonization. They became an outcast people, religiously marginalized, pushed to the periphery of society, cast outside the universe of moral obligation, beyond the boundaries of normal care and concern.

Jules Isaac opened my eyes to this underside of Christian theology and history, and during the years I was engaged in graduate study, I read everything I could get my hands on about antisemitism, Christian-Jewish relations, and anti-Judaism in Christian theology, even though it had nothing to do with the courses I was taking at the time. I became familiar with the work of scholars like Edward Flannery, *The Anguish of the Jews: Twenty-three Centuries of Antisemitism;* Rosemary Ruether, *Faith and Fratricide;* James Parkes, *The Conflict of the Church and the Synagogue;* Charlotte Klein, *Anti-Judaism in Christian Theology;* Samuel Sandmel, *Anti-Semitism in the New Testament;* and Franklin Littell, *The Crucifixion of the Jews,* among others. In the midst of trying to sort my way through this labyrinth, I discovered the work of Gregory Baum, a Canadian Catholic theologian.

His book *Religion and Alienation: A Theological Reading of Sociology*[6] had a profound impact on me. Baum helped me to understand that behind the straightforward aims of religion and culture are hidden trends that exercise a powerful influence on society and sustain the authority of existing institutions. Often these features are so closely interwoven with the true content of a religion and have so affected the inherited consciousness of a religion that it is not easy for adherents to see how the original message has been distorted. Religion, however spiritual in appearance, has a social impact that may be hidden from its adherents, including theologians. I began to understand a little more clearly why so many Christians were indifferent to the fate of the Jews during Hitler's Third Reich and the Holocaust. They could not discern the difference between German nationalism and Nazi ideology, which had become inseparable from racial antisemitism and traditional anti-Judaism in Christian theology.

In the fall of 1977, having completed a master's degree and with an almost completed doctorate, I accepted an administrative position at Mercy College of Detroit. Subsequently I was invited to teach a course on the Holocaust in Mercy's new Department of Interdisciplinary Studies. I readily accepted, as it gave me an opportunity to explore the questions and issues that had consumed my free time during the previous six years. To my surprise, twenty-five students, almost all of them Detroit metropolitan area policemen (no women here!), signed up for the course, "Encountering the Holocaust." Most students who registered for the class did so because it was cross-referenced with Religious Studies, and every student—whether Catholic or not—was required to take at least three credits in Religious Studies in order to graduate.

I began lecturing, and students began reading—Lucy Dawidowicz, *The War Against the Jews;* Franklin Littell, *The Crucifixion of the Jews;* Terrence Des Pres, *The Survivor;* Simon Wiesenthal, *The Sunflower;* Elie Wiesel, *Night;* and, of course, Viktor Frankl, *Man's Search for Meaning.* Nothing engaged student interest more compellingly, however, than the April 1978 broadcast of the NBC docudrama, "Holocaust." Elie Wiesel found it "Untrue, offensive, cheap . . . an insult to those who perished and those who survived,"[7] but my students found it riveting. What TV program could ever convey the horror of Auschwitz? Still, my students found "Holocaust" instructive. It imprinted upon their memories an evil beyond comprehension, and they wanted to know more. My questions became their questions, and vice versa. Together we struggled to find answers—or at least a way into the questions. They wanted to speak to Holocaust survivors, and I discovered there were many living in the Detroit area.

I remember a husband and wife, survivors of Auschwitz, who came to that first class. They were Greek Jews, originally from Salonika. He was short and stocky; she was slim and elegant as a reed. I remember how she began to shake as she started to speak, and how her husband gently coaxed her to continue. I remember my students sitting perfectly still, absorbed in her words, touched by her pain. Eighteen years later, I still remember how respectfully those policemen asked their questions about the kingdom of night, and I remember the searing honesty of this Greek Jewish couple who tried to speak about the unspeakable. The shared experience of listening to these Holocaust survivors was like no other experience I had ever had.

We read *Night,* Elie Wiesel's "exodus" experience into Auschwitz and beyond. It began toward the end of 1941, before the Nazis came to Sighet, with a pious young Jewish boy proclaiming that he "believed profoundly."[8] It ended four years later, after Auschwitz and in Buchenwald, with that same young Jewish boy, his world and faith now shattered, gazing into a mirror from which "a corpse gazed back at me. The look in his eyes, as they stared into mine, has never left me."[9] One student called Wiesel's book, "the most eloquent statement of despair" he had ever read. Could I not invite him to class so that they could talk to him, just as they had talked to the Greek couple from Salonika? I told them I doubted if Elie Wiesel would be able to come to our class, but perhaps he might be persuaded to participate in Mercy's lecture series on contemporary issues during the next academic year.

I knew Wiesel taught at Boston University, so one day I called the university and was connected to his assistant, Martha Hauptman, who discretely inquired about the purpose of my call. She put me on hold, then passed my call through to Elie Wiesel himself. I told him who I was, that I was teaching a course on the Holocaust at Mercy College of Detroit, that I was a Sister of Mercy, and that my students wanted to meet him. Would he ever be willing to give a lecture at Mercy? To my delight, he said he would, if we could find a workable date. I assured him I would find such a date. Elie Wiesel kept his word. Six months later, he came to Mercy College of Detroit, and thus began a relationship that has marked my life in many ways.

When Wiesel came to Mercy College of Detroit, he came as a messenger to humanity, to borrow Robert McAfee Brown's phrase, and the message he brought was one of solidarity and hope. He challenged us: Do not be indifferent to evil. The Holocaust is the benchmark against which to judge and oppose continuing acts of genocide in our world. To remember the Holocaust, he said, is to commit oneself to action on behalf of others. To remember the past is to commit oneself to the future.

In September 1980, Wiesel again visited Mercy College, this time to participate in the program "After Auschwitz: Vision or Void?" We had time to talk. He asked me about my projects; I asked him about his work as the chairman of President Jimmy Carter's Commission on the Holocaust. He told me about a conference he was organizing in Washington, D.C., that would bring together Holocaust survivors and former Allied soldiers who had "liberated" Nazi concentration and death camps. He wanted to bring them together in our nation's capital so that *together* they could bear witness to what had happened. And he wanted to provide an opportunity so the survivors could thank their "liberators."

After Wiesel's visit, I returned to my own projects and to my research and teaching, inspired and challenged by this man who had emerged from the abyss of the death camps, speaking words of hope, not words of despair. I continued struggling to understand the pathologies of Nazi leaders like Hitler, Himmler, and Eichmann, but increasingly, I focused my attention on those who tried to help Jews during the Holocaust rather than harm them.

I knew millions of people had been swept into the Nazi net of death, Jews and non-Jews alike. I also knew there were a few good people who did not stand idly by while their friends and neighbors were rounded up and shipped off to Nazi death camps. I wanted to know more about them. What motivated them to risk their lives to help Jews? For so many years, I had explored the mystery of evil, but now I wanted to explore the mystery of goodness.

During the summer of 1982, I spent a month in Jerusalem, going almost every day to Yad Vashem, Israel's memorial to the 6 million Jews who perished in the Holocaust. I worked in the library and archives, trying to discover more about these so-called "Righteous Gentiles." One day as I was walking through the "Avenue of the Just," reading the names on the plaques in front of the carob trees planted to commemorate those who risked their lives to help Jews during the Holocaust, I decided to organize an international conference about rescue during the Holocaust.

A year later, I wrote to Elie Wiesel, briefly outlining my idea for a conference. Within a week, he called me. Could I come to Washington to discuss the idea further? I flew to Washington, and after a meeting of the United States Holocaust Memorial Council, explained my idea and said I was confident I could get the money to organize such a conference, if he would participate in it. He asked me to prepare a proposal. Less than a year later, September 1984, in the auditorium of the Department of State and under the sponsorship of the United States Holocaust Memorial Council, Elie Wiesel convened the opening session of the international conference, "Faith in Humankind: Rescuers of Jews during the Holocaust."

When I think about the question, "What do you regard as your most important contribution(s) to interpreting/understanding the Holocaust?" I immediately think about that conference, and about the book and documentary film, *The Courage to Care,*[10] which resulted from it. These, I think, are important contributions I have made to interpreting the Holocaust. Why? Because at a time when few people were focusing attention on the *challenge of the exception,* that is, on the challenge presented by people who tried to help rather than to harm Jews during the Holocaust, I focused attention on them. Today there are many conferences, many books, and many articles written about the "Righteous Gentiles," about altruism, and about moral courage under stress. Ten years ago there were only a few.

The rescuers do not provide us with answers. On the contrary, they compel us to ask ourselves: Why do some people, during the meanest political times and under the most terrible political threats of reprisal, act in a morally correct way? Seeking an answer to that question demands a double inquiry into the human potential for caring and the rare summoning of courage to show concern and compassion for others in extreme danger. That so few summoned the courage to care during the Holocaust is clear from the historical evidence, and we must not avoid the terrible implications of that evidence even as we explore the dynamics of rescue. Those who tried to help Jews during the Holocaust demonstrate that there is always an alternative to passive complicity with evil, and therein is a lesson for all of us.

After the conference, I returned to Detroit and to my work at Mercy College. I continued my own research and teaching about the Holocaust and stayed in contact with Elie Wiesel. He appointed me an advisor to the United States Holocaust Memorial Council. This meant that from time to time I sat in on meetings of the council, which was in the midst of a struggle to develop an appropriate and suitable Holocaust memorial in our nation's capital. The council had a delicate and difficult task: to preserve the unique aspect of the Jewish tragedy during the Holocaust without neglecting the other victims of the Nazis—Poles, Gypsies, Soviet prisoners of war, Jehovah's Witnesses, homosexuals, and others swept into the Nazi net of death. Wiesel himself had addressed this challenge when he was chairman of President Jimmy Carter's Commission on the Holocaust, the precursor organization to the United States Holocaust Memorial Council: "Our Commission believes that because they were the principal target of Hitler's Final Solution, we must remember the six million Jews and, through them and beyond them, but never without them, rescue from oblivion all the men, women and children, Jewish and non-Jewish, who perished in those years in the forests and camps of the kingdom of night."[11]

In early 1986 I proposed another conference to Wiesel. I knew he had devoted his life to writing and speaking, with extraordinary power and eloquence, about the Holocaust, but I also believed that he did not want to neglect non-Jews who had suffered and died at the hands of the Nazis and their collaborators. I suggested he think about convening a conference on "the other victims," the phrase I so often had heard for non-Jews persecuted and murdered by the Nazis. If he convened it, I told him I would organize it.

As a Jew, a survivor of Auschwitz, and as a scholar, Elie Wiesel knew there were risks. Such a conference, for example, might blur the unique aspect of the Jewish tragedy during the Holocaust, might simplistically but conveniently group the various victims together, might dump them all into the same file—Jews and Resistance fighters, Jews and anti-Nazis, Jews and political prisoners, Jews and homosexuals, Jews and Gypsies, Jews and Jehovah's Witnesses, Jews and Soviet prisoners of war, Jews and social deviants, Jews and. . . . Still, he opted to convene the conference and asked me to direct it. It took almost a year to put it together, and in the intervening months, Wiesel was awarded the 1986 Nobel Peace Prize and also resigned as chairman of the United States Holocaust Memorial Council. Nevertheless, in the midst of one of Washington, D.C.'s worst snowstorms, the conference opened with an address by then-Secretary of State George Shultz, who said that "while the attention of civilized humanity has been focused, and rightly so, on the unprecedented Nazi murder of six million European Jews . . . the acts of unspeakable evil committed by Nazi Germany against non-Jewish people also deserves to be studied, to be condemned, and above all to be remembered."[12]

This conference is another contribution I think I have made to interpreting/understanding the Holocaust. Michael Berenbaum, a scholar whose sensitive and astute advice proved invaluable during the months I worked organizing the conference, said at the closing session,

Years from now, as we look back at this conference, at the communities that were represented and the issues that were raised, we may see that it pointed the way for solving the problem of uniqueness and universality. It showed us how to include the other victims of Nazism without distorting history or backing away from the Judeo-centric nature of the Holocaust itself. . . . Only by understanding the fate of others who suffered, where it paralleled the Jewish experience and, more importantly, where it differed, can the distinctive character of the Jewish fate as a matter of historical fact be demonstrated.[13]

In the spring of 1987, a few months after Wiesel received the Nobel Peace Prize in Oslo, Norway, he established The Elie Wiesel Foundation for Humanity and invited me to be the foundation's first director. With the approval of the Sisters of Mercy, I accepted and set to work organizing the foundation. During my three and a half years as director, I also helped to organize four international conferences in France (Paris), the United States (Boston), Israel (Haifa), and Norway (Oslo), each of which focused on some dimension of "The Anatomy of Hate." These were challenging, exhilarating, exhausting years, but satisfying as well. I learned a great deal working with Elie Wiesel, but when I was asked to take on a less demanding assignment in Scranton, Pennsylvania, I did so, as it provided me with an opportunity to refocus my energies, get back into teaching, and also to do some writing.

During my years at The Elie Wiesel Foundation, I interacted and worked with many people from different parts of the world. Few, however, were as impressive or generous as John Roth, a Holocaust scholar and the Russell Pitzer Professor of Philosophy at Claremont McKenna College in California. John brings to his scholarly endeavors an incisive mind, a humane spirit, and a questing faith. He has been a major influence on my thinking, teaching, and writing, evident in the several books we have worked on together, particularly *Different Voices: Women and the Holocaust.*[14]

Our first collaborative writing effort was an edited book on the Auschwitz convent controversy, *Memory Offended,*[15] an issue still not completely resolved. A few months after our book appeared, I received a copy of a volume Michael Berenbaum and John had published, *Holocaust: Religious & Philosophical Implications.*[16] It is a collection of "now classic essays" about the Holocaust, essays repeatedly referred to by scholars, and required reading for anyone serious about studying this event. It is a good collection, a valuable resource for teachers and students, but when I reviewed it, I felt it suffered from a serious flaw. Of the twenty-three "classic essays" in the book, only one is written by a woman, Lucy Dawidowicz, "Thinking about the Six Million: Facts, Figures, Perspectives."[17] When John and I spoke, I mentioned to him that women seemed to be invisible in his book. Anyone studying the Holocaust, I said, knows women were everywhere—in the ghettos, in the trains, in the camps, in resistance, in hiding, in places of refuge—and they also know there are many fine books and essays by female authors. We agreed that another book was needed. Two years later, *Different Voices: Women and the Holocaust* was published.

I think I can speak for John as well when I say *Different Voices* is an important contribution to interpreting/understanding the Holocaust. Why? As one reviewer commented, "Yes, women's voices are missing, but this book, the first anthology of its kind (at least, in English), portends the beginning of more rediscoveries, more narratives of women's courage and caring, and more research into the catastrophe that haunts our memory and shapes our paths to the future."[18]

When John and I proposed our idea for *Different Voices,* scholars were just beginning to call attention to the particular experiences of women, *as women,* during the Holocaust. Today, scholars increasingly are writing about the particularities of women's experiences during the Holocaust. Growing numbers of scholars—women and men—are elucidating women's experiences, drawing attention to how their experiences compare and contrast with those of men. Today, there are more books by and about women during the Holocaust, but many more need to be written, and many more need to be rediscovered.

What are some challenges facing us as we move into the twenty-first century? Nearly twenty-five years ago, Elie Wiesel wrote, "It was at Auschwitz that human beings underwent their first mutations. Without Auschwitz, there would have been no Hiroshima."[19] I have always wondered what Elie Wiesel meant when he wrote that. Did he mean to suggest that there was a cause and effect relationship between Auschwitz (the Holocaust) and Hiroshima? Was he suggesting that there existed a parity of horror between Auschwitz and Hiroshima? As we face the twenty-first century, with its threats and promises, I think we need to examine again, to "unpack" and explicate Wiesel's statement, as well as to encourage Elie Wiesel himself to confront anew the profundity of his insight.

On June 13, 1960, two years before the first session of Vatican II, Pope John XXIII received in audience the Jewish historian Jules Isaac. Their conversation lasted a mere twenty-five minutes, but it began one of the most profound renewals of the Catholic Church's two thousand year history. In his presentation to the pope, Isaac outlined centuries of Christian "teaching of contempt" against Jews and Judaism. He presented the pope with a carefully prepared program designed to rectify the negative aspects of Christian teaching. Toward the end of their meeting, the old Jewish scholar asked Pope John XXIII, "whether there was any hope of ridding Christian teaching of the many anti-Jewish myths that had become encrusted on it like barnacles on a ship." John replied with characteristic honesty: "You have every right to more than hope."[20]

I have had many "teachers" who have helped me to confront the historical catastrophe of the Holocaust: Jules Isaac, Gregory Baum, Elie Wiesel, and John Roth, among others, but the teacher whose lesson I am still trying to learn is Pope John XXIII. It was this old man, faithful to his church yet unafraid to confront its past, who taught me that I have "every right to more than hope" that the future will be different, if I am not afraid to take history seriously, to engage in dialogue with my brothers and sisters in the human family, to learn from them, and to change.

NOTES

1. Viktor E. Frankl, *Man's Search for Meaning: An Introduction to Logotherapy* (New York: Simon & Schuster, Inc., 1984).

2. Alvin H. Rosenfeld, "Popularization and Memory: The Case of Anne Frank," in *Lessons and Legacies: The Meaning of the Holocaust in a Changing World,* ed. Peter Hayes (Evanston, Ill.: Northwestern University Press, 1991), 248–49.

3. Jules Isaac, *Jesus and Israel* (New York: Holt, Rinehart and Winston, 1971).

4. Gregory Baum, *Is the New Testament Anti-Semitic? A Reexamination of the New Testament,* rev. ed. (Glen Rock, N.J.: Paulist Press, 1965), 12.

5. In 1990, when John Roth and I were preparing our edited volume, *Memory Offended: The Auschwitz Convent Controversy* (New York: Praeger, 1991), I spoke to Mme. Huchet-Bishop by telephone to invite her to contribute an essay to our volume. She spoke passionately about the work of her friend, Jules Isaac.

6. Gregory Baum, *Religion and Alienation: A Theological Reading of Sociology* (New York: Paulist Press, 1975).

7. Quoted in Lance Morrow, "Television and the Holocaust," *Time,* 1 May 1978, 52.

8. Elie Wiesel, *The Night Trilogy* (New York: Hill and Wang, 1987), 14.

9. Ibid., 119.

10. Carol Rittner, R.S.M. and Sondra Myers, eds., *The Courage to Care: Rescuers of Jews during the Holocaust* (New York: New York University Press, 1986); and *The Courage to Care,* produced and directed by Robert Gardner, 29 min., United Way Productions, 1986.

11. See further, Elie Wiesel's letter to President Jimmy Carter, which serves as the preface of the *Report to the President* (Washington, D.C.: President's Commission on the Holocaust, 1976), iii.

12. George Shultz, "Remarks" at the conference, "The Other Victims: Non-Jews Persecuted and Murdered by the Nazis" (Washington, D.C.: U.S. State Department, #45 [mimeographed]).

13. Michael Berenbaum, ed., *A Mosaic of Victims: Non-Jews Persecuted and Murdered by the Nazis* (New York: New York University Press, 1990), xiv.

14. Carol Rittner and John K. Roth, eds., *Different Voices: Women and the Holocaust* (New York: Paragon House, 1993).

15. Carol Rittner and John K. Roth, eds., *Memory Offended: The Auschwitz Convent Controversy* (New York: Praeger, 1991).

16. John K. Roth and Michael Berenbaum, eds., *Holocaust: Religious and Philosophical Implications* (New York: Paragon House, 1989).

17. See further, Roth and Berenbaum, eds., *Holocaust: Religious & Philosophical Implications,* 51–68.

18. Helen Brent, "Different Voices: Women and the Holocaust," *Belles Lettres* 9 (Winter 1993/94): 46.

19. Elie Wiesel, *One Generation After,* trans. Lily Edelman and the author (New York: Avon Books, 1972), 220.

20. Eugene Fisher, *Faith Without Prejudice: Rebuilding Christian Attitudes Toward Judaism* (New York: Paulist Press, 1977), 5–6.

Part Three

CHALLENGES

11

The *Shoah*-Road to a Revised/Revived Christianity

Alice L. Eckardt

In 1974, when my first paper dealing with the impact of the Holocaust on Christian and Jewish faith was published,[1] I had been teaching a university undergraduate course on the history of Jewish-Christian relations ("The Christian-Jewish Encounter") for two years[2] and was about to initiate an additional course, "The Holocaust: Its History and Meaning." Both subjects, so irrefutably interrelated, have been central to my thinking for so many years that it is with difficulty that I have attempted to retrieve the exact course of that concern.

My first awareness of the terrible hatred of Jews being enacted in governmental decrees and actions was during the late 1930s—my high school years. I recall my mother remarking that a neighbor, who had come to the United States from Bavaria a good many years before, was speaking in total support, even enthusiasm, for Hitler's then-current restrictions on the Jews of Germany. I was shocked to hear that someone I thought I knew rather well could take such a point of view.

By contrast, at Oberlin College, to be Jewish was not an issue, any more than being black was—at least so it seemed to me as an "Anglo." In short, I was extremely fortunate in that milieu, as in my prejudice-free childhood.

But I soon discovered that on the broader scene prejudices and hatreds abounded. While racial attitudes toward blacks were obviously dealt with in American history courses covering certain eras, historical antisemitism was, to the best of my recollection, almost never mentioned in any of my courses, except with reference to Nazi Germany. (The one exception was the period of the medieval Crusades.)

My learning about that ignored long history—identified variously as the *adversus Judaeos* tradition, Christian anti-Judaism, or Jew-hatred/*Judenhass* before the nineteenth-century coining of the term *Antisemitismus*/antisemitism—was prompted largely by the Holocaust, my husband's doctoral dissertation work[3] in the immediate aftermath of World War II, and my own interest in tracing the historical trail. The more I uncovered, the more I became committed to exposing the dreadful and shameful past of the Christian community and its contribution to modern day secular and political antisemitism including, ultimately, the Nazi Final Solution; and equally committed to helping free Christian teachings of this poison. My teaching, writing, speaking, and thought have never ceased being influenced by the *Shoah* and the long history of antisemitism (and anti-Judaism)[4] that preceded it. And I am convinced that the Christian community must live with this awareness for many years to come as it struggles to free itself from the theological and sociological consequences of absolutizing its faith, and, even more particularly, of holding in contempt or defect the people of the faith community out of which it originated.

As I struggled with the questions raised by all of this, I found that I had to reconsider other fundamental issues, such as suffering, power and powerlessness, the State of Israel, and repentance and forgiveness,[5] both in the ways that the two faiths had dealt with them in the past and how we have to rethink them now post-*Shoah*. I came to conclude that the God of history commands us to reshape Christianity in the light of learning from history. The authentic Christian message is not just a repletion of previous teachings but a creative process of reinterpretation and reformulation in obedience to God's word *in the present*.

In 1974 when I evaluated the contemporary scene, I insisted that "Christianity has [still] failed to grasp the crucial nature of the questions raised by the Holocaust for its own theology and future, just as it generally has refused to admit any responsibility for the death camps." I went on to say that "those Christians who have grappled with the reality and implications of the Holocaust see a church in vast apostasy, involved not only in the murder of Jews but also of God through his people, still linked to a supersessionist theology that bears the genocidal germ, in danger of repeating its complicity in criminal actions, and without credibility because of its failure to understand that everything has been changed by Auschwitz."[6] We need to learn that the Third Reich's laws and actions regarding Jews had Christian precedents going back to the earliest centuries. (Only the death camps were new.) Thus we Christians have a weighty tradition to overturn, not only that of low-level suspicion and hatred but also of high-level systematic theology.

Can there be a theology *of* the Holocaust? No. There can only be a theology *before* the Holocaust, and one *after* the Holocaust.

Clearly, in 1974 I believed that the various church statements that had begun to emerge after World War II and even after the Second Vatican Council's *Nostra Aetate* (1965) had not had a significant or wide enough impact to put needed judgment into effect. Yet the rock had *begun* to be pushed up the hill, slowly, and with much effort due to the weight of the past centuries' teachings and events.

Today many more Christian scholars, clergy, and church governing bodies—at least in this country[7]—have some awareness of the history of Christian mistreatment of Jews, the churches' negative teachings about Judaism, and the very serious challenge these factors pose to their proclaimed gospel. Even so, the worldwide Christian community in particular, as well as large portions of American and European Christianity, remain either largely ignorant of that history or disinterested in its pertinence to the Church's message, and this is the main challenge for Christian faith. Indeed, some Christians are so incensed at any challenge to the absolute primacy of the Christian faith and its obligation to convert all other peoples that they will not consider the fundamental challenges of this long history. Moreover, pre-*Shoah,* anti-Jewish preaching can still be heard from some clergy in all branches of the Church.[8]

Even those who are aware of the problem remain largely baffled about how to purify the "good news of Christ Jesus" of its built-in anti-Jewish aspect and how to deal with some of the New Testament's texts. And the task of rethinking and revising Christian theology from the ground up has still not received major attention, especially from those considered "leading" theologians, that is, those holding prestigious appointments and writing most of the books used in the field. The German Catholic theologian Johannes-Baptist Metz is one of the few who fully acknowledges this: "There is no truth for me which I could defend with my back turned toward Auschwitz . . . in the final analysis, [it is] a matter of revising Christian theology altogether."[9]

To be sure, since 1965 a fairly large number of official and laudable Church statements addressing various aspects of the Christian-Jewish relationship in the past and the present have been issued by international Church bodies and officials (the Vatican and several popes, worldwide Lutheran and Anglican assemblies), multidenominational organizations (World Council of Churches, National Council of Churches), national denominations, regional groups, and dioceses.[10] While little reference was made to the Holocaust in many of the earlier documents (especially the Roman Catholic ones), frequent mention is made of it in the later documents. Thus the grounds for the needed changes have been prepared and the seeds planted. But unless properly cultivated and fertilized, the seedlings can be crowded out by the prolific old plants.

Two United Church of Christ (UCC) documents (1987, 1990) contain some of the most forthright admissions of past failures by the Christian community along with clear recognition that "God's covenant with the Jewish people has not been rescinded or abrogated by God, but remains in full force. . . ." The 1990 follow-up "Message to the Churches" by the UCC Theological Panel acknowledges that the "new context for the very old question of the relation of Jews and Christians is the epochal event of the twentieth century. . . . The Holocaust has sent Christians back to their texts and traditions to re-examine their theology and to ask about their own complicity in the anti-Semitism that gave rise to this horror." Perhaps most importantly the "Message" reaffirms the denomination's constitution, which calls it "to make the faith its own in each new generation" and recalls its Reformation founders' call to let "new light and truth break from God's holy Word."[11] Unfortunately many in the denomination, including its clergy, oppose these path-breaking assertions, thus demonstrating the residual theological problem.

Even more of a problem arises when the State of Israel is considered. Nevertheless the "Message" appreciates "the compelling moral argument for the creation of modern Israel as a vehicle for self-determination and *as a haven for a vicitimized people.* . . ."

Another particularly significant document—and one that refers to the State of Israel—comes from the Protestant churches in the Rhineland (1980). It acknowledges Christian coresponsibility and guilt for the Holocaust, and recognizes that the "continuing existence of the Jewish people, its return to the Land of Promise, and also the creation of the State of Israel, are signs of the faithfulness of God toward His people."[12]

Why did it require the Nazis' "Final Solution of the Jewish Question" for Christians to begin to look at and question their centuries-long "teaching of contempt" toward the Jewish people and Judaism? And why do we find Christians still refusing to concede that there is a problem for their faith community? Is it mere stubbornness? Or is it a too deeply inculcated hatred of, or conviction about, the evil they believe Jews and Judaism represent? Is it fear of the loss of security their traditional faith has provided them and therefore resistance to any change in it, the yearning for an absolute that holds all the answers and does not require difficult decision making? Whatever the reasons may be, unremitting work is required to overcome the resistance they engender. And unless that resistance is overcome, Christian society and persons may continue to contribute to harming those outside their own community. That would hardly be a future to look forward to. Having gazed into the abyss of the *Shoah,* I am compelled to try to alert and arouse fellow Christians to the life-and-death issue of so much of our inherited teaching.

In addition to the danger of the *adversus Judaeos* continuum, I gradually came to discern two foundational issues that required attention: the need to rediscover God in a radically new understanding, and to apprehend more fundamentally the essential role of humankind in history. These issues require a good deal of rethinking and have led me to tackle some difficult and troubling issues facing us, both apart from the *Shoah* per se and yet given a demanding prominence by the events of that deadly twelve-year period.

Suffering and evil have always challenged the thinking of any system of ethical thought or of believers in a good creator, and hence any number of explanations or justifications have been constructed to meet the problem. Usually the victims are said to be at fault, even though no one but God may know what wrongdoing they have committed. Alternatively, the sufferers are told they must endure their pains and sorrows because it somehow fits into the divine scheme.

Suffering of the worst sort, both psychologically and physically, is epitomized in the Nazis' Final Solution program. Inevitably it raises questions about God's "goodness" or God's action in history, for if that evil did not call forth divine response, what would? Neither the long-held Jewish view that God expects them to bear the role of "suffering servant" until the world accepts and lives by God's Torah, nor the traditional Christian view that Jesus' suffering was God's way of offering humankind salvation from "original sin" helps us when we see such vast and *useless* suffering. We are convinced that God would not wish any people to have to endure this. And we begin to wonder whether we have misunderstood. Has God deprived Herself/ Himself of absolute power and made Godself vulnerable to powerlessness, suffering, even possibly death? If so, what are the ramifications of that action?

Having pondered over these interrelated questions for quite some years, and having given them and various attempted answers lengthy attention, I came out where I began, convinced that suffering is not part of God's will or wish for the creation.[13] I reached much the same conclusion (however tenuous it may be) as did Hans Jonas: that God cares about all those in the creation and wishes only good for all its creatures; but that God has left the future in the hands of those She/He created and consequently God is indeed vulnerable and subject to being hurt and diminished. However, when God suffers, the world shares that pain until it relieves the divine agony by relieving the agony of fellow humans and other living creatures.[14]

In an earlier article[15] I had already considered the prevailing views about power and powerlessness that prevailed in the Jewish community over the centuries, noting that during times when the Jewish people had a state of their own, prophets, sages, and rabbis emphasized the community's responsibility for the total well-being of all its members. Power was natural and necessary. But it had to be exercised with restraint. Even the Creator had set a limit to divine power by creating a finite universe and by giving humankind responsibility for helping to perfect the unfinished, imperfect world. I noted that for Judaism the covenant of society is formed by the check and balance of power and counterpower. Evil can only be neutralized by the use of counterpower refined by *mitzvot,* legislation, and constitutions.

With the onset of the long centuries of powerlessness, accommodation to those in power became the primary method of Jewish survival. However, extreme circumstances were to be met with martyrdom (*kiddush ha-Shem*). In the Nazi era the utter degradation of powerlessness was fully revealed as Europe's Jewish communities experienced the reality of total vulnerability and helplessness. During these years resistance began to be seen as a moral obligation. (In a later essay I specifically insisted that Christianity must stop exalting suffering and sacrifice. "Suffering servant" may have a heroic sound until one is faced with the reality. But it is particularly immoral to recommend it for *others.*[16])

It is not surprising that both the survivor community and the smaller Jewish community living in Palestine (Eretz Israel) refused to accept the pre–World War II British determination to end the experiment with Jewish statehood. For if Jewish survival is a first requirement, their own country appeared to be a necessity. Jews had learned that they had to risk their very lives—and suffer inordinate losses—in order to survive as a free people. The State of Israel came into being out of the recognition that hope without power is not a hopeful position in a world where power dominates. (Nor was the State of Israel viewed as a fulfillment of messianic promise.) Thus Israel reflects the "courage of a people who dared to embody 2,000 years of hope in the fragile vessel of a state."[17]

While more Christians and churches in the West are now prepared to take the *Shoah* and antisemitism into consideration for Christian theology and preaching, that is less true for the State of Israel. I asked why this was the case. "Is it because with the Holocaust the Jewish people remain victims, and thus fit the traditional stereotype, whereas Israel turns Jews into victors?" (I observed that even with their own state, Jews remain victims in many ways, though that is not generally acknowledged.) Or can it be "simply that so many Christians see [the State of] Israel *only* in political terms?" And yet we Christians are not unwilling to make relative moral and political distinctions about others, including the Palestinian people and the Arab states. I concluded that "Israel bears the burden of the Bible, with both the negative and positive aspects that involves, and the aura of a 'special' people and nation of whom extra-ordinary behavior is expected (either good or evil) and of whom good or even exceptional behavior is even demanded." Among seven basic ingredients of Christianity's anti-Judaic theology at least three need to be noted for their relevance to the land/state issue: that God abrogated the old Covenant as proven by the destruction of the Temple and the city of Jerusalem in 70 C.E.; that Christianity took the place of Judaism in the city and former kingdom of David by right; and that Jews were exiled forever from their land by God to serve as negative witnesses to the truth of the Christian gospel.[18]

I ended my article on suffering with a number of my own judgments pertinent to this issue, including: the establishment of Israel was a responsible religious and political commitment; radical evil must be resisted; martyrdom can no longer be considered as the ideal religious or responsible political method by which to respond to tyranny and evil; our ultimate goal must be peace and community but not by making a sacrificial offering of some nation or people, especially the one people that tried for two millennia to live without sovereignty and paid the price of six million lives twice over.[19] Indeed, the State of Israel may well be the ultimate test question for non-Jews.

It is time for Christians to acknowledge that this reborn nation is, or at least can be, a *beginning* of *tikkun,* of restoration or healing of the world, even though only fragmentary. For it enables the Jewish people as a collectivity some control over their lives and destiny, and offers a new possibility of survival to the people so decimated and dismembered. In fact, Israel is the only practical step taken so far to protect Jews from another genocidal attack. Furthermore, the Jewish state represents its people's effort not to be cut off from the nations of the world but to be an integral part of the community of nations. For the Christian world, the State of Israel offers a unique opportunity for repentance and reconciliation with brothers and sisters in the Covenant, as well as participation in the process of *tikkun.*

In 1988, at the Oxford conference, "Remembering for the Future," I struggled with the question of forgiveness, particularly as it was highlighted near that time in several publicized events in Britain, Germany, and the Netherlands. (Repentance was singularly overlooked in most of the episodes, while forgiveness was either treated sentimentally or made into an absolute.) I also looked at the thought-provoking views of thirty-two public figures and scholars (Jews and Christians) who were asked by Simon Wiesenthal to consider forgiveness in a specific *Shoah* situation that he set out for them. It is a complex paper and does not lend itself to a brief summary.[20] However, a few final observations can be made here: First, time is a most important factor. There is a time to ask for forgiveness and there is a time to wait to ask. The Jewish people as a whole need time to absorb the enormous pain and loss they have sustained in this century, and they need to be able to feel safe for an indeterminate period of time before they should be called on to assist others with their problems of guilt and remorse. Second, the *Shoah* must be incorporated into collective memory so that it can influence the future. The only possibility of its having a positive and restorative impact on world history—one that will turn us away from the evils the *Shoah* so totally represented—lies in remembrance. Third, compassion and understanding for others—trying to comprehend what it is like to walk in another's shoes—not only may make us more responsive to their needs, but are also more likely to produce sympathy if and when we ourselves may need it.

In a very recent paper considering the denial of both the Armenian geno-cide (by the Turkish government) and the *Shoah*[21] I contended that ignoring such terrible destruction of human lives en masse is a form of complicity *even if* that is not intended. Therefore, remembering is both a way of pre-venting complicity and a way of counteracting those who seek to obfuscate, diminish, or deny such events. Moreover, it is important to realize that time does *not* necessarily heal all wounds, especially when the sense of a morally ordered universe is challenged.

A full rethinking of Christian theology, which the *Shoah* demands, must take all of these issues into consideration,[22] not only because of the prob-lems we now discern in our tradition(s) but also because of the new reali-zation that God is working, however indirectly or slowly, to entice us onto untried paths. The *Shoah* was the terminus of the previous Christian age and it forced us into the age After the Final Solution (AFS). Will we be able to bring about a noticeably reformed era? Or will we move on to ever more murderous and self-destructive actions?

NOTES

1. Alice L. Eckardt, "The Holocaust: Christian and Jewish Responses," *Journal of the American Academy of Religion* 42 (1974): 453–69.

2. I took over this course from A. Roy Eckardt, who had initiated it a few years earlier. It dealt with the long history of the relationship and the theological teachings undergirding it.

3. See Chapter 9, A. Roy Eckardt, "Once and Not Future Partisan: A Plea for History," in this volume.

4. There is no hard-and-fast line between anti-Judaism and antisemitism.

5. Other issues I have dealt with at some length but have not mentioned in this retrospective include the Reformation (historically reviewed and criticized), biomed-ical issues, denial (of the Armenian genocide as well as the Holocaust), and teaching a course on the Holocaust.

6. "The Holocaust . . . ," 453–54. A few other Christians who wrote to express a similar view at that time include the American Protestant William Jay Peck (1973) and the French Catholic Claire Huchet-Bishop (1975).

7. In 1985, both the Christian *and Jewish* communities of Britain opposed Bishop Hugh Montefiore's attempt to arrange for the showing in Birmingham of the Auschwitz Exhibition. The international conference "Remembering for the Future" (1988) was held in Oxford and London precisely because of this attitude. And only in that same year (1988) did the Lambeth Conference of the worldwide Anglican communion produce its first document dealing with antisemitism and the *Shoah*.

To be sure, European churches had, in the early 1970s, issued statements con-fessing the fallacious and harmful teachings of the past centuries, and acknowledged the terrible happenings of the 1930s–1940s. But since the Third Reich's Final Solu-tion had decimated the European Jewish communities there was less insistence from neighbors to face the issues fully and fewer interfaith groups than in the United States.

8. In fact, some widely read scholars (such as Wolfhart Pannenberg) forcefully reiterate the traditional anti-Jewish charges and reassert Christianity's replacement of Judaism (see A. Roy Eckardt and Alice L. Eckardt, *Long Night's Journey into Day: A Revised Retrospective on the Holocaust* (Detroit: Wayne State University Press, 1988), 129–31. A relatively new pastoral edition of the Bible, *The Bible of the Christian Communities,* which was first published in South America in 1972 and is now being published in France (as of 1994), is found to have notes and comments that "represent all the variants of anti-Judaism which official texts of the Roman Catholic Church since Vatican II have fought against." Throughout, the texts "echo the ancient substitution theology" and confuse historical times with the present (*ICCJ News* 16 [1995]: 2–3).

9. Metz, "Facing the Jews: Christian Theology After Auschwitz," in *The Holocaust as Interruption,* ed. Elisabeth Schüssler Fiorenza and David Tracy (Edinburgh: T. & T. Clark, 1984), 28, 29–30.

10. I evaluated the Protestant documents of 1975–83 and considered how much attention was given to seven fundamental questions; see "A Christian Problem: Protestant Documents" in *More Stepping Stones to Jewish-Christian Relations,* compiled by Helga Croner (New York: Stimulus Books & Paulist Press, 1985), 16–23. For the complete Christian documents see that volume and *Stepping Stones to Further Jewish-Christian Relations* (covering 1965–75), (New York: Stimulus Books & Paulist Press, 1977); *Stepping-Stones to Further Jewish-Lutheran Relationships,* ed. Harold H. Ditmanson (Minneapolis: Augsburg Press, 1990); and *The Theology of the Churches and the Jewish People: Statements by the World Council of Churches and Its Member Churches,* commentary by Allan Brockway, Paul van Buren, Rolf Rendtorff, and Simon Schoon (Geneva: World Council of Churches, 1988). None of these books includes two documents from the United Church of Christ (1987, 1989), one from the Disciples of Christ/Christian Church (1988), nor the very significant "Declaration of the Evangelical Lutheran Church in America to the Jewish Community" (1994). Nor are some of the later interfaith statements included.

The most recent Roman Catholic statements from Polish and German bishops on the anniversary of Auschwitz's liberation (1995) may have been more of a response to the world's attention to the commemorations than to genuinely changed views within those churches.

Almost nothing has emerged from the Eastern Orthodox churches, where the traditional liturgy for Holy Week is replete with odious and hateful references to Jews while equating Jesus Christ fully with God. See Charlotte Klein, "The Image of the Jew in Oriental Liturgies," *Christian Attitudes to Jews and Judaism* 28 (1973): 12–15.

11. "The Relationship Between the United Church of Christ and the Jewish Community" (1987) confesses that the "Church's frequent portrayal of the Jews as blind, recalcitrant, evil, and rejected by God has found expression in much Christian theology, liturgy, and education [and] has been a factor in the shaping of anti-Jewish attitudes of societies and the policies of governments. The most devastating lethal metastisis of this process occurred . . . during the Holocaust." This document and its successor, "A Message to the Churches," are published in *New Conversations* 12:3 (Summer 1990): 67–68, and 5–7.

12. Many of the other statements avoid the subject of the State of Israel. In my 1985 analysis of thirteen Protestant church documents I noted that five of them

included positive references to the State of Israel, with three giving the subject fairly extensive coverage (see "A Christian Problem: Protestant Documents," 20–21).

13. Alice L. Eckardt, "Suffering, Theology and the Shoah," in *Contemporary Christian Religious Responses to the Shoah,* ed. Steven L. Jacobs (Lanham, Md.: University Press of America, 1993), 34–57. This essay looked at and rejected most Jewish and Christian "solutions" to the problem of suffering. We Christians need to acknowledge that the cross was not and is not the ultimate in suffering, and that suffering does not have purifying power.

14. See Hans Jonas, "The Concept of God After Auschwitz," in *Out of the Whirlwind,* ed. Albert H. Friedlander (New York: Schocken Books, 1976), 465–76.

15. "Power and Powerlessness: The Jewish Experience," in *Toward the Understanding and Prevention of Genocide,* ed. Israel Charny (Boulder, Colo.: Westview Press, 1984), 183–96. See also "A Christian Problem," 20–21.

16. Alice L. Eckardt, "Post-Holocaust Theology: A Journey Out of the Kingdom of Night," *Holocaust and Genocide Studies* 1:2 (1986): 238.

17. David Hartman, "The Moral Challenge of Israel," *Jerusalem Post,* June 20, 1988, 8.

18. Alice L. Eckardt, "The Place of the Jewish State in Christian-Jewish Relations," *European Judaism* 25:1 (1992): 4, 8.

19. "Suffering, Theology and the Shoah," 50; also my article "Yom Ha-Shoah Commandments," *Midstream* 28:4 (1981): 39. The unrecognized antipathy against the Jewish people epitomized in hostility to the Jewish state was the motivation for my first article on Christian attitudes toward the State of Israel: "The Arab-Israel Conflict," *Lutheran Forum* 5:6 (1971): 16–17.

20. "Forgiveness and Repentance: Some Contemporary Considerations and Questions" in *Remembering for the Future,* Vol. 1, ed. Yehuda Bauer, Alice Eckardt, et al. (New York: Pergamon Press, 1989), 571–83.

21. Alice L. Eckardt, "The Significance of Denial," in a forthcoming volume of the conference "Genocide and Holocaust: Armenian and Jewish Perspectives," April 1995.

22. This will require related changes in Christian worship materials, including hymns and anthems, as well as very significant changes in the way the Scriptures are used and taught.

12

From Anger to Inquiry

David R. Blumenthal

"Some people think of me as the Jewish James Bond. But I am really an old Jew with a heart condition who survived the holocaust and who feels that justice, however inadequate, must be done." These words, spoken by Simon Wiesenthal as he stood on a stage at Emory University surrounded by enormous Georgia Bureau of Investigation agents, changed my life. Up to that point I had, like many Jews, avoided the subject of the holocaust. My Christian colleague, the late Jack Boozer, had tried to persuade me that I owed it to the dead, to the survivors, and to God to teach it, but I was not willing to listen. Jack couldn't understand how a young, serious Jewish person, and a scholar at that, could not feel compelled to deal with the holocaust, but I was in deep denial—until Wiesenthal spoke. Then, I knew I must confront it. (As a matter of theological principle, I do not capitalize *holocaust*. Only words referring to God—or otherwise conforming to the usual English rules of capitalization—are so treated.)

My first efforts were really primitive, as was natural. By 1964, I had studied in Jewish parochial schools, majored in Oriental studies at the University of Pennsylvania, been ordained at the Jewish Theological Seminary of America, and spent two years at the Hebrew University in Jerusalem. In that time, I had heard one lecture on the holocaust that was all numbers, no experiential approach. I also knew that I had an Uncle Max who was a survivor, but, like many survivor relatives, he had been kept out of our way as children. So when I decided to study and teach the holocaust after Wiesenthal's visit, I was ill prepared, to say the least. Only Jack Boozer's moral vision sustained me.

"Professor Blumenthal, why are you snapping at us?" the undergraduate woman asked, at once surprised and aggressive. After hemming and hawing, I apologized and confessed that the material upset me as a person; that, even though I was an instructor, I was also a human being and I was angry, confused, and deeply hurt by what we were studying. It was a revelation to the students, and to me, but it was true. We shared our own upset and then we began to analyze the myriad defense mechanisms we were using to push the material away from us. Even several years of psychoanalysis had not prepared me for the sheer creativity of the human being in the face of data that undermines our basic human self-image. We learned that defense mechanisms are a sign of our humanness, but that we did need to try to get beyond them to the data.

"Be a little paranoid." "Get organized and stay organized." "Educate." "Support the institutions of freedom." "Reproduce." "Confront your opposition." And "Be prepared even with violence." These were "The Seven Commandments for Jewish Survival in the Post-Holocaust World."[1] The last one always aroused opposition. Was I really advocating social violence? Did I really approve of assassinating a potential future Hitler? The lecture became known as "Blumenthal's Brass Knuckles Lecture." Violent as it was, I thought then, and think now, that it does represent a considered and perhaps intelligent response to racial hatred. Jack Boozer did not agree, nor did many Jews, but they did learn to think: Where would I go if I had to flee? How much cash do I need to have on hand to rescue my family? Whom would I really trust with my children? How early would I resist? And, how far would I let my resistance go? These were emotional responses to studying the holocaust, as much as they were reflections of popular Jewish attitudes and possible, if not probable, contingencies for a future that all Jews knew could happen again.

Slowly, I tried to sort out the data and the emotions. I wrote "Scholarly Approaches to the Holocaust" as an attempt to put the data field into some order.[2] It is still a good guide. I also wrote "On Teaching the Holocaust" to share with other instructors the affective problems of this material.[3] And I began reading and reviewing books in the field.

The holocaust, however, must be seen to be experienced. So, I began acquiring and using films. We also organized the first of what became a long series of exhibits on the theme of the holocaust. "Danzig 1939," prepared by The Jewish Museum, came to Emory, and we organized a wide range of sponsors, lectures, national television coverage, a film series, and docents for organized tours. Over twenty thousand people saw the exhibit in the short time it was at Emory.[4] We also began to ask survivors to speak in the classroom. I could introduce them, but I was always too upset to thank them; Jack took care of that.

Slowly, the circle widened. The late Fred Crawford, a colleague and American POW, persuaded me to work with him on the Witness to the Holocaust

Project, which interviewed primarily liberators (Fred, as an Army person, had a special rapport with these people) as well as survivors. We republished booklets issued by the Armed Forces as they liberated the camps. We made tapes for public television, including one with a liberator and a survivor who were at the same camp, and we examined the Jewish and Christian press.[5] When Fred died, the Witness to the Holocaust Project continued. One result was that Robert Abzug was designated a Project fellow, and he wrote an important book on the early American reaction to the holocaust.[6] In addition, Elie Wiesel was awarded an honorary degree by the Emory School of Theology. Other exhibits came to campus, including "Auschwitz: A Crime Against Mankind," the Anne Frank exhibit, "The Value of the Human Being; Medicine in Germany: 1918–1945," and more recently, "The Rescuers: Portraits in Moral Courage during the Holocaust." Graduate students also began to take an interest and several went to Yad Vashem in Jerusalem for training, taught the holocaust course, and published articles on the subject. Undergraduates, too, wrote publishable articles and one even coedited a book. Meanwhile, I continued to read and write articles and reviews.

Having broadened my inquiry and involvement from near denial to teaching, publishing, organizing exhibits, and sustaining students and colleagues in their work, I began to feel the need to focus, to develop a more formal inquiry. My interests and training are primarily in the area of theology. I had already begun to express this interest by looking into the area of Jewish and Christian spiritual resistance. But the most important theological problem still remained: How can one account for the active, loving, and covenantal presence of God in the holocaust? Human beings are, to be sure, responsible for the holocaust, but, in a theological perspective that asserts God's presence in history, what can one say? This is the question that motivated the writing of *Facing the Abusing God: A Theology of Protest,* which appeared in 1993.

The most recent stage of my work on the holocaust was the realization that, with Jack Boozer and Fred Crawford no longer among the living and with my own interests becoming more focused, I needed a colleague who could effectively guide the university's efforts in the area of holocaust studies, giving direction to our scholarship in the area, teaching the courses, directing the Witness to the Holocaust Project, and providing direction for future exhibits. We hired Deborah Lipstadt and we received a chair to support her work.[7]

For me, personally and morally, Emory University's activity in holocaust studies reached a high point in May 1995 when it awarded an honorary degree to Mr. Alex Gross, the survivor in the Atlanta area who has been most active in speaking about the holocaust, not only at the university but also in the entire state of Georgia. The degree, awarded to a man who never formally graduated from high school but who has shown unbelievable courage in continuously exposing himself and his story, was a deeply moving moment, one that brought a certain closure to the years of intellectual, emotional, and administrative wrestling with the issues of the study and teaching of the holocaust.

In retrospect, I see that I moved from denial to involvement. At first, it was very difficult because I was so upset by the material and by my own reactions. During that period, I encouraged everything: exhibits, speeches, articles, reviews, classes, projects, interviews. Slowly, however, I moved toward my own focus, the theological question. I began with emotional indignation and broad investigation and gradually gave more disciplined consideration to my work without ever losing the passion that had brought me to it.

THE FIRST FOCUSED INQUIRY

My extensive training in Jewish theology did not give me an adequate answer to the question of theodicy. It is really not morally permissible to say that the holocaust was punishment for the sins of the Jewish people, even when one admits that the people have been sinful. Nor is it really cricket to say that God was not responsible at all, that God was "hiding God's face," or "in eclipse," or "present but not causal." God is, and must be, present in our personal and national lives. Following the example of medieval Jewish theologians who went outside Jewish tradition to study philosophy and then returned to the Jewish sources to elaborate a philosophical theology, I too turned to sources outside the theological tradition. I worked in child abuse, particularly in the area of psychotherapy with adult survivors of child abuse.

There, I acquired much human wisdom. I learned, first and foremost, that abuse is never, never the fault of the child no matter what the child is told or how she or he blames herself or himself. Abuse is force used against a person when that force is disproportionate to the alleged wrongdoing. I learned, too, how abused persons behave—their inability to trust, their wariness in love, and their towering anger, their rage. Finally, I learned that some healing is possible. One is never fully "cured" of child abuse, but one can learn to live a more trusting and a more productive life. The wounds do heal, but they leave scars.

Returning to the Jewish situation, I noted that the Jewish people exhibit many of the symptoms of adult survivors of child abuse—innocence of the violence of the holocaust, hypervigilance, and inability to trust others. I reasoned that we might learn something from therapy with adult survivors of child abuse that would yield insight into reconfiguring our relationship with God after the holocaust. It was a very difficult book to write, emotionally and theologically, but I was able to conclude first that, since we were innocent of the violence of the holocaust, we were "abused" and, therefore, that God was the Abuser. Second, unpleasant as that realization is, we owe it to ourselves, to the dead, to the survivors, and to God to speak that truth—theologically and liturgically. Hence, I called up the long tradition of protest, beginning in Psalm 44 and carrying through to post-holocaust Hebrew poetry, as the proper response to the problem of God and the holocaust. I also pushed this protest into traditional rabbinic liturgy, creating inserts into the prayerbook as well as new prayers.

The whole is very powerful. My own faith, real faith, is stronger for having faced the facts, and God, honestly and for having evolved a no-nonsense answer, even going so far as to modify the received prayers. These inserts into the prayerbook are not easy to recite but they say what needs to be said.

No one, so far, has agreed with me; the response has been enthusiastic but very wary, resistant. Still, I think I am right, theologically and morally, and I have no regrets. As a follow-up, I would like to see a conference of psychotherapists who deal with adult survivors of child abuse and those who deal with survivors of the holocaust. I think they would have much to say to one another. I would also like to see a conference of holocaust and child abuse survivors. These people, too, would have much to say to one another. How *does* one put Humpty-Dumpty back together again?

THE SECOND FOCUSED INQUIRY

The mystery of the holocaust is not its sadism, or its antisemitism, or its scale. Each of those factors is known. To me, the real mystery is a double mystery. The first half lies in how so many people were persuaded to go along with the holocaust. Tens of millions of people went along with the holocaust. It was not only terror, though terror played its role. Christopher Browning's book *Ordinary Men: Reserve Police Battalion 101 and the Final Solution in Poland* embodies this aspect of the problem best. The other side of the mystery lies in how a few were persuaded to resist the overwhelming force and consensus that generated the holocaust. A few thousand did resist. It was not just politics or ideology, though these were factors in some cases. Samuel and Pearl Oliner's book *The Altruistic Personality: Rescuers of Jews in Nazi Europe* presents this apsect of the problem best— conformity and obediece, on the one hand, and resistance and disobedience, on the other.

The implications are enormous: Why do people conform? Disobey? If we knew, could we cultivate resistance? How? Can we "prevent" another holocaust or at least mitigate its effects? Suppose more people had resisted . . .

My current work is in examining the social psychological data on obedience and altruism and comparing it with historical data drawn largely, but not exclusively, from the holocaust. Eventually, I will need to work out a field theory that will account for the commonalities and disjunctions in obedient and altruistic behavior. When that is done, I will have acquired some wisdom from outside the tradition, and I shall be ready to return to the tradition with that wisdom. I will, then, need to confront the fact that preaching good and studying it, which is what religious traditions usually do, is not effective. I will need to figure out what would be effective in cultivating a morally resistant stream within Judaism. That, too, will be a focused response to the holocaust.

I WISH

I wish I didn't have to teach the holocaust. It tears me apart each time. It hurts my students and my Christian colleagues. It also distorts the values of Jewish civilization and survival.

I wish I didn't have the sense of identification with those who were murdered. I was born in late December 1938 in Houston, Texas. Had I been born in late December 1938 in Warsaw, Poland, the little brown-eyed child in *Night and Fog* would have likely been me.

I wish I didn't feel so responsible for the decisions that my generation is now making that will ensure, or endanger, the State of Israel and Jewish survival in the exile. But I do, and I am responsible. I am "on watch" now, as those before me were "on watch" in the late 1920s or early 1930s.

I visited Dachau in the summer of 1962; I've never been back to a concentration camp. I've never taken my children. There are plenty of opportunities, to go alone or with colleagues or with groups. I know more now. But I am afraid to go. I have enough defense mechanisms to deal with it, or at least I think I do. But the horror is too strong. I understand why students prefer *The Yellow Star* (a film based on holocaust paintings) to *Night and Fog.*

I wish I didn't have to recite the prayers I have written. Sometimes, I skip prayers on Mondays and Thursdays to avoid saying them.

And I wish I didn't have to get out on a limb in academic areas in which I have no special training, earlier with psychotherapy with adult survivors of child abuse and, now, with social psychology. Writing theology is difficult enough but writing it with wisdom garnered from elsewhere exposes one to claims of incompetence. Also, while this interdisciplinary process generates new theology, it does force one, and others, to question the old theologies. This too exposes one to criticism. Still, if we are to face the holocaust as directly as we can and if we are to do more than pin down the loose historical details or just react emotionally, we must be able to go from anger to inquiry, to develop the questions that that moment in human history poses, and to search diligently for answers—not just out of curiosity, but out of a deep moral impulse to confront evil with as much courage as we can and to fight that evil whether it be in theology or in society. This, it seems to me, is the task at hand, always, but especially so in holocaust studies. My own contribution has been small, but at least I know that I have tried.

NOTES

1. See David R. Blumenthal, "In the Shadow of the Holocaust," *The Jewish Spectator* (Winter 1981): 11–14.

2. See David R. Blumenthal, "Scholarly Approaches to the Holocaust," *Sho'ah* 1 (1979): 21–27.

3. See David R. Blumenthal, "The Popular Jewish Response to the Holocaust: An Initial Reflection," *Sho'ah* 2 (1980): 3–5.

4. See " 'Danzig: 1939'—An Exercise in Interfaith Understanding," in *Emory Studies on the Holocaust,* Vol. 1, ed. David R. Blumenthal (Atlanta: Emory University Press, 1985), 136–45.

5. A full catalog of publications and tapes is available from the Fred R. Crawford Witness to the Holocaust Project, Emory University, Atlanta, GA 30322.

6. See Robert Abzug, *Inside the Vicious Heart: Americans and the Liberation of Nazi Concentration Camps* (New York: Oxford University Press, 1985).

7. Deborah Lipstadt is the author of important books on the Holocaust, including *Beyond Belief: The American Press and the Coming of the Holocaust 1933–1945* (New York: Free Press, 1986) and *Denying the Holocaust: The Growing Assault on Truth and Memory* (New York: Free Press, 1993).

13

A Twentieth-Century Journey

Richard L. Rubenstein

I began this essay one day short of my seventy-second birthday. Although healthy and actively engaged in the most demanding position of my entire career, I believe I have arrived at a time in life at which the essential profile of my abiding intellectual and spiritual interests is clear to me. One fact stands out: No historical event is remotely comparable to the Holocaust in the dominant role it has played in shaping those interests and concerns.

In an earlier autobiographical study, I noted that I first became aware of Adolf Hitler in 1932 at the age of eight when I learned that he wanted to become chancellor of Germany and that he had promised to get rid of Germany's Jews.[1] Although my family had no close relatives in Europe, I followed the events in Germany as if they were neighborhood happenings.

I became fifteen and entered my senior high school year in January 1939. World War II began nine months later. It was clear to me that religion, although largely absent from my home, was an overwhelmingly important force in human affairs and that being Jewish constituted my greatest potential hazard. As an adolescent ignorant of my own tradition, I initially tried to flee the perceived danger of Jewishness by joining Manhattan's All Souls Unitarian Church and setting out to become a Unitarian minister. Fortunately, flight was followed by a more authentic response. When a well-meaning Unitarian leader suggested that I change my name, I quickly decided that I could only live a life of honor and dignity by accepting and affirming my Jewish identity.

I began my studies for the reform rabbinate at the Hebrew Union College in September 1942 at a time when European Jews were being systematically murdered. My turn to religion appears in retrospect to have been very largely a quest for self-understanding in a world in which the Holocaust was unfolding. Nevertheless, I did not grasp the full horror of National Socialism until the fall of 1944 when word came that advancing Soviet troops had captured Majdanek, a huge extermination camp near the Polish city of Lublin. Majdanek was the occasion of my first theological crisis. I simply could not reconcile the optimistic Reform Jewish ideology I had superficially accepted and the gruesome facts of the extermination project. By the spring of 1945 I decided to leave the Hebrew Union College. Some of my motives were personal, reflecting my emotional turmoil at the time; others were theological, the latter being of greater weight.[2]

After leaving the college, I decided to train for a career in secular philosophy but soon abandoned that idea. In the face of the greatest catastrophe in all of Jewish history and the first tentative steps toward *tikkun* or restoration, I came to see secular philosophy as morally uncommitted, a way of being in the world I found unacceptable. In 1947 I returned to rabbinical studies. I received private instruction in Talmud at the Mesivta Chaim Berlin, an important Orthodox Yeshiva, during the year 1947–48. I entered the Jewish Theological Seminary in September 1948 and graduated in May 1952. During that period three of my four children were born. Aaron and Hannah have grown to adulthood, each now having a child. Nathaniel died at age three months. Their mother, Ellen van der Veen, was born in Amsterdam about the same year as Anne Frank. Unlike Anne Frank, Ellen's parents left the Netherlands for England as soon as the German invasion began on May 10, 1940. My children grew up with the knowledge that, but for a split-second decision of their grandfather, their mother would have perished as did Anne.

Upon graduation, I was accepted by Harvard for the joint doctoral program of the Divinity School and the Graduate School of Arts and Sciences in the History and Philosophy of Religion. Initially, I was more interested in Kierkegaard, Sartre, and Freud than the Holocaust but that was soon to change. I was painfully aware of the role the depiction of Jews and Judaism in Christianity had played in creating a rationale for genocide.

Because of the necessity of supporting my family, it took eight years to complete my doctoral studies. During that period my relations with my first wife were deteriorating. Divorce was precluded by the need to care for three young children and by occasional periods of reconciliation. Keenly aware of my inner turmoil, I entered psychoanalysis in 1953 and continued in it until 1958 when I left Cambridge for the University of Pittsburgh. Along with the more intimate personal issues with which I was trying to cope, my feelings about the Holocaust, antisemitism and the need to find an emotional *modus vivendi* in my relations with Christians figured largely in the analysis.

The encounter with psychoanalysis greatly influenced my research. My doctoral thesis was entitled "Psychoanalysis and the Image of the Wicked in Rabbinic Judaism." A revised version of the thesis was published in 1968 as *The Religious Imagination*.[3] At one level, the work is a study of the rabbinic response to the twin defeats inflicted upon Israel by the Romans under Vespasian and Hadrian in the wars of 66 to 70 C.E. and 131 to 135 C.E. At another level, I was asking psychological and theological questions about the roots of an even greater modern debacle. Just as the rabbis used Nebuchadnezzar's conquest of Jerusalem in 586 B.C.E. as a vehicle with which to reflect upon the fall of Jerusalem in their own time, so I used the fall of Jerusalem in 70 C.E. the better to understand the Holocaust. Among the questions explored in the thesis were the religious and psychological responses of individual Jews and the Jewish community to the experience of catastrophic defeat and powerlessness. I came to see the religious civilization of Rabbinic Judaism as a functional means of coping with the consequences of that defeat. I later concluded that in the post-Holocaust world the normative rabbinic response was no longer credible or functional.

I have often reflected on the Judaeo-Roman War of 66–70 C.E. and its aftermath. Given the overwhelming preponderance of Roman power in ancient times and German power during World War II, I asked myself: What was the difference between the historical situation and culture of these two peoples that led to unmitigated genocide in the one case but not the other? Was it the advent of modernization with its by-product of a redundant population willing to exterminate the competing stranger? Were Europe's Jews made to pay with their lives for Germany's defeat in the First World War? Was it the fact that, unlike Rome, Germany's fundamental culture remained Christian under National Socialism, thereby intensifying the animus against Jews and Judaism? Was it the consequence of the impact of the personality of Adolf Hitler on the people he led? Was it some mixture of the above and much else besides? In the course of time all of these questions were subsumed in my mind in a single question: *Why did it happen in the twentieth century?* This led to a further, related question, *What does the Holocaust tell us about humanity in the twentieth century and beyond?*

In the conclusion to both the thesis and *The Religious Imagination*, I argued that the creators of Rabbinic Judaism had bestowed "the gift of meaning" on the Jewish people in the aftermath of their ancient defeat. By interpreting the defeat as the consequence of their own and their people's shortcomings, the rabbis enabled the Jewish people to avoid falling into a condition of radical meaninglessness or *anomie*. The rabbis' interpretation of events also gave the community a program of goal-oriented personal and group behavior which, they opined, would ultimately reverse the devastation they had experienced at the hands of the Romans. They argued that a want of conformity with God's commandments had been the cause of Jewish misfortune and that uncompromising commitment to the fulfillment of the commandments would ultimately reverse the misfortune. In essence, I offered a *functional defense* of the normative prophetic-rabbinic response to the communal catastrophe. Nevertheless, a functional defense of a religious belief is by no means a defense of its credibility.

Initially, my functional defense of tradition was strongly Freudian. Nevertheless, at no time did I reduce the motivation of historical actors to the categories of individual depth psychology. My first explicit attempt to interpret the Holocaust, "Religious Origins of the Death Camps: A Psychoanalytic Interpretation,"[4] was, as the title indicates, strongly psychoanalytical. When I wrote this essay, I was strongly impressed by the psychological truth, but not the historical veracity, of Freud's "primal crime" hypothesis. Impressed by Freud, I saw crucial links between the biblical doctrine of covenant and election, sibling rivalry, and the deicide accusation. By proclaiming that the Creator had taken human form and experienced the vicissitudes of human existence, including excruciatingly painful death upon the cross, Christianity introduced a radically novel element in the biblical understanding of both the Creator and the covenant. By equating obedient faith in Jesus Christ with fidelity to the covenant with Abraham and by accusing the Jews of full responsibility for his death, Christianity introduced the ideas of sibling rivalry and deicide into its complicated relations with the older tradition.

Christianity accused the Jews of a crime more radical and destructive than any ever before imputed to a human community. As alleged God-murderers, the Jews were depicted as utterly beyond all law and moral restraint. This is effectively expressed by symbolically and ritualistically identifying the Jews with Satan, Satan's spawn, and the Anti-Christ. The deicide accusation also imputed magic and demonic powers to the Jews. The Jews were depicted as possessing a terrible magic potency, both as the people in whose midst God-in-the-flesh had been born and as His murderers. The gravity of the accusation was intensified by the identification of Jews with Judas, *the disciple who betrays his savior with a loving kiss.* The Judas identification characterizes the Jews as betrayers whose actions can never be trusted even when their behavior is exemplary. The Judas identification served as a crucial component in the "plausibility structure" that rendered credible such diverse but related antisemitic phenomena as the accusation that Captain Alfred Dreyfus had indeed betrayed France, that the Jews were responsible for the alleged "stab in the back" by which Germany was defeated in World War I, and that the Bolshevik Revolution was the fruit of a Jewish conspiracy for world domination. The infamous forgery known as *The Protocols of the Elders of Zion* was often offered as "proof" of the latter claim. Far from being a crime, radical antisemites saw extermination of the Jews as a purifying act on behalf of civilization.

At the time, I regarded the National Socialist quest for an homogenous *Völkisch* culture as a flight from and revolt against modernity. By contrast, a principal thesis of *The Cunning of History* (1975) was that the "Holocaust was an expression of some of the most significant political, moral, religious and demographic tendencies of Western civilization in the twentieth century. The Holocaust cannot be divorced from the same culture of modernity that produced the two world wars and Hitler."[5] In *The Age of Triage* (1983) I expressed the view that the quest for cultural homogeneity is no less an expression of modernity than pluralism and diversity.[6] That is not a happy opinion, for, if correct, it means that we are likely to witness more attempts at "ethnic cleansing" in the years ahead. In any event, in the aftermath of World War I, a thoroughly modern quest for cultural homogeneity in Germany and elsewhere was an important element in the eventual destruction of Europe's Jews. Combined with the paranoid myth of the Jew as the Judas-like magic betrayer, the quest made the elimination of the Jews a widely shared objective in Germany.

My encounter with Dean Heinrich Grüber in Berlin on August 17, 1961, four days after the erection of the Wall, was one of the most important of my entire life. It was the catalyst that brought to full expression theological concerns that went back to my reaction to the Russian entry into the extermination camp at Majdanek in the fall of 1944. After Dean Grüber declared to me that it was God's will to send Hitler to punish the Jews for their sins, I could no longer avoid openly discussing the theological problem of God, Israel, and the Holocaust. There was absolutely no malice in Grüber's assertions about God, Israel, and the Holocaust. He was firmly convinced of the truth of the biblical theology of covenant and election. Any number of Orthodox rabbis have held similar views save that they offer a different catalogue of transgressions to account for Israel's misfortune. His terrible statement, uttered in the apocalyptic atmosphere in which Berlin was initiated into the travail of the Wall, had a ring of authenticity if not truth to it.

After the meeting with Grüber, I could not avoid the conclusion that if one accepted Israel's fundamental understanding of its relation to the Lord of the Covenant, it followed that the Holocaust was a decisive and, in all likelihood, a punitive expression of the Divine Will. I was unable to accept the idea that Auschwitz was either providential or punitive. This is not the place to enter into my ideas concerning "God after the death of God."[7] I would, however, add that my rejection of covenant and election was as much the result of my experience in psychoanalysis as it was the theological difficulty of seeing Hitler as in any sense an instrument of Divine Wrath. As a result of my personal analysis, I had come to regard any claim of *privileged* distinctiveness as a compensatory mechanism for low personal esteem. I regarded all claims of a distinctive relationship between Israel and God as such a claim. I had no interest in rejecting my Jewish identity, an impossible task in any event as I had learned early on, but I saw no special virtue in being born Jewish or anything else. Nor did I see myself charged with any divinely appointed role such as serving as a "light unto the nations." I had been cast into the world with one set of parents and grandparents with their distinctive histories. Others had been shaped by very different families and their memories. In attempting to overcome a measure of personal narcissism, I had come to understand that group narcissism is no less problematic.

My radicalism was closer to Orthodox Judaism than to liberal interpretations of the tradition. The liberals wanted to affirm the covenant and Israel's election while at the same time evading the logical consequence of such an affirmation. Today, I have greater sympathy for the liberal compromise than in the 1960s. The entire corpus of Jewish religious literature—the Bible, the Talmud, the prayer books, the writings of the mystics—is impregnated with the idea that God chose Israel. To excise that idea from Judaism would be to destroy that entire corpus. Jews have no choice but to read from Scripture and utter words of prayer in which God's election of Israel is insistently affirmed. It is, so to speak, the price of admission to participation in Jewish religious life. Jews have inherited a liturgy that their historical experience has contradicted. Nevertheless, it is their inheritance. They can invent no other. Admittedly, the Holocaust has greatly intensified the dissonance between Jewish experience and the corpus of Jewish religious literature, and dissonance is a painful state. A possible consolation is that all religious traditions must contend with the problem of dissonance in some measure.

Another memorable encounter was my dialogue with Elie Wiesel at the International Scholars' Conference on the German Church Struggle and the Holocaust held at Wayne State University in the spring of 1970. In addition to offering a deeply personal expression of my religious views at the time, my observations anticipated the thesis of *The Cunning of History*:[8] "Auschwitz can be seen as the first triumph of technological civilization in dealing with what may become a persistent human problem, the problem of the waste disposal of superfluous human beings in an overpopulated world."[9] Two related themes dominate *The Cunning of History*, the problem of technologically induced population redundancy and the role of bureaucracy in facilitating its elimination. The problem of population redundancy arises when, as in modern times, ever fewer people are required for an ever greater workload. *The Cunning of History* dealt in large measure with the "fate of those who were rendered politically or economically redundant" in the early decades of the twentieth century. In 1996 that problem has once again become acute as electronic technology replaces an ever greater number of human beings in the workplace. In Europe the problem became acute in the nineteenth century with the ongoing rationalization of agriculture. It was partly solved, at least for a time, by the greatest human migration in history, the emigration of Europeans to the New World, and by the imperial expansion of the European powers throughout the world. In *The Cunning of History* I argued that the mass slaughter of World War I and of the Russian Civil War was facilitated by a surplus of human beings for whom no place could be found in the labor markets of their native lands. I pointed to the incredible carnage that attended the Battle of Verdun and the Second Battle of the Somme. I saw the casualties that the Allies and the Germans were willing to sustain as anticipations of the Holocaust and suggested that political leaders who were willing to sacrifice the lives of millions of their own countrymen could hardly be expected to manifest concern for those they regarded as alien in both nationality and religion.

Both emigration and war can serve as mechanisms to eliminate a redundant population. Modern, rationalized genocide is a more precisely targeted method. One of the questions implicit in both *The Cunning of History* and *The Age of Triage* was, "Given the strength of antisemitism throughout the history of Europe and the overwhelming power of European Christendom vis-à-vis the Jews, why did the Holocaust happen in the twentieth century and not before?" In the process of formulating a tentative answer, I became convinced that the modernization of Europe's economy and society was an indispensable precondition of the extermination of Europe's Jews. Without modernization there would have been pogroms and expulsions but no systematically organized, industrial-style, state-sponsored mass murder. I was strongly influenced by Max Weber's reflections on instrumental rationality, bureaucratic or "rational-legal" domination, and the character of the modern era.

As I read Weber, I was struck by the extent to which the SS conformed to his description of the "ideal type" of bureaucrat, although, in retrospect, I tended to see the SS more in "ideal-typical" terms than its history warrants. Weber insisted upon the inherent rationality of bureaucratic organization and saw the triumph of instrumental or functional rationality as the dominant method of economic and social organization in the modern period. Under Weber's influence I came to see the Holocaust as a prototypically modern, rationally implemented event. This put me at odds with historians such as Lucy Dawidowicz, who argued that the Holocaust was an irrational outburst on the part of those who would turn the clock back to the Middle Ages.

The Age of Triage was the promised sequel to *The Cunning of History.* As such, it was a continuation of my attempt to comprehend the Holocaust in terms of "the economic, social and cultural forces at work in modern society that make for both unemployment and genocide." I had come to see the Holocaust as the most extreme, but by no means the only, example of a state-sponsored program to eliminate a population deemed unwanted or redundant. In *The Age of Triage,* I sought to understand the Holocaust in the context of such examples of population elimination as the enclosure movement in England, English policy during the famine years in Ireland, the Armenian genocide, the forced rationalization of agriculture in the Soviet Union during the Communist Revolution, the Pol Pot massacres in Kampuchea, and the Vietnamese boat people. By attempting to understand what the Holocaust had in common with these catastrophic events, I was able to see wherein the uniqueness of the Holocaust was to be found.

The common element lay in the fact that in all of these disasters the lives of millions of human beings "were either blighted or lost because they were unable to find a viable role in the economy and society in which they were born."[10] I saw the Holocaust as related to these other events. The rationalization of hygiene produced a quantum increase in the number of human beings who survived the hazards of childbirth and childhood to become reproductive adults. The rationalization of agriculture provided the food that nourished the increased population. The same agrarian revolution rendered millions of peasants vocationally redundant and compelled the peasants and their families to leave the countryside for the cities of Europe or for new habitations overseas. As a result, the Jews ceased to be a complimentary economic class and became the competitors of an insecure class of urbanized peasants and their descendants, especially those who had achieved some measure of petite bourgeoise status. Alien to both the ethnic and religious consensus of the communities into which they were born, it was only a matter of time before the Jewish situation in Europe became utterly untenable. In retrospect, it seems clear that the fate of the European Jews was sealed long before the advent of Adolf Hitler.

During the 1980s I tended to stress economic, social, and demographic roots of the Holocaust, but these factors could not account for the uniqueness of the event. I was especially impressed by the overwhelming response to the United States Holocaust Memorial Museum. There have been other large-scale, demographic catastrophes perpetrated by human beings in the twentieth century. Nevertheless, it is unlikely that a museum devoted to Stalin's murders or the Armenian genocide of 1915 would consistently draw so large a number of visitors as the Holocaust Museum.

It is religion that accounts for the persistent interest in the Holocaust half a century after the end of World War II, especially the pervasiveness in Western civilization of what Stephen R. Haynes has called the "witness people myth," the belief that whatever happens to the Jews, for good or for ill, is an expression of God's providence and, as such, is a sign "for God's church."[11] According to Haynes, the witness people myth is "a deep structure in the Christian imagination . . . a complex of ideas and symbols that, often pre-critically and unconsciously, informs ideas about Jews among persons who share a cultural heritage." The myth has its roots in the biblical idea of God's election of Israel. Given the enormous weight Judaism and Christianity place upon the interpretation of Jewish disaster as an expression of God's justice, it was inevitable that the place of the Holocaust in God's providence would be a matter of interest and concern to Jews and Christians alike. The uniqueness of the Holocaust is not dependent upon the number of the victims or the manner in which they were slain, but rather upon the uniquely religious meanings given to Jewish history in the biblical religions.

As I became convinced that religion accounted for the uniqueness of the Holocaust, I also came to see religion as a profoundly important motivating factor for genocide. Recently, I have characterized the Holocaust as a Holy

War whose fundamental objective was the elimination of the Jews as a religious, political, cultural, and demographic presence in Christian Europe. I now believe the Holy War hypothesis offers the most plausible account of the so-called Final Solution. To understand the Holocaust as a modern Holy War, we must keep in mind the fact that, apart from the Jews, in the formative centuries of Europe's development those who rejected baptism were either expelled or exterminated.[12] Although there was a geographical location we today can identify as Europe long before the advent of Christianity, *European civilization* did not exist before Christianity, and the price of admission to full participation in that civilization was membership in the Christian Church.

For a variety of reasons—some economic, others theological—Jews were permitted domicile in different parts of Christian Europe at different times, but they were never Europeans. Ironically, their hazard was intensified after their emancipation. For the first time in the history of European Christendom, members of a group that denied the most fundamental affirmation of Christianity, that Christ is Lord, were permitted to influence European civilization *from within.* With the success of the Bolshevik Revolution, widely seen by conservative Europeans as a Jewish assault on Christendom, whatever minimal tolerance existed for Jewish emancipation disappeared. By the 1930s most European Christian leaders were convinced that the greatest threats to the integrity of their symbolic universe came from two sources— Bolshevism and unconverted Jews—whether religious, socialist, Zionist, secular, or assimilationist. Moreover, these same leaders thought of Bolshevism as largely Jewish in origin and spirit. In their minds the two often merged into one.

The overriding importance of the struggle against godless communism was a continuing theme in the Vatican throughout the decade of the twenties.[13] As the world was to learn, that fear was not unjustified. By May 1919 at the latest, Archbishop Eugenio Pacelli, who later became Vatican secretary of state and then Pope Pius XII, came to regard the German Right as Europe's most dependable bulwark against communism. Having served as a Vatican diplomat in Germany from 1917 to 1929, Pacelli was known to be pro-German but not pro-Nazi. Nevertheless, despite strong reservations about National Socialism's underlying neopaganism, he was impressed by Hitler's anticommunism.[14]

Antisemitism was another area of agreement between the National Socialists and the leaders of the Christian Church, both Catholic and Protestant. Church leaders were heartily in accord with the initiation of anti-Jewish measures by the Nazis in 1933.[15] However, it is important to keep in mind that only retrospectively can the antisemitism of the 1930s be seen as leading to Auschwitz. In 1933, the overwhelming majority of Europe's Christian leaders wanted to revoke the emancipation of the Jews. The Nazis wanted to expel the Jews from Germany. The churches had no objection as long as baptized Jews and the Jewish spouses of Christians were exempt. There had been expulsions before—England in 1290, France in 1306 and 1394, Spain in 1492. In each case church leaders regarded the expulsions as a gain, a cleansing of the Christian heartland. Moreover, the idea of expelling the Jews was popular in pre-World War II Europe.[16] There were, however, differences in the response of the German Evangelical Church and the Catholic Church. There were a few attempts at rescue by Catholics but almost none by German Protestant institutions or their leaders. Apart from a few exceptions, John Conway's evaluation of the German Protestant response to the extermination of the Jews is essentially correct, "all save a handful of German churchmen continued to turn a blind eye on events, retreated into apathetic indifference, *and even manifested a sort of sympathetic acquiescence.*"[17] Hitler gave them what they wanted but not necessarily by methods they would have chosen independently.

There have been many attempts to explain the pope's public silence concerning the Holocaust. His unwillingness to do anything that might weaken the Third Reich's defense of Europe against Bolshevism is often cited by historians. Nevertheless, I have come to believe that the motives for the pope's silence were more deeply rooted in his religious beliefs, especially the role of the Jews in God's providential ordering of history, than most observers credit. *What I find especially surprising is the relative absence in the literature of the possibility that the pope and his subordinates may have taken the elimination of the Jews from Europe to be as important as the elimination of Bolshevism.*

Let me be absolutely clear about what I am NOT suggesting: I am not suggesting that the pope or the Roman Catholic Church as an institution actively sought the extermination of the Jews, although some clerics did.[18] I am also cognizant of the selfless attempts at both protest and rescue by some Christians, both lay and clerical, during the war. Nevertheless, one must ask whether Pope Innocent III's World War II successor regarded Jews and Judaism as Innocent regarded the Cathar Church in 1208, namely, as a cancer in the body of Christendom.[19] Of one thing we may be certain, by the nature of his office, Pope Pius XII, like his thirteenth-century predecessor, was compelled to think institutionally rather than personally.

One may object that the Roman Catholic Church regarded the Cathars as heretics and, as such, an *internal threat,* whereas the Jews were external to the body of Christendom. In reality, as Jews entered the ranks of intellectuals, writers, journalists, publishers, and other opinion makers, they came to be regarded as dangerously subversive internal enemies. Long before the Bolshevik Revolution, Church leaders concluded that ideas from Jewish sources could have negative moral and political consequences.[20]

There is also, I believe, a tendency among scholars to underestimate the extent to which the Bolshevik Revolution changed the perception among European elites of Jews as strangers to Jews as enemies. The belief that

Judaism had spawned Bolshevism was widely held throughout the interwar period and even later.[21] No political threat to Christianity comparable to that of the Bolshevik Revolution, and its derivatives—Béla Kun's Soviet regime in Hungary and the Munich Soviet—had ever before erupted in the midst of Europe. Insofar as the European symbolic universe was Christian, the impressive sacrifices made by German Jews on the battlefield during World War I counted for nothing. Instead, they were blamed both for Germany's defeat and for Bolshevism. As such, they were regarded as agents of corrosion, disorder, and decay.

In such a climate, the call for their "removal," *Entfernung,* was welcomed by European elites everywhere. There was, of course, an important difference between the Christian and the National Socialist approaches to *Entfernung.* However we date Hitler's decision to exterminate the Jews, he did not ignore the problem of implementation.[22]

During the war, Christian leaders became privy to the secret that was no secret, that the Jews were being slaughtered in the east.[23] At that point they were caught between their desire for a wholly Christian Europe and the fact, clearly understood by Hitler, that this could only be accomplished by systematic genocide. A small minority responded by endeavoring to shelter or rescue Jews. Others responded by blessing the work of the perpetrators. The vast majority kept silent. Those who wanted to rid Europe of Jews knew that nothing more was required of them to finish the job. Nor were Europe's religious leaders alone in wanting Europe free of Jews. There is no other way to explain the refusal of the American and British governments to take even the slightest direct action to hinder the Final Solution in the face of the exact knowledge they had of the program. Many historians argue that the Allied refusal to take action was due to their "indifference" to the fate of the Jews. In reality, something far worse was involved. When political leaders know that a massive atrocity is taking place that they have the power to hinder at little or no cost and they refuse to take action, they are not indifferent; they are silent partners.[24]

Over time I have become convinced that during World War II Pope Pius XII and the vast majority of European Christian leaders regarded the elimination of the Jews as no less beneficial than the destruction of Bolshevism. Moreover, as the head of the oldest continuous corporate institution in the Western world, the Roman pontiff understood that great historical transformations are seldom, if ever, bloodless. He did not have to be instructed in the history of the terrible wars, crusades, and inquisitions that were necessary to complete the Christianization of Europe. The pope neither was nor could have been an Oskar Schindler, who could not ignore the personal consequences of the Final Solution for the individuals working for him. In addition, the Final Solution could be rationalized by Christians as Divine punishment of obstinately unfaithful Israel.

The most plausible explanation of the behavior of church leaders in Rome and Berlin during World War II seems to me to be that they had a view of those responsible for the Final Solution not unlike the Roman Catholic Church's view of the *routiers* during the Albigensian Crusade. Let us recall that in the assault on Béziers in 1209, the crusader army consisted primarily of knights from the north and *routiers.* The latter did most of the killing. The typical *routier* was described as a "godless, lawless being, who . . . showed no mercy . . . a living emblem of Hell on earth."[25] Although neither religious nor lay authorities had any illusions about these men, they also understood that the Crusade could not have succeeded without them. And so, they were used not only at Béziers but also throughout the Languedoc region to uproot Latin Christendom's most serious internal threat. Actually, the Roman Catholic Church took a much more benign attitude toward the perpetrators of the Final Solution. An enormous effort was made by some Church officials in Rome immediately after the war to rescue Nazi war criminals, including death and concentration camp commandants such as Franz Stangl of Treblinka and Alois Brunner of Drancy, and to help them find new lives.[26] Wartime acts of extermination became easily pardonable offenses as yesterday's war criminals became heroic fighters against godless communism.

Innocent did not flinch from prescribing the sword.[27] Pius XII was responsible for no such incitement. Nevertheless, both Pius XII and Innocent III believed their church was confronted by dangerous external and internal threats. As leaders of their ancient institution, both were committed to doing whatever was necessary to overcome those dangers. In the case of Pius XII, this meant doing nothing to impede a German victory in the east as long as there was any likelihood of such a victory. In and of itself, that decision spelled the physical destruction of Europe's Jews. The Holy War against the Jews was an unparalleled success.

Thus, there has been both continuity and change in my view of the Holocaust. The continuity is to be found in the view that the Holocaust was an expression of the dominant trends in Western civilization rather than a wholly exceptional event. The change has come in my growing conviction that the Holocaust was religious in motivation to a far greater extent than I had initially believed and that its outcome, if not its method of implementation, was welcomed by a far wider circle of bystanders than I had initially imagined. Germany can now afford to banish the swastika. The Nazis have made their contribution to the Fatherland and Europe as far as the Jews are concerned.

Already in *The Cunning of History,* I saw a potentially genocidal strain running through the civilization of the West that will be difficult if not impossible to eradicate. In the ensuing years that view has been immensely fortified, but there has been little sense of alienation or resentment on my part. As a Jew, there is much in Western civilization that rejects me and in World War II would have destroyed me. Nevertheless, I am the heir of the principal components of that civilization, Jewish, Christian, and Graeco-Roman alike. On balance, I have far more reason for gratitude and thanks-giving than for estrangement.

Over time, my theological views have changed, especially concerning cov-enant and election. I still reject both ideas, but I have gained much appre-ciation for the idea of a religious calling or vocation that derives from the idea of covenant. I have also acquired considerable sympathy for religious liberals who insist upon retaining belief in the election of Israel while de-nying God's involvement in Auschwitz.

In conclusion, I would like briefly to respond to a few of the questions that have been suggested to me by the editors of this volume:

- I regard my most important contribution to Holocaust studies to have been the raising of the *theological* issue of the God of covenant and election and the Ho-locaust at a time when the subject was largely ignored in contemporary Jewish thought. I also raised the related issue of the *theological* significance of the rebirth of Israel at a time when few Jewish thinkers acknowledged that this was an issue.

- Have there been questions that I have been afraid to confront? I do not think so.

- Is there yet work that I hope to complete? Most certainly. I was totally surprised when I was invited to become president of the University of Bridgeport, arguably one of the most complex positions in American higher education. The invitation was extended in October 1994 for a term commencing January 1, 1995, and ending December 31, 1999, when, if all is well, I shall be seven days short of my seventy-sixth birthday. When I accepted the post, I had finished about two-thirds of a book entitled *Holy War and Ethnic Cleansing,* which deals with such phenomena as religiously motivated communal conflict, population elimination, and genocide in the current era. If my good health continues, I will return to writing and research for the book as soon as my present duties permit or when they are completed. I have no regrets about this hiatus. To paraphrase the young Karl Marx, it is not enough to understand the world, one must seek to change it for the better. The arena in which I have been called to attempt that enterprise is an international university with one of the most religiously and ethnically diverse constituencies of any American institution of higher education. Should it be given to me to complete *Holy War and Ethnic Cleansing,* it is my hope to write a sequel to my earlier autobiography, *Power Struggle: An Autobiographical Confession,* published in 1974. Such a work would, if completed, be the story of one thinker's journey through the twentieth century.

NOTES

1. Richard L. Rubenstein, *Power Struggle: An Autobiographical Confession* (New York: Charles Scribner's Sons, 1974), 74.

2. I discuss the motives in *Power Struggle,* 74–76.

3. Richard L. Rubenstein, *The Religious Imagination: A Study in Psychoanalysis and Jewish Theology* (Indianapolis: Bobbs-Merrill, 1968).

4. Richard L. Rubenstein, "Religious Origins of the Death Camps: A Psychoanalytic Interpretation," *Reconstructionist*, May 5 and 19, 1961.

5. Richard L. Rubenstein, *The Cunning of History: Mass Death and the American Future* (New York: Harper and Row, 1975), 6.

6. Richard L. Rubenstein, *The Age of Triage: Fear and Hope in an Overcrowded World* (Boston: Beacon Press, 1983), 17–19.

7. See my essay "God After the Death of God," in Richard L. Rubenstein, *After Auschwitz: History, Theology and Contemporary Judaism* (Baltimore: Johns Hopkins University Press, 1992), 293–306.

8. Richard L. Rubenstein, "Some Perspectives on Religious Faith After Auschwitz," in *The German Church Struggle and the Holocaust,* ed. Franklin H. Littell and Hubert G. Locke (Detroit: Wayne State University Press, 1974). The exchange with Wiesel is included with insightful editorial comments in *Holocaust: Religious and Philosophical Implications,* ed. John K. Roth and Michael Berenbaum (New York: Paragon House, 1989).

9. Rubenstein in *The German Church Struggle and the Holocaust,* 264.

10. Rubenstein, *The Age of Triage,* 1.

11. See Stephen R. Haynes, *Jews and the Christian Imagination: Reluctant Witness* (Louisville: Westminster/John Knox Press, 1994), Introduction, 8ff.

12. On this point, see Robert Bartlett, *The Making of Europe: Conquest, Colonization and Cultural Change 950–1350* (Princeton: Princeton University Press, 1993).

13. For example, in 1922 Count de Salis, the British Minister to the Holy See, reported to the Foreign Office: "Everything in the Vatican is dominated by the Pope's fear of Russian Communism, that the Soviets may reach Western Europe." See Anthony Rhodes, *The Vatican in the Age of Dictators 1922–1945* (London: Hudder and Stoughton, 1973), 18.

14. Rhodes, *The Vatican in the Age of Dictators 1922–1945,* 165.

15. The shortwave radio address by Bishop Otto Dibelius, general superintendent of the Lutheran Church in Prussia, on April 4, 1933, was typical of mainstream Protestant response. Beamed at the United States, the address was the bishop's answer to protests by American Protestants against Nazi treatment of the Jews. Dibelius expressed approval of both the boycott and the measures being taken "to remove Jews from the public administration, particularly from judicial offices." (See John S. Conway, *The Nazi Persecution of the Churches 1933–45* [New York: Basic Books, 1968], 342–44.) This was not a new position for Dibelius. In 1928 Bishop Dibelius sent an Easter greeting to the clergy of Prussia that read in part, "Despite the ugly sound which often attached itself to the word, I have always regarded myself as an anti-Semite. The fact cannot be concealed that the Jews have played a leading part in all the symptoms of disintegration in modern civilization. . . . May God bless our Easter and our Easter message." (Conway, *The Nazi Persecution of the Churches 1933–45,* 410–11.) Dibelius' was no minor figure. He was a major church leader from the 1920s to the 1960s. He was strongly opposed to National Socialism because of its neopaganism and its attempts to compromise the authority of the Christian Church in spiritual matters, but not because of its treatment of nonconverted Jews. In 1937 the Nazis almost sent him to a concentration camp. (Conway, *The Nazi Persecution of the Churches 1933–45,* 208–12.) From 1954 to 1961 he served as a president of the World Council of Churches.

16. On September 20, 1938, Hitler told Josef Lipski, the Polish ambassador, that

he was thinking of shipping Europe's Jews to a colony and hoped that Poland, Hungary, and Romania would cooperate. Lipski replied that if the *Führer* could solve the problem, the Poles would build a monument to him in Warsaw. The incident was reported to Col. Jozef Beck, the Polish foreign minister on September 20, 1938. See Jozef Lipski, *Diplomat in Berlin, 1933–1944* (New York: Columbia University Press, 1968), 411ff.

17. Conway, *The Nazi Persecution of the Churches 1933–45*, 261, italics added.

18. On this point, let us recall the participation of a few Lutheran clergymen in the *Einsatzgruppen* and some Catholic priests in *Ustasa* mass murder.

19. The use of biological terms denoting agents of internal decay to describe the Jews and justify their elimination was widespread in the Third Reich and elsewhere in Europe. See Robert J. Lifton, *The Nazi Doctors: Medical Killing and the Psychology of Genocide* (London: Macmillan, 1986), 15ff.

20. The connection between highly visible Jewish intellectuals and revolutionary politics, which directly threatened his life, must have made an indelible impression on Papal Nuncio Eugenio Pacelli during his stay in Munich. On November 7, 1918, the eight hundred-year-old Wittelsbach dynasty, the royal house of Bavaria, was overthrown and Kurt Eisner, a socialist Jewish writer, found himself at the head of the provisional revolutionary government of Bavaria. In addition to Eisner, a number of other Jewish intellectuals, *literati,* and revolutionaries took leadership roles in the three successive revolutionary regimes. They included Gustav Landauer, Eugen Leviné, Ernst Toller, and Towia Axelrod. On the revolution in Munich see Allan Mitchell, *Revolution in Bavaria, 1918–1919* (Princeton: Princeton University Press, 1965); Ruth Fischer, *Stalin and German Communism* (Cambridge: Harvard University Press, 1948); Charles B. Maurer, *Call to Revolution: The Mystical Anarchism of Gustav Landauer* (Detroit: Wayne State University Press, 1971); Rosa Leviné-Meyer, *Leviné the Spartacist* (London: Gordon and Cremonesi, 1978); Richard Grunberger, *Red Rising in Bavaria* (New York: St. Martin's Press, 1973).

Eisner was assassinated by Count Anton von Arco Valley, a right-wing extremist of partly Jewish descent. After his death, a Bavarian Soviet Republic was established without the Communists. A second Soviet Republic led by Eugen Leviné, a Russian-born, Jewish-educated Communist, was established in April. On Palm Sunday 1919, posters signed by Leviné appeared all over Munich proclaiming: "Finally today Bavaria has also elected the dictatorship of the proletariat. The sun of world revolution has risen: Long live the world revolution!" Grunberger, *Red Rising in Bavaria,* 116.

To frighten the bourgeoisie into submission, the Munich Soviet's action committee announced an indefinite general strike. The police were disbanded and replaced by Red Guards. When the Whites declared a blockade, the Reds ordered the confiscation of all hoards of food, wherever found. When the milk supply was reduced to a tenth of the normal amount, Leviné declared: "What does it matter if for a few weeks less milk reaches Munich? Most of it goes to the children of the bourgeoisie. We are not interested in keeping them alive. No harm if they die—they'd only grow into enemies of the proletariat." Grunberger, *Red Rising in Bavaria,* 124–25.

The revolution ended in a right-wing bloodbath, but not before the Reds had entered Pacelli's compound, pointed a gun at his head, and threatened to kill him. Pacelli never forgot this incident and often alluded to it as long as he lived. In the eyes of the victorious Right, the Bavarian Republic and the two subsequent Soviet Republics constituted a "pogrom against the German people staged by Jews." Karl

Dietrich Bracher, *The German Dictatorship* (New York: Praeger, 1973), 82. A violent wave of antisemitism ensued in Munich, then becoming the birthplace and spiritual capital of the National Socialist movement.

For Archbishop Pacelli, the Communist Revolution was not something that happened in distant Russia. He experienced it directly. He also had experienced the forces of right-wing German nationalism as the defenders of Christian civilization against the assault of rootless, godless Communists. That lesson was never to leave him. If he was not convinced of the destabilizing consequences of the entrance of Jews into European intellectual and political life before Munich 1919, he was thereafter. Let us also recall that the infamous forgery, *The Protocols of the Elders of Zion,* with its myth of a Jewish conspiracy for world domination, was introduced into Munich during this decisive period by the Baltic German Alfred Rosenberg and White Russian *émigré* refugees. It was their "proof" that the Bolshevik Revolution had been the result of a Jewish conspiracy for world domination. Unfortunately, the events of 1919 greatly enhanced the credibility of the forgery in the minds of conservative Germans.

21. On the enormous influence of the *Protocols* in Japan, see Richard L. Rubenstein, "The Financier and the Finance Minister: The Roots of Japanese Anti-Semitism," *Continuum* 2 (1993).

22. Richard L. Rubenstein and John K. Roth, *Approaches to Auschwitz: The Holocaust and Its Legacy* (Atlanta: John Knox Press, 1987), 343ff.

23. See Walter Laqueur, *The Terrible Secret: Suppression of the Truth about Hitler's "Final Solution"* (New York: Penguin Books, 1982), 17–40.

24. See David Wyman, *The Abandonment of the Jews: America and the Holocaust 1941–1945* (New York: Pantheon Books, 1984), 105 and Wyman, "Why Wasn't Auschwitz Bombed?" in *Anatomy of the Auschwitz Death Camp,* ed. Yisrael Gutman and Michael Berenbaum (Bloomington: Indiana University Press, 1994).

25. Zoé Oldenbourg, *Massacre at Montségur: A History of the Albigensian Crusade,* trans. Peter Green (New York: Pantheon Books, 1961), 104.

26. This subject is covered in some detail in Gitta Sereny, *Into That Darkness: An Examination of Conscience* (New York: Vintage Books, 1984) and Mark Aarons and John Loftus, *Unholy Trinity: The Vatican, the Nazis and Soviet Intelligence* (New York: St. Martin's Press, 1992).

27. After persuasion failed to convert the Cathari, the pope wrote to the king of France, "Those who hold cheap the correction of the Church must be crushed by the arm of secular power." Innocent III, "Letter to Philip II of France and the French Nobility," in *Chronicles of the Crusades,* ed. Elizabeth Hallam (New York: Weidenfeld and Nicolson, 1989), 229.

14

Transforming the Void

Michael Berenbaum

My confrontation with the Holocaust began in silence, in the unspoken, the unsaid.

Born in 1945, some three months after the liberation of the camps, I entered Yeshiva of Central Queens in 1951—just six years after the Holocaust. During the early years, we were taught both religious and secular studies, Hebrew and English as we called it then, by women. The English faculty were unaccented, American-born or at least American-bred. The Hebrew teachers were European-born but long Americanized. They taught us in Hebrew because the Yeshiva of Central Queens was a Zionist school, and in the early 1950s the content of their Zionism was the Hebrew language, not the land of Israel and not yet the State of Israel. As we grew older our Hebrew teachers became more foreign, more Eastern European, and almost all men.

Images stick in my mind. A seventh grade teacher could not move his left hand. It stayed in his pocket all day long, every day. There was some talk about an experience in Russia. Where and when, I still do not know. Another teacher who taught us the Prophets of Israel had no fingers on his right hand, only a fearsome fist. He was the first to put us on the honor system for exams. We stared at that fist and wondered. Of our Talmud teacher, Rabbi Moses Feifer, it was said that he was in the camps together with his wife. They had lost a child. The word *camps* was spoken; so, too, *loss*. Beyond that no explanation was offered. Silence.

My younger cousin Larry came to live with us for a time—whether it was a week, or several months I do not remember. Larry was also known as

Paul. His name kept changing. His parents had been in the camps. His mother was sick so he came to live with us. No explanations. His parents were called refugees; so, too, were my aunt's neighbors who later became prominent in causes of remembrance. Only much later did they become known as survivors.

And then there was our synagogue, Adath Jeshurun, the Kew Gardens Synagogue, founded in 1939 by European refugees, an odd assortment of German, Belgian, and Dutch men who found a haven in the United States during the late 1930s, and who subsequently moved from Manhattan, Brooklyn, or the Bronx to Queens. My father was one of the few "Americans," one of the very few who knew baseball and not soccer. The services were traditional, the decorum Germanic, as were the melodies and the pronunciation of prayers. The president, Jacques Schwalbe, was a benevolent despot; he ruled the synagogue with an iron hand, strong, fair, and decisive. He was not only the wealthiest—or most generous with both time and money—of the lay leaders, but also the volunteer cantor. Unchallenged, he led the community for more than two decades. He taught us to chant the prayers, and to this day, each of his boys still uses those melodies, recalling with admiration and nostalgia the intensity and the intentionality of those melodious prayers.

Each Shabbat after services, one could hear different languages; some German and Dutch, less Yiddish than at any other Orthodox synagogue I knew, French and even Persian. Only decades later in the 1990s did I learn the background of these men and hear of their stories.

They were displaced. Their synagogue was modeled after a community I knew not, yet they were confident in their transplanted culture. Still nothing was said.

For high school, I attended Ramaz, an elite, moderately Orthodox day school. Our teachers were better educated, less European, and less directly impacted by the Holocaust. Nothing of the Holocaust was taught, and little was said. Only at Camp Ramah, where I spent summers, was the Holocaust mentioned. It became central to the observance of *Tisha B'av*, the fast day commemorating the destruction of the first and second temples, the exile from Spain, and other tragedies in Jewish history. The Holocaust was added as yet another event in the long litany of Jewish anguish.

When I was sixteen, I went to Israel for the first time and visited Yad Vashem, the Jewish national memorial to the *Shoah*. I was moved to tears and touched in the indelible way that high school students can be touched by tragedy. That summer, the Eichmann trial was being conducted in Israel and we spent one morning watching the trial on what I imagine was closed circuit television. From then on I listened attentively, rising at 6:30 each morning to hear a special NBC radio report by Martin Agronsky, reading accounts of the trial from the *New York Times, Life,* and *Look*.

I don't remember reading about the Holocaust until college. Only as an adult did I read *The Diary of Anne Frank.* I was a junior or senior in college before I read Elie Wiesel's *Night,* and a graduate student before I really tackled Raul Hilberg's, *The Destruction of the European Jews.*

Still I was fascinated by two questions that were to serve as my entry point to Holocaust studies. One was the question of theodicy, "Why do the innocent suffer?" and the other was a question of communal resilience, "What happens on the tenth of Av, the day after destruction?" How do communities respond to catastrophe, rebuild on the morrow, overcome catastrophe?

I was enthralled by the thundering of the Prophets, by Hosea's sense of betrayal, Isaiah's vision of justice, his outrage at the false religion of those insensitive to widows and orphans, of fasts that do not feed the hungry; I was moved by his teaching to clothe the naked, shelter the homeless. My favorite prophet was Jeremiah, who for four decades preached the destruction of Judea, and then when his prophecy was realized preached the words of consolation. Those words were altogether contemporary in the sixties when the fight for civil rights and opposition to the war in Vietnam galvanized my generation, and the battle for Israel and struggle for Soviet Jewry were the Jewish responses for those of us who were determined to right the wrongs done to Jews.

Only decades later did I understand that part of my preoccupation with undoing injustice was a response to inequality at home. The favored son of my father, I had been the chosen one—the *Kaddish*—and I had remained silent as my sister struggled to achieve appropriate recognition in a home where men were important and women were not, as father and daughter clashed and father and son bonded.

I was intrigued by a religious question, what happens in the aftermath of defeat? How does one rise on the morrow of catastrophe? Thus, not only did the 9th of Av interest me but also the scroll of Lamentations, which is read on the evening of *Tisha B'av* (the 9th of Av) and the morning after, as well as the chapters of consolation in the book of Jeremiah. I was also fascinated by the story of Yochanan ben Zakkai, who reconstituted the Jewish people at Yavneh and whose religious teaching transformed a land-centered, Temple-centered people, whose destiny was linked to the fate of Jerusalem, into a Torah-centered, synagogue-centered portable community that could move from place to place and reestablish itself with a synagogue and an academy. The Torah could move with the people.

Little did I realize how contemporary was the clash of myths and that such an ancient struggle was being reenacted at that very moment. When I first traveled to Israel in 1961 with a Yeshiva University group, as we ascended Masada we heard the voice of continuity in Jewish history, of return, but not revolution. Only later did I recognize that contemporary Jews were undoing the teaching of Yochanan, by rediscovering the God of space, and reconstituting a religion of land. Secularists were avowed revolutionaries, but what W. D. Davies has called the "territorial dimension of Judaism" would emerge most deeply within the religious community in the decades that followed the Six Day War.

I never made it to my college graduation on June 4, 1967. The first of my family to graduate from college, it was to be a splendid occasion. My grandfather was to join us. And unlike high school, where I had to return the diploma upon receipt as I had not completed all my courses, I had done well in college and had earned my degree with hard work.

I went to Israel instead. For three weeks, the signs of war were everywhere. Israel was surrounded on all sides. The Gulf of Aquba was closed. United Nations troops were withdrawn from the Sinai. The United States would not test the Egyptian blockade. Israel was alone and isolated. For Jews everywhere, the tension was high.

Ahmed Shukiery, Yasser Arafat's predecessor, then threatened to drive the Jews into the sea; and suddenly the Holocaust and Israel were linked as never before. Something in the archetypal memory of the Jewish people had been touched. We remembered the High Holiday prayer: "On Rosh Hashanah it is written and on Yom Kippur it is sealed. Who shall live and who shall die? . . . Who by fire and who by water? The last generation was consumed by fire, shall this generation perish by water?"

It is difficult to forget the anxiety that afflicted the American Jewish community. My friend Art Green, whose turn toward religion had alienated him from his father, was suddenly quoting his father: "We must at least evacuate the children." Israel seemed doomed. And American Jewry at least had to do what it had failed to do a generation earlier, at least rescue the next generation. I knew—as deeply as I knew anything—that I had to go to Israel. I did not want to be on the sidelines, a bystander—whether passive or active—as Jewish history was being lived. I had to be with my people. In the dramatic way that only an adolescent can think, I felt that if they were to die, then so would I.

I went to synagogue that Shabbat morning with my father and heard the rabbi's anguish. I listened more attentively as Rabbi Gerson Appel preached what could have been my eulogy; extolling the decision to go to Israel, fully expecting that I, and two other young men who had also volunteered, would never return alive.

I also remember feeling that if Israel were destroyed and Jews led to the slaughter, I would be the last Jew in my line. I could not convert and probably could not have abandoned Jewish practice, but if there was to be no Jewish future in Israel, if two generations of Jews were to be murdered, then I would certainly not be responsible for a third. My reaction was antithetical to all that I had been taught by the heirs of Yochanan ben Zakkai, by those who thought of Jewish survival as religious survival. Still, it was clear in my mind.

So I left for Israel on the last plane before the Six Day War. But before I left, I went to the graduation ceremonies of the Jewish Theological Seminary and the ordination of my friends Art Green and Neal Kaunfer. It was then that I heard Elie Wiesel for the first time. He was being given an honorary doctorate. He was the graduation speaker. He was—as usual—masterful, but given the anguish of the moment, we hung on every word. He challenged the world, he stormed the heavens, he pleaded on behalf of the Jewish people in their hour of travail. In truth, I less remember what he said that day than that he spoke. Yet I fully knew then what had led Steven Schwarzschild to describe Wiesel as "the de facto high priest of our generation, the man who spoke most tellingly of our time, of our hopes and fears, our tragedy and our protest." And only when I boarded the plane filled with Israelis returning home to fight did I sense that they fully expected to win.

My role in the Six Day War was tangential at best. I drove a garbage truck in the Old City, filling in for the mobilized men, but I was in Israel for the euphoric announcement that "The Old City is in our hands." I was in synagogue on the Friday evening of the war when the president of Israel, Zalman Shazar, spoke: "Clothe yourself with the clothing of your majesty Jerusalem," he said, as if the words of Isaiah had been written for that moment alone!

And I was in Israel when on Shavuot—the festival of revelation—hundreds of thousands of Jews walked to the Western Wall under Jewish sovereignty for the first time in 1,897 years, where miniskirted women danced with caftan-clad Hasidim in the ecstasy of reunion.

I had prepared for the evening in the traditional manner. I studied Torah at night. En route to the Wall, I took pride in the fact that we were walking on the pope's path, a special road that had been designed to accommodate Pope Paul VI's visit to the Holy City. He had not wanted to recognize Israel, to enter the country at an established crossing, so the Jordanians had built a special road on Mt. Zion. I joined a minyan and wanted to pray with the intensity warranted by the occasion, but could not.

The words I knew by heart, but the *kavana*—the intentionality—did not come until we recited the words of the *kaddish d'rabanan,* the *kaddish* with the special insert "for Israel and for her rabbis and for their students' students and all who study Torah." At that moment I saw teachers and masters, rabbis and prophets, Moses and Jeremiah, Rabban Yochanan and Rabbi Akivah, the rabbis who had taught me and saw themselves as part of that unbroken chain, all chanting *ashrecha sh'zachita,* happy are you who have been deemed worthy (of this moment).

I had a sense of continuity and discontinuity. While others were returning, rediscovering their roots, their links to the past, I, who had for so long been rooted in the past, grasped the transformation of tradition that after Auschwitz and after Jerusalem we were a different people. Something awesomely significant had happened in Jewish history, in my generation, and I wasn't quite sure what. I was a different type of Jew than my father and his father before him.

That summer in Jerusalem, I did not experience the blessing of Israel reborn alone; I had encountered Israel alongside the destruction of the Jewish people. Nearly successful twenty-two years earlier, it had almost been reenacted yet again.

I wonder if I had stayed in Israel and not returned to graduate school in the United States whether I would have come to see the Holocaust as so dominant an event. Or would I have seen the significance of the Jewish revolution purely in terms of Israel as does David Hartman, whose every thought is influenced by American pluralism and the interchange of diverse cultures in this country, and yet who sees Israel as the novum in Jewish history, the sole transformative event for contemporary Jews? Emil Facken-heim, Elie Wiesel, Richard Rubenstein, Irving Greenberg, and I among so many others see Auschwitz and the return to Jerusalem as revolutionary events. My own thought has been deeply influenced by Israel and the em-powerment of the Jewish people.

But I didn't stay. I came home again, and home was America. I was at home in a country that was undergoing its own cultural revolutions that were to shape me during this formative period. The struggle for civil rights had given way to the antiwar movement and the sexual revolution, as surely as beer had given way to marijuana and the neatly trimmed boys of the early sixties to the unshaven long-haired men of the last third of that decade. Girls had not become young ladies as we and they had expected them to become, but women in the process of seeing themselves and being per-ceived as equal—expecting careers of their own and their spouses to share fully in the responsibility for the children and home. I was one such long-haired man who soon was to marry a woman transformed by the women's movement. And as a Jew, the counterculture found expression is our alien-ation from the conventional synagogue and our gravitation toward *chavurot*.

I studied philosophy, but kept reading theology. I read Richard Ruben-stein's *After Auschwitz* and recognized in Rubenstein a kindred spirit, the man who was asking all the right questions, insisting that Auschwitz and Israel are the two revolutions of modern Jewish history and that "no Jewish theology will possess even a remote degree of relevance to modern life if it ignores the question of God and the death camps." It is the question for Jewish theology in our time. I was so completely comfortable with his ques-tions that I couldn't comprehend the controversy that his book had gen-erated in the Jewish community.

And I read Elie Wiesel. I devoured his books; one by one, as he wrote them, I read them—I still do, but with diminished fervor. *Night* was the journey into the abyss, the young boy's loss of faith, the confrontation with the anti-God and the antiman at Auschwitz, the revelation of the "other side." *Dawn* was the Israel option, seen in revolutionary terms, in discontinuity with the past; it required a deliberate shattering of the past. *The Accident*, as *Le Jour,* was incorrectly translated (only in a recent release of the trilogy is it entitled *Day*), was the struggle for life, to embrace life, to chose life, to turn away from the dead. And *The Town Beyond the Wall* was a partial, fragmentary means of rebuilding in a world without faith in humanity or divinity. I still teach these books each year in a seminar on the Holocaust at Georgetown University. Rereading them in middle age I remain grateful for the way in which Wiesel's questions shaped my maturation.

I first studied philosophy in graduate school, but the questions I was asking, the issues that really stirred my soul, were theological: the problem of evil, how to speak of God's presence in a time of absence, how to speak of God at Auschwitz and to God after Auschwitz, the ongoing meaning of Jewish tradition. I took two years off from formal study to teach at Colby-Sawyer College in New Hampshire, teaching philosophy and sociology to freshmen and sophomore women, some four or five years my junior. A long-haired and bearded New York Jew, I lived in New London, a rural town with less than a minyan of Jews, more than thirty miles from the nearest synagogue. Interstate 89 had only opened a year before and though Boston was less than ninety miles and ninety minutes away, it was a different world. It was in New Hampshire, so very distant from my past, that I rediscovered myself as a Jew. Being the representative Jew, and most often the only Jew, made me feel more rooted in the past, more at home in tradition.

The question of my future could not be deferred. A failed philosopher, should I try law school or return to a Ph.D. program to confront the issues that really haunted me? The law was too conventional, too staid, too much my father. So theology it was, and the choices were few. Temple University was a place where the Christian theologians were raising all the right issues for Christianity, but would they have a place for a Jewish theologian and could one be credentialed by them to do the work that I wanted to do? Something kept attracting me to Richard Rubenstein, though neither *The Religious Imagination* nor *Morality and Eros* quite touched me as had *After Auschwitz*.

But Rubenstein the man did! I still remember meeting him in the elevator for the first time. Strikingly handsome, distant and fierce, he was intent on reaching his office and did not take to the distraction of a student easily. In class, I began to see the Holocaust in a much larger context, as part not only of Jewish history, but of the history of Europe. I learned Jewish theology from him, but in a wider context. The angle of vision was different. Freud and Hegel, Marx and Peter Berger. I began to read texts differently and to understand their subtexts. The issues that concerned Rubenstein were also radically different than any I had even imagined relevant—status and power, class and social structure. He was at the transitional moment in his own career when he supplemented a psychoanalytical approach with a sociological and structural one that was soon to give rise to *The Cunning of History.* More important, as we reread *After Auschwitz,* I began to understand that within each chapter were bold struggles, difficult questions, tentative answers. Over time, we grew quite close, but not without difficulty. Rubenstein was hesitant, and I was fearful of becoming a disciple or, worse yet, a groupie. I also learned that Rubenstein's questions were my own. His answers were his own; I was more rooted in the Jewish community, more religiously observant, more socially tied. After all, I had grown up in an intensely Orthodox community and he in an assimilated Reform home. I was a product of yeshivot and he of Townsend Harris high school.

What is the difference between a good master and a great master, a Hasidic rebbe was once asked: "A good master teaches you his way; a great master allows you to discover your own." According to these criteria, Rubenstein was indeed a great master. He taught me to be authentic to my own experience.

I wrote my dissertation on Elie Wiesel. The decision was easy; the field was open. Everyone had been speaking of Wiesel's significance, no one had yet analyzed his thought. I wrote of Wiesel as a religious thinker, not quite sensing what I later understood quite well: that Wiesel's symbolic role— dare I say iconic—in the American Jewish community was as significant as his intellectual contribution. I was also able to mask many of my own thoughts as commentary on Wiesel as thinker. I had not yet mastered the ability or the courage to speak in my own voice, nor had I learned John Roth's technique of meditations that allow the personal to be expressed so clearly in dialogue with analysis.

My central conclusions about Wiesel's corpus—most especially his early works—still form the cornerstone of my own sense of God, the Holocaust and the Jewish people. Wiesel, I wrote, was a theologian of the void, writing of absence where presence had been. Authentic Jews had to confront that void. In *God's Presence in History,* Emil Fackenheim had recognized the void and backed away because of the consequences. His form of affirmation was dependent on the fear of consequences. The central word was *lest—lest* the memory of the victims perish, *lest* the Jewish people perish, *lest* Judaism perish, *lest* we turn the world over to the forces that made for Auschwitz. Thus fearful, we are commanded to remember the victims and to survive as Jews; we are forbidden to despair of the God of Israel and of humanity. Fackenheim's notion of the Holocaust as rupture, which he developed in *To Mend the World,* is much closer to the void. In *Faith after the Holocaust,* Eliezer Berkovits masterfully constructed a philosophy that deferred the question of the void until the end of history. Why was there something rather than nothing? became his central question, more important than the question of why the innocent suffer and the wicked prosper. And Richard Rubenstein had looked at the void and moved beyond. The past was broken; it allowed no reconstruction. Wiesel had the courage to face the void and to offer a tentative answer as to how to live and create despite the void.

In his early work, Wiesel struggled to find meaning for his suffering, to endow his destiny and the history of the Jewish people with a transcendent purpose. Only in *The Town Beyond the Wall* did he succeed. The major character is a young Holocaust survivor who has made his way to Paris after the war. His mentor, the man who teaches him the meaning of survival, is not a Jew with memories of Sinai and Auschwitz, but a Spaniard who learned of death and love during the Spanish Civil War. From Pedro, the young survivor learns two lessons that have shaped Wiesel's writings ever since. Pedro told the young man:

You frighten me. . . . You want to eliminate suffering by pushing it to its extreme: to madness. To say "I suffer therefore I am" is to become the enemy of man. What you must say is "I suffer therefore you are." Camus wrote that to protest against a universe of unhappiness you had to create happiness. That's an arrow pointing the way: it leads to another human being. And not via absurdity.[1]

And I understood Wiesel's corpus as offering an additional covenant to re-place the one shattered at Auschwitz—or to supplement it for those to whom the traditional covenant was still credible, a covenant not between God and Israel, but between Israel and its memories of pain and death, God and meaning.

The content of that covenant was solidarity, witness, and sanctification. The content of solidarity was easy to articulate. An authentic post-Holocaust Jew had to embrace all Jews and all of Jewish history. Toward the Jewish experience, one must say ours, toward the Jewish people, one must say we, and toward Jewish destiny, one must say it is mine. So too, witness. All Jews stood at Sinai were received the Torah; Jewish history was in part a response to that moment. And all Jews were condemned to Auschwitz where the anti-God and the antihuman were revealed in this world. In the post-Holocaust world, the Jew must bear witness to both in all their conflicting, dialectical dimensions. Jewish continuity was to be found in the act of sanctification; making the secular sacred, making life holy. There were many ways to sanc-tify life, and unlike more Orthodox (or conservative in a nondenominational sense) friends, I was willing to entertain these many ways, but the very commitment to sanctification, the reach for the holy was essential then to my understanding of Judaism. I have not abandoned these views, indeed I have embraced them so much that they seem commonplace, essential but obvious, a natural part of my religious life.

After graduate school, I went to teach at Wesleyan University where I served as university Jewish chaplain and for the first time worked profes-sionally as a rabbi. In the world of the early seventies, swirling with prophets, my students needed a priest who would not only coax them and place additional demands on them, but confirm and embrace them, accept them for what they were and discover with them what they could be. Wesleyan had a wonderful tradition of academic freedom and intellectual innovation. I taught virtually what I pleased and could therefore experiment with material that I wanted to study. Thus, as I was working through the Wiesel material, I taught a seminar on his writings. As I wrestled with Midrash as theology, I taught Midrash, and as I sought to learn more intellectual history, I could teach more Jewish intellectual history.

I had grown closer with Irving Greenberg over time. I first met him when he delivered a splendid address at the Cathedral of St. John the Divine in New York City, later published as "Cloud of Smoke, Pillar of Fire: Judaism, Christianity, and Modernity after the Holocaust,"[2] his masterful articulation of post-Holocaust thought. I worked with him, coordinating a conference that was to take place in December 1976 in the Soviet Union where I spent the summer of 1976 working to redeem Soviet Jewry. It was the first of many trips to the Soviet Union, an expression of my generation's determination to rescue imperilled Jewish communities. I was so taken by Greenberg's thought that in the fall of 1978 I accepted a position at Zachor: The Holocaust Resource Center, which was a central part of his vision for a national Jewish conference center, later evolving into CLAL, the Center for Learning and Leadership. No sooner had I settled in at Zachor when Elie Wiesel was named chairman of the President's Commission on the Holocaust, inviting Greenberg to be director. Since he could not devote the day-to-day time required, Greenberg invited me, with Wiesel's consent, to be deputy director and to move to Washington.

Trained in theology and history, I began to think institutionally. Trained as a Jewish thinker in America, I was to work at creating an American institution—it became the United States Holocaust Memorial Museum in Washington, D.C.—that would deal with Jewish memory and transmit to the American public what could have remained the parochial memories of a bereaved people.

As such, the questions that began to preoccupy me were rather different than any of those I had faced in graduate school or in my first years of teaching. It was no longer possible merely to arrive at an intellectual solution, but one had to achieve a consensus behind that conclusion among people for whom the questions were of little interest and the information strange.

Two central questions became of immediate concern even during my work for the President's Commission on the Holocaust and for its successor organization, the United States Holocaust Memorial Council. They remain of central concern today. The first has to do with the Americanization of the Holocaust; that is, the presentation to an American audience of an event that occurred on the European continent decades ago. How does one represent this past? How does one represent this past to an American public that thinks in other categories of interpretation? How to bridge the gap of understanding—to engage, motivate, and move an audience? More importantly, does the process of Americanization falsify the presentation of the Holocaust? What is legitimate and illegitimate, appropriate or inappropriate? And must the Americanization of the Holocaust inevitably lead to vulgarization and dejudaization?

The second question related to the uniqueness and universality of the Holocaust. How are all the victims of Nazi terror to be included in a memorial without misrepresenting the fact that Jews were the central victims. There was a strong fear, primarily among survivors and Israelis, that the inclusion of non-Jewish victims of Nazism would dejudaize the planned United States Holocaust Memorial Museum and thus falsify the event. Wiesel expressed the fear when he spoke to the President's Commission on April 24, 1979: "Today they speak of six million Jews and five million others. Soon they will speak of 11 million victims, 6 million of them Jews; and soon thereafter of 11 million victims."[3] His less fearful and more poetic solution to the problem was that "while not all victims were Jews, all Jews were victims." Yehuda Bauer was similarly concerned. In an article entitled "Whose Holocaust?" he wrote: "The memorial as seen by the President [not the commission] should commemorate all the victims of Nazism, Jews and non-Jews alike, and should *submerge* the specific Jewish tragedy in the *general* sea of atrocities committed by the Nazi regime."[4]

Bauer attributed the "submersion" of the specific Jewish tragedy to pressure from American ethnic groups and warned that an Americanized, non-Jewish memorial would misrepresent the Holocaust. He then marshaled three highly emotional arguments to foster his claim. First was the Russian attempt to deny the Jewishness of the Holocaust, resulting in the abominable memorial at Babi Yar where, until 1991, no mention of Jews was made either in the content of the sculpture or in the inscription on the memorial. Second, Bauer referred to the Western denial of the "War Against the Jews," which led to the failure to rescue. Third, Bauer alluded to international antisemitism, which seeks to deny the Holocaust altogether.

Edward Linenthal has dealt with the politics of this clash, and perhaps at another time and place I will comment on those politics, but it is ideas and issues that are of interest to us in the context of this essay.

Intuitively, I understood that there was a historically authentic and intellectually truthful way to navigate among the conflicting needs and competing groups. Thus, I wrote "The Uniqueness and Universality of the Holocaust," which argued that only by the inclusion of all victims of Nazism can we document and illuminate the uniqueness of Jewish fate. It was not politics but the requirement of education and scholarship that mandated—necessitated—the inclusion of non-Jewish victims of the Nazis. Perhaps because, unlike Bauer and Wiesel, I was born and raised in America and felt at home in America as a Jew, I was less fearful of the process of Americanization and more confident that uniqueness could survive the process of absorption. Furthermore, I had greater empirical experience in seeing the Holocaust taught in American high schools. In a report on the teaching of the Holocaust, I concluded:

As an event of this magnitude is incorporated into the American educational system, the lens through which the data is seen is necessarily an American one. The categories relate to the experience of American students throughout the country and also to their teachers. There is no way of resisting this tide, and indeed from our research, we find that the uniqueness of the Holocaust is underscored by this process of filtration and absorption. Indeed, its specialness is its own best witness, communicating itself most profoundly, most clearly and incontrovertibly.[5]

Even after I left the employ of the Holocaust Memorial Council for a time, I kept writing about the issues central to the formulation of the museum, the role of Holocaust commemoration, the place of the Holocaust in American Jewish consciousness and American national consciousness, what we should tell our children, and how we should teach the Holocaust. Published separately, they formed the Holocaust section of my work *After Tragedy and Triumph: Modern Jewish Thought and the American Experience*, chronicling my intellectual work during the mid-eighties. I also edited a collection of essays that I deliberately entitled *A Mosaic of Victims: Non-Jews Persecuted and Murdered by the Nazis*. The word *mosaic* replaced the word *other* since the world was not to be divided between Jews and others.

In 1987, I had the opportunity to work again on the United States Holocaust Memorial Museum and to help shape its permanent exhibition and the intellectual content of the entire institution. I had the rare privilege of uniting my professional and intellectual work and writing the conclusions on a scale writ large. In essence, the issues that concerned the creation of the museum became of central concern to me. Thus, the questions that preoccupied me were how to tell the story of the Holocaust to the American people. I became less concerned with theology and more with history; in truth I also became less engaged with the victims and more focused on the perpetrators and the structures that facilitated the perpetration of so vast a crime and over such a long duration. It was ironic that with Wiesel's resignation as chairman I was invited, at the initiative of the survivors, to return to protect the Jewishness of the Holocaust and the integrity of Jewish memory.

I understood that in order to create the museum with the integrity of Jewish memory that Wiesel demanded, we had to reject Wiesel's notion of the Holocaust as mystery and resist all efforts at mystification. Wiesel had taught that "only those who were there will ever know and those who were there can never tell." If he was right, then there was no way for a nonsurvivor to contribute to the project or to approach the event. Furthermore, he portrayed the Holocaust as the "Kingdom of Night," a world apart that permits no comparisons, a universe that is impenetrable. If the Holocaust is the sacred mystery that cannot be understood—or understood solely by the survivor—then the efforts of the nonsurvivor are futile. In truth, there may be a dimension of understanding that eludes us—all of us, survivor and nonsurvivor alike—but that should face us only at the end of a confrontation with the Holocaust and not at the beginning.

However, it was not only professionally that the theological became deemphasized for me, but personally as well. As a young man I asked questions that could not be answered and I had begun to live with these questions and to build a positive traditional religious life despite the questions. Surely, my religious life changed. For example, the divine drama of sin and atonement, reward and punishment, guilt and judgment that were so central to the Yom Kippur observance as a child and adolescent became impossible to reenact in a post-Holocaust world, and thus became less relevant to my religious life. Yom Kippur became a celebration of opportunity and renewal—I don't have to be tomorrow what I was yesterday. All the vows and commitments of the past year, all the achievements and failures of the past year were subject to reexamination. On Yom Kippur I recited some prayers without belief. I, who wrestled with the God who did not answer, would read prayers and indeed lead prayer that spoke to the God who answered. I found a kindred soul in David Blumenthal, who wrote one of the most honest and difficult books in post-Holocaust theology, *Facing the Abusing God.* He transformed the liturgy and wrote new prayers to force an honest confrontation with the God of the Holocaust, as I had many years earlier in a far less sophisticated and poetic way.

Passover too became less a celebration of God's saving power, for like Fackenheim, I know the redeeming God was absent at Auschwitz. It was more of a celebration of the possibility of liberation—self-liberation in which the divine is encountered, but the human community is the prime initiator. Holidays were transformed, gently but not boldly, and I could share with my children the richness of traditions and the contemporary questions that Jews today must ask. Thus, there was a sense of coherence in what I practiced and surely in what I preached, and an inner truth allowing a measure of peace. As my daughter worked on her senior thesis at Brown University on the Passover Haggadah, I was pleased to see that she understood the questions and lived with them as well.

Ironically, I believe that it was my theological training that allowed me to navigate the issues of the museum. If one reflects upon the museum's permanent exhibition, one will see that we have walked a narrow ridge, to use Buber's phrase; we have balanced the uniqueness and the universal precisely in the manner that was formulated more than a decade ago. All of the victims are included in the museum—each story is told—yet the Jewish story is paramount, for such was the experience of the Holocaust.

I had been deeply mistaken when I thought that the issue was intellectual and that the question was how to include the other victims. In actuality there were three very different positions at odds with one another. There were those who deeply—and often subliminally—felt that to speak of the Jewish experience was to parochialize the institution and, therefore, they embraced the inclusion of all other victims so as not to focus on the Jews. Even after the museum became so very successful by walking the narrow ridge, they were convinced that the Jewish was parochial.

There were others who were adverse to mixing Jews and non-Jews and felt that the very inclusion of the non-Jews was to somehow misrepresent the status of the Jews in the Holocaust. Inclusion was a question of status, by speaking of other victims we were diminishing the status of the Jews.

There are many among my generation who believe, as I do, that the deeper and more authentically one explores Jewish experience, the more universal it becomes, the more it echoes and touches on the experience of others. In essence, these differences could not be bridged because they were a window as to how one felt *as* a Jew in America or as to how one felt *about* Jews in America and will remain a perpetual dilemma within the leadership and the staff of the museum.

We have walked the narrow ridge between presenting the horror of the Holocaust without softening it and still not becoming a museum of horrors. We have told of the noble and the good, but in a context where it appears as a mere glimmer of light in a world of darkness. We resisted the temptation in the permanent exhibition—though not in all aspects of the museum—to heroize the American liberator who by happenstance encountered the camps en route to battles elsewhere, or to make the survivor the moral hero. In short, we refused to offer easy answers, simple resolutions.

Clearly, the United States Holocaust Memorial Museum is an integral part of the Americanization of the Holocaust. Contrary to Alvin Rosenfeld and Yehuda Bauer, I believe that the Americanization of the Holocaust is appropriate, perhaps inevitable.

"By the Waters of Babylon we sat and we wept as we remembered Zion," the psalmist wrote. The place from which an event is recalled shapes the content of that act of remembrance. So what has occurred in Israel is the Israelification of the Holocaust as Tom Segev has shown in *The Seventh Million;* and in Washington, what results is Americanization. There is one essential difference between the two processes. If not properly done the process of Americanization can—but need not necessarily—lead to dejudaization. Israelification of the Holocaust may lead to a falsification of the history, but is somewhat protected against dejudaization.

But the pitfalls of Americanization have been avoided. Thus, the uniqueness of the event is not treated within the context of American social problems or even the history of genocide. But by its presence on the Mall, and in contrast to its neighbors, memorials to the power of government—museums celebrating human achievement in art, science, literature, technology—the Holocaust is presented as the other side of government and civilization, the event that instructs us about the dark side of culture and civilization—dare I say even divinity. It becomes the touchstone of evil, paradigmatic, absolute evil.

The American role is examined in detail and in specifics. The origins of the Holocaust are detailed. More space is dedicated to origins than in any other museum of the Holocaust, most especially since one of the questions that American visitors specifically want answered is how a democratic society becomes a totalitarian dictatorship.

Yet, in a most important way, the history of the Holocaust cuts against the grain of the American ethos. We are a nation of new beginnings, of eternal hope. We believe that tomorrow will be better than yesterday. Our founding fathers proclaimed that human equality was a self-evident truth. The most pressing demand for falsifying the event came from those who wanted a happy ending. That pressure was resisted. So in the United States Holocaust Memorial Museum, the visitor learns of evil unredeemed, of death, of destruction. The Holocaust offers no happy ending, no transcendent meaning, no easy moralism. And even if we pause occasionally to learn of courage and valor, of heroism and decency, the overriding theme of the Holocaust is evil perpetrated by individuals, organizations, and governments. Consider the allocation of space and place to rescuers in the museum as contrasted to *Schindler's List* or the Jewish Foundation of Christian Rescuers, or Yad Vashem's exaggerated language as it honors "The Righteous Among the Nations of the World."

Exaggerated language is a reflection of our exaggerated needs, genuine needs, appropriate needs, all too human needs to find the noble and thus preserve a sense of the nobility of the human spirit. But again and again, if we heed carefully the words of those who saved Jewish lives, we hear a very different story. Father Louis Celis, a Roman Catholic priest who saved the Rotenberg children in Belgium, said of himself: "You insist on considering me a saint because I was unfortunately able to save only a few Jewish lives. But was this not an urgent and serious obligation of every person, Jew, Christian, or atheist, still worthy to be considered human?"[6] Eva Hermann, a German woman who hid a Jewish couple, wrote of her canonization: "I am fully conscious of the fact that my late husband and I did nothing special; we simply tried to remain human in the midst of inhumanity."[7] Righteousness, she said, "cannot have another meaning than the attempt to do what is right and to live humanly even during times of inhumanity."

And so it is. We overstress the word righteousness as we mystify goodness. The good was natural, routine, commonplace. But given the dialectic of the Holocaust, the good was ordinary, commonplace behavior—but the ordinary was anything but ordinary. It was extraordinary. In this case the sum total of banal deeds is not banality, but nobility.

The central theme of the story of the Holocaust is not regeneration and rebirth (as it is in Yad Vashem), goodness or resistance, liberation or justice, but death and destruction, dehumanization and devastation, above all, loss. Millions were murdered, worlds were shattered, cities were without Jews, and soon even without the memory of Jews. And behind each loss was a person whose life was ended tragically and prematurely. And for those who survived, there were the burdens of memory—to use Lawrence Langer's words, haunting memories, nonheroic memories—of worlds shattered and destroyed, of defeat, and of life in its aftermath. We meet those people in the museum in the identity cards the visitors carry, in the hall adjacent to the Birkenau barracks where we hear survivors describe a day in the death camp, in the final film *Testimony,* and in thousands of oral histories available at the touch of a button in the Learning Center.

For our visitors, the bulk of whom are Americans, confronting this European event brings a new recognition of the tenets of American constitutional democracy: a belief in equality and equal justice under law; a commitment to pluralism and tolerance particularly at a time when our society is becoming more diverse than ever before; a determination to restrain government by checks and balances and the constitutional protection of "inalienable rights"; and a struggle for human rights as a core national value and foundation for foreign policy. That is what they bring to the experience of visiting the museum, not what the museum gives to them.

And for American Jews it is a place of pilgrimage and a source of pride. In many important respects the museum represents the arrival of the American Jewish community as confident and self-assertive in America. A generation ago, the museum would have been built in New York, not in Washington. American Jews—the primary constituency for the museum's creation—would have preferred to keep their bereaved memories private, parochial, or feared that if the museum had been built in Washington, it would have, as Elie Wiesel suggested, muted the Jewishness of Holocaust victims. A generation ago, Jews had internalized the rule of emancipation, "be a Jew in your house, a man in the street." No public life as Jews was permitted to them. Now in pluralistic America, the most painful of Jewish memories can be brought to the center of our national life. The museum includes the totality of Nazi victims without falsifying the event, without distorting, neglecting, minimizing, or deemphasizing the fact that Jews were the central target of Nazi genocidal deeds.

Apart from the museum, in my own scholarship, I have become more interested in the killers and in their motivations, more anxious to probe the scope of the evil and the dimensions of responsibility. Thus, in the work that Israel Gutman and I edited, *Anatomy of the Auschwitz Death Camp,* almost all the essays deal with the killers and the crime. We devote adequate but not major space to resistance at the camp, less to the experience of the camp and much more to the structure of evil from its architecture to its economics. So too, in an anthology I recently edited, I was surprised by how much documentation of the killers I included and how little of victim material. Still, I continue to read memoirs, I continue to view oral histories, I remain engaged with the survivors, but the killers are of increasing interest.

Working with this material has taken its toll. It has had an emotional cost that is difficult to measure. When my children were young I would often wake them and play with them late at night after a day confronting difficult material. It was essential to touch the source of life, to balance immersion in death by life. From time to time, I write of baseball and seek the pleasure of sports as a diversion. Several of my colleagues have had cancer. I went through the breakdown of a marriage followed by a difficult divorce. It is impossible to gauge the impact of working with this event, but no one who enters the darkness emerges unchanged. Perhaps Rabbi Nachman is right when he says that nothing is as whole as a heart that has been broken, but I do not yet know it.

Perhaps.

NOTES

1. Elie Wiesel, *The Town Beyond the Wall,* trans. Stephen Becker (New York: Holt, Rinehart and Winston, 1964), 118.

2. Irving Greenberg, "Cloud of Smoke, Pillar of Fire: Judaism, Christianity, and Modernity after the Holocaust," in *Auschwitz: Beginning of New Era?,* ed. Eva Fleischner (New York: KTAV, 1977) and abridged in *Holocaust: Religious and Philosophical Implications,* ed. John K. Roth and Michael Berenbaum (New York: Paragon House, 1989).

3. Transcript of meeting of the President's Commission on the Holocaust, April 24, 1979.

4. Yehuda Bauer, "Whose Holocaust?" *Midstream* 26:9 (November 1980): 42 [emphasis added].

5. Mary T. Glynn, RSM and Geoffrey Bock, *American Youth and the Holocaust: A Study of Four Major Curricula* (New York: Zachor: The Holocaust Resource Center, 1982).

6. Mordecai Paldiel, *The Path of the Righteous: Gentile Rescuers During the Holocaust* (Hoboken, N.J.: KTAV, 1993), 76–77.

7. Ibid., 155.

15

It Started with Tears: The Holocaust's Impact on My Life and Work

John K. Roth

The Holocaust demands interrogation and calls everything into question. . . . All must be revised in the shadow of Birkenau.

—Elie Wiesel

Fresh from graduate study at Yale University, I headed for California and joined the Claremont McKenna College faculty in 1966. Writing these words thirty years later makes me realize more than ever that I could scarcely have imagined then how the Holocaust would affect my life and work. I can start to explain what I mean by noting that during my 1995–96 sabbatical a Fulbright fellowship took me to Norway. That country's chapter in the Holocaust's history may seem small, even insignificant, but neither of those descriptions fits for me. True, Norway's Jewish population was minuscule compared to Poland's. Still, the destruction of Jewish life was more thorough in Norway than in many other Nazi-occupied countries.

CHANCE ENCOUNTERS

In 1995–96, my Oslo apartment was down the street from Kirkeveien 23. Since a relatively new building stood at that address, Kirkeveien 23 meant little to me until I learned that hundreds of Norwegian Jews were sent there when roundups took place around the country in the early morning of Monday, October 26, 1942. Later some of those Jews were imprisoned at

Grini, a concentration camp that was located only a few minutes by train from my flat.

While pursuing Holocaust studies in Norway, I visited the country's secondary schools to consult with teachers who have responsibility for teaching American history and literature to Norwegian students. Those schools often contain memorials to Norwegians who were killed by the Nazis. The memorials sometimes include the names of Jewish students—Feinberg and Jaffe, for example—who were taken from their schoolrooms by Norwegian police while their classmates and teachers stood by.

Some of those children were in the largest transport of Norwegian Jews that left Pier 1 in Oslo on November 26, 1942. Those Jews sailed aboard the *Donau,* a German troop ship that became available for the deportation. Their Norwegian citizenship was revoked the moment the ship departed. It was intended that none of these people would see Norway again. Few did. There were less than twenty survivors. Most of the deported Norwegian Jews were gassed at Auschwitz-Birkenau instead.

Some Americans visit the Resistance Museum in Oslo, but probably few Americans who spend time in Norway know very much about the places I have mentioned or the history they contain. It is almost by chance that I have come to care about them myself. Yet not a day of my life—in Norway or anywhere else—now passes without feelings, thoughts, and visions that intensify my encounters with the Holocaust. As I think about how easily my experience could have been different, I wonder how it turned out the way it has. As I wonder, I also know that I must try to find out more about the Holocaust, its history and implications, because that event teaches me more than any other part of human history.

A STALKED SOUL

Although a generation younger, I identify with Stingo, the fictional but not unreal American character who narrates *Sophie's Choice,* William Styron's controversial novel about the Holocaust. Stingo hailed from the Presbyterian South. For a time, he never heard of Auschwitz, but gradually he found that Auschwitz stalked his soul. Like so many of my American peers, I grew up Christian in the United States—a Midwesterner born in 1940, the son of a Presbyterian minister, too young to be much aware of World War II, barely hearing of Auschwitz afterward, and knowing practically nothing about the Holocaust for a long time. Yet I increasingly think of myself as a post-Holocaust American Christian. Auschwitz stalks my soul, too.

My academic training in philosophy and theology at Pomona College and Yale University in the late 1950s and 1960s stirred my interest in questions about evil, suffering, and injustice. Valuable though it remains, that excellent scholarly training was too divorced from history, too abstract to excavate in depth what Holocaust survivor Ida Fink would call "the ruins of memory."[1]

There was, however, an early and decisive exception to that pattern. As I finished my graduate work, which concentrated on American philosophy and the thought of William James in particular, I was deeply affected by Richard L. Rubenstein's *After Auschwitz: Radical Theology and Contemporary Judaism,* a work first published in 1966 and then updated and revised in 1992.[2] That book introduced me not only to some of the most penetrating post-Holocaust thought ever written but also to a man who would become a mentor, friend, and colleague—one of the three interpreters who have most deeply informed my perspectives on the Holocaust.

After Auschwitz led to my first published writing about the Holocaust. In *The American Religious Experience,* coauthored with Frederick Sontag in 1972, I reflected on Rubenstein's place in the so-called "Death of God" movement that attracted much attention in the United States at the time. This effort to connect American culture and reflection on the Holocaust anticipated concerns that became major themes in my work. I had not yet experienced, however, the Holocaust turn that would reorient my professional and personal life. It took tears for that to happen.

TEARS AND ELIE WIESEL

In 1973–74, an earlier Fulbright appointment took me to the University of Innsbruck, Austria, where I lectured on American culture. That year proved to be immensely important for me. I tried to interpret American life to Austrians by exploring the American Dream, a topic that has occupied much of my scholarly life. During that Innsbruck year, I also worked on the writings of Elie Wiesel.

Following Frederick Sontag's suggestion, I had begun serious reading of Wiesel's works in the summer of 1972. In what now seems more like destiny than the chance it involved at the time, my study of Wiesel was under way when my second child was born on the Fourth of July. The collision I experienced then between my good fortune—fatherhood, a promising academic career, soon a Fulbright appointment—and the destruction of family and hope explored in Wiesel's Holocaust reflections left lasting marks upon me.

My wife, Lyn, and I named our newborn daughter Sarah. In more ways than one, my entry into Sarah's world coincided with my entry into Elie Wiesel's. For in the latter, I would meet another Sarah, a Holocaust survivor whose part in *The Accident* led Wiesel to write, "Whoever listens to Sarah and doesn't change, whoever enters Sarah's world and doesn't invent new gods and new religions, deserves death and destruction."[3] Tensions created by the contrast between my joy as Sarah's father and the despair of "Sarah's world" portrayed in that early novel by Wiesel were among the catalysts that make me continue to respond to his words in writing of my own.

The first essay I published in that vein appeared in late 1972, not long before I departed from Claremont to Innsbruck. It was called "Tears and Elie Wiesel." My reflection began: "Lately something has been puzzling me. I do not think of myself as an emotional person, so why do I sometimes find myself about to weep? Nobody notices, but why is it that especially in church on Sunday mornings tears well up in my eyes?"[4]

That experience continues. It is one reason why I still go to church. In writing that initial article some twenty-five years ago, I began to understand that my tears were partly a response to the Holocaust and to Elie Wiesel in particular, an awareness that has become all the more poignant with the passing of time.

To this day, I still do not know how Wiesel happened to read my initial essay about him, but not long after it had appeared, I received an encouraging note from him. I wrote back; soon we met, and even though we live on opposite sides of the United States, we continue to keep in touch with one another. Thanks to tears and Elie Wiesel, my life and work had taken a decisive Holocaust turn.

HOLOCAUST MEETINGS

Having returned to California from Austria in 1974, I immersed myself in research and began to teach the Claremont McKenna College course on the Holocaust that I have offered annually ever since. Those commitments deepened in 1976–77, when I became a Fellow of the National Humanities Institute at Yale University. That year contained six significant experiences. First, living in Connecticut meant that I was close to New York City and thus able to meet with Elie Wiesel more often than I had done before. Second, Richard Rubenstein, who had just published another influential book, *The Cunning of History*, was also a Fellow at the National Humanities Institute. Not only did we meet and work together for the first time during that year, but, third, it was Rubenstein's urging that led me to immerse myself in the study of Raul Hilberg's magisterial work, *The Destruction of the European Jews*, which has taught me more about the history of the Holocaust than any other single book. Fourth, Rubenstein introduced me to another young Holocaust scholar, Michael Berenbaum, who had completed his doctoral studies at Florida State University under Rubenstein's direction and was then on the faculty at nearby Wesleyan University. As my meeting with Berenbaum illustrated, Holocaust studies were bringing me into contact with an amazing group of people—scholars, survivors, and students as well—who have encouraged, supported, and challenged me in more ways than I can acknowledge. Fifth, when Berenbaum and I first met, we were both writing books about Elie Wiesel. *Vision of the Void* was what Berenbaum called his distinguished work. It explored Wiesel's impact on Berenbaum's post-Holocaust understanding of his Jewish tradition. I called my book *A Consuming Fire*. With special emphasis on Wiesel's theme of protest against God and inhumanity, it explored how Wiesel both challenged and deepened my understanding of my own Christian tradition. Sharing Rubenstein and Wiesel as mentors, Berenbaum and I became friends and soul mates. Sixth, our fellowships at the National Humanities Institute enabled Rubenstein and me to receive grants from the National Endowment for the Humanities to implement on our home campuses the model courses on the Holocaust that we had devised during our year together.

A few years later, in November 1979, the American Academy of Religion held its annual meeting in New York City. I participated in a panel that Rubenstein had organized, "Academic Teaching and Study of the Holocaust." During that discussion, he observed that it would be useful to have a book that did not then exist: an interdisciplinary volume that could be a unifying text for the growing number of college and university courses that concentrated on the Holocaust. When I asked if he was writing such a book, Rubenstein said no. When I asked if he would consider writing such a book with me, he said yes.

WRITING AND TEACHING

Books are conceived more easily than they are written. But eight years later *Approaches to Auschwitz: The Holocaust and Its Legacy* appeared. To the best of our knowledge, it is the first book about the Holocaust coauthored by a Jew and a Christian. My contributions to this volume were significantly influenced by the fact that I did some of my research and writing in 1982 while serving as visiting professor of Holocaust studies at Haifa University in Israel. While there I explored Christian sites around the Sea of Galilee, where a Jew named Jesus called Andrew and Peter, James and John, to follow him. I walked the streets of Jerusalem, where Roman—not Jewish—power so fatefully sentenced Jesus to death by crucifixion. My work always brought me back to my university office, which had a magnificent view of Mount Carmel, where tradition holds that the prophet Elijah defeated the prophets of Ba'al by calling on "the God who answers by fire."[5] In that place I especially studied and wrote about the responses—or more specifically the lack of them—that Christian churches made to the Holocaust. To explore that subject as I did in Israel was an experience that was as humbling as it was awesome. It haunts me still and always will.

My contributions as a Holocaust scholar have been deeply informed by my Christian identity, by my training as a philosopher, and by my long-standing interests in American experience. Thus, it is not surprising that my writing has explored themes such as Jewish-Christian relationships; the theological implications of the Holocaust, especially as they affect Christianity; the challenges that the Holocaust poses for philosophy and for ethics in particular; and America's encounters with the Holocaust.

Some of my most significant work, however, has simply been to develop books that can enhance teaching about the Holocaust. *Approaches to Auschwitz* is one example. Another is a book conceived in December 1987, when Michael Berenbaum and I had dinner together at the Old Ebbitt Grill in Washington, D.C. The result, *Holocaust: Religious and Philosophical Implications,* collected classic writings by Holocaust survivors such as Elie Wiesel and Primo Levi and by scholars such as Raul Hilberg and Yehuda Bauer. Although these writings were referred to repeatedly by interpreters of the Holocaust, many of the essays we selected were scattered widely, some in books and journals that had gone out of print. Our book made them newly accessible to students.

When my friend Carol Rittner received a copy of *Holocaust,* she telephoned congratulations and raised a question as good as it was pointed: "Where are the women?" Her question was justified because the contents of *Holocaust* were male dominated. Her inquiry also echoed questions that I had been getting from some of my Claremont students. Commonly, women are a majority of the students who take my courses on the Holocaust. Nudged by my students, encouraged by Carol Rittner, I found my understanding challenged, expanded, and revised by extensive listening to women—especially survivors and scholars who focused attention on the particularity of women's Holocaust experiences. One outcome of that research was *Different Voices: Women and the Holocaust,* which Carol Rittner and I published in 1993. Meeting an unfilled teaching need, this book made easily available to students significant Holocaust testimony and scholarship by and about women. My work on this book, plus the reception it has received, persuade me that it is one of my best contributions to Holocaust interpretation.

Different Voices was not the first project on which I collaborated with Carol Rittner, who is another of the exceptional friends I have made through encounters with the Holocaust. Elie Wiesel brought us together, and we met in the late 1980s when Rittner helped to organize a conference about people who had rescued Jews during the Holocaust. That work led to her award-winning documentary film and book called *The Courage to Care.* A dedicated member of the Religious Sisters of Mercy, Rittner uses her religious calling more creatively and imaginatively than almost any other Christian I know. She was, for example, the first executive director of The Elie Wiesel Foundation for Humanity, which Wiesel established after receiving the Nobel Peace Prize in 1986. That role gave me the chance to work with her on a series of conferences that Wiesel led in Boston, Haifa, Israel, and Oslo. They focused on "The Anatomy of Hate." In addition, I worked with Rittner to organize an essay competition for American undergraduates, The Elie Wiesel Prize in Ethics, which the Wiesel Foundation has sponsored for nearly a decade. During most of that time, I have chaired the reading committee that selects the finalists for the jury that ultimately awards the prizes.

In the late 1980s, moreover, when post-Holocaust Christian-Jewish relations were jeopardized by the convent that Carmelite nuns had established at Auschwitz, it was Carol Rittner who called me again. That conversation originated another shared project, *Memory Offended: The Auschwitz Convent Controversy,* a 1991 book that documented the controversy's history and contained honest and sensitive debate about it by an international group of Christian and Jewish Holocaust scholars. As indicated by the book in which this essay appears, as well as by the series "Christianity and the Holocaust" of which this book is a part, Rittner's partnership in my Holocaust studies continues. Often, Holocaust teachers and writers must and should work alone. But I have also learned that Holocaust teamwork in teaching and writing can and should take place, too. By working together, especially when different traditions or disciplines are represented, people can often do more good work than one person can do alone. That understanding seems especially fitting where encounters with the Holocaust are concerned.

Not all writing about the Holocaust shows up in books or articles, journals or diaries. Some of it can be found in the exhibits and on the walls of Holocaust museums. Of the words I have written about the Holocaust, the most widely read are likely to appear in such places. In the summer of 1994, Michael Berenbaum, who for some time had been the director of the Research Institute at the United States Holocaust Memorial Museum in Washington, D.C., facilitated the formation of a team that linked me with Ralph Appelbaum Associates, the firm that had carried out the design for the Washington museum, and the Holocaust Education Center in Houston, Texas, which was developing a Holocaust museum for the fourth largest city in the United States. It became my responsibility to write the permanent exhibition text for Holocaust Museum Houston, which opened in March 1996. As demanding as any writing I have ever done, those modules went through draft after draft as I aimed to relate the Holocaust's complex history in publicly accessible language that would be as accurate and detailed, yet as compact and understandable, as the museum's educational purposes required. Those purposes include the hope that tens of thousands of school children from the Houston area will visit the museum every year. Linking that aim with the experiences of some three hundred Holocaust survivors who have made Houston their home, this distinctive museum and my contributions to it underscore the belief that it is especially important for Americans to encounter the Holocaust. In particular, the Holocaust should warn us Americans to take nothing good for granted. The Holocaust's "truths" denied basic human equality and human rights. Nazi Germany's antisemitism and racism identified "life unworthy of life" and then targeted it for annihilation. Those policies were the antithesis of life, liberty, and the pursuit of happiness.

QUESTIONS AND DILEMMAS

Earlier I mentioned that three writers have influenced my perspectives on the Holocaust more than any others. Although each one is Jewish—indeed perhaps *because* each one is Jewish—they think very differently, even in ways that may be in conflict. It is fitting that this meditation should conclude by amplifying how each of them continues to influence immensely my Holocaust thinking.

At the beginning of *Night,* the classic memoir that details his experiences as a man-child in Auschwitz, Elie Wiesel introduces one of his teachers. His name was Moshe, and the year was 1941. Although the Holocaust was under way, it had not yet touched Wiesel's hometown directly. One day the twelve-year-old Wiesel asked his teacher, "And why do you pray, Moshe?" The reply Wiesel heard was, "I pray to the God within me that He will give me the strength to ask Him the right questions." Wiesel adds, "We talked like this nearly every evening."[6]

I am a philosopher, and I believe that philosophy, first and foremost, thrives on questions. Immanuel Kant was on the mark when he defined philosophy as the inquiry that pursues three questions in particular: What can I know? What should I do? For what may I hope? Those are some of the right questions for human beings to wonder about.

Wiesel's brief description of his conversation with Moshe in 1941 stands out for me, for Holocaust studies have driven home to me how some questions are much more important than others. Specifically, I began to discover, questions do not give us the insight they can provide when they are posed abstractly and without reference to real human experiences and their histories. The writings of Elie Wiesel showed me that. So have Raul Hilberg's.

A few years ago, the University of Vermont honored Hilberg by holding a major symposium on his work. Among the many distinguished speakers was the filmmaker Claude Lanzmann, whose epic *Shoah* is a cinematic counterpart to Hilberg's monumental book, *The Destruction of the European Jews.* Hilberg plays an important part in Lanzmann's film. In a segment on the Warsaw ghetto, for example, he discusses the dilemmas faced by Adam Czerniakow, the man who headed the Jewish Council there. Czerniakow documented his role in the diary he kept until he took his own life on July 23, 1942, the day after the Germans began to liquidate the Warsaw ghetto by deporting its Jews to Treblinka. Hilberg knows the details of Czerniakow's life because he helped to translate and edit the Czerniakow diary, which survived the Final Solution.

In another segment of Lanzmann's *Shoah,* Hilberg studies a different kind of document: *Fahrplananordnung 587.* This railroad timetable scheduled death traffic. Conservative estimates indicate that *Fahrplananordnung 587,* which outlines a few days in late September 1942, engineered some ten thousand Jews to Treblinka's gas chambers.

Raul Hilberg has spent his life detailing how such things happened. Thus, in his first appearance in the Lanzmann film, he observes that, "In all of my work I have never begun by asking the big questions, because I was always afraid that I would come up with small answers; and I have preferred to address these things which are minutiae or details in order that I might then be able to put together in a gestalt a picture which, if not an explanation, is at least a description, a more full description, of what transpired."[7]

As a philosopher who keeps encountering the Holocaust, I also keep in mind Hilberg's statement—indeed his warning—about "big questions." He does not deny that the Holocaust raises them—first and foremost the question *Why?* Contrary to much human expectation, however, the fact that a question can be asked does not mean that it can be answered well, if at all, particularly when the questions are "big"—fundamental and sweeping ones of the kind that typically characterize philosophical and religious inquiries. So Hilberg concentrates on details instead. Those minutiae, however, are much more than minutiae. Their particularity speaks volumes and forms a terribly vast description. So full of life distorted and wasted, its accumulated detail makes the "big" questions less easy and simple to raise but all the more important, too.

Put into perspective by work like Hilberg's, the "big questions" become what Elie Wiesel's teacher, Moshe, called the "right questions," and thus they command the respect they deserve. That respect enjoins suspicion about "answers" that are small—inadequate for the facts they must encompass. That same respect also focuses awareness that the big questions raised by the Holocaust nonetheless need to be kept alive. For the political scientist's detail and the historian's minutiae, far from silencing the big questions, ought to intensify wonder about them. Otherwise we repress feeling too much and deny ourselves insight that can only be deepened by asking the "right questions."

There is another statement that keeps me thinking about questions that are properly big and right: "The Holocaust demands interrogation and calls everything into question. Traditional ideas and acquired values, philosophical systems and social theories—all must be revised in the shadow of Birkenau."[8] Used in this essay's epigraph, those words are Elie Wiesel's.

One of the important points those words make is this: Whatever the traditional ideas and acquired values that have existed, whatever the philosophical systems and social theories that human minds have devised, whatever religions have been believed or gods have been worshiped, they were either inadequate to prevent Auschwitz or, worse, they helped pave the way to that place.

There are a few of us philosophers, but not too many, who work on those particular problems. Philosophy, and perhaps the world, would be better off if there were more. But at the same time, when Holocaust scholars from the fields of history, religious studies, or literature, political science or sociology, ask the right questions, they move into the area that too many philosophers have ignored. How can they fail to do so, for Kant's big questions remain: What can I know? What should I do? For what may I hope? Fortunately, when scholars who do not identify themselves primarily as philosophers get around to the big questions, they often do so with immense philosophical sensitivity and insight.

But what about philosophers and the discipline of philosophy in relation to the Holocaust and Holocaust studies? I think philosophers and philosophy have avoided the Holocaust and Holocaust studies because so much history is involved. To encounter the Holocaust philosophically, one must study what happened, to whom, where, when, and how. Reckoning with detail and particularity of that kind is not what philosophers are trained or naturally inclined to do. So it is likely that relatively few of us philosophers— maybe those who have grown impatient with the abstraction and distance from history that most contemporary philosophy reflects—will immerse ourselves in this field of study. Once there, however, we are unlikely to want to be anywhere else, for the work is so intense and important.

Think of the big questions that now and forever will need to be explored and that must be handled with great care if they are to be the right questions: How did the Holocaust happen? Who is responsible for it? How can we best remember this history? What can words say? What about God and religion after Auschwitz? What about human rights and morality in a post-Holocaust world? What can I know, what should I do, for what may I hope in the shadow of Birkenau?

Philosophers should ask the right questions. At least some of us should let our questioning be informed by the Holocaust in ways that heed Raul Hilberg's warnings about "big questions." We should join scholars in other fields, using the insights that philosophy can bring, to revise traditional ideas and acquired values, philosophical systems and social theories, even religions and views about God. Then we might have a better picture, which, if not an explanation, is at least a description, a more full description, of what transpired and how its repetition might be checked and even avoided.

As I think about all the Holocaust study that still needs to be done, Richard Rubenstein's work continues to loom large. I am particularly concerned about what I call "Rubenstein's dilemma." This dilemma is important for every person and for every community, but it is especially provocative for us Americans, who have a tradition that speaks of "self-evident" truths about "inalienable rights" to life, liberty, and the pursuit of happiness.

The Holocaust's evil appears to be so overwhelming that it forms an ultimate refutation of moral relativism. No one, it seems, could confront Auschwitz and deny that there is a fundamental and objective difference between right and wrong. Nevertheless, the Final Solution paradoxically calls into question the practical status of moral norms. Thus, the dilemma I have in mind is underscored by statements in *The Cunning of History,* Ruben-stein's small but seminal book about the Holocaust and the American future.

As Rubenstein assesses the situation, the Holocaust, genocide, and related instances of state-sponsored population elimination suggest that "there are absolutely no limits to the degradation and assault the managers and tech-nicians of violence can inflict upon men and women who lack the power of effective resistance."[9] A key implication of that point of view, adds Rub-enstein, is that "until ethical theorists and theologians are prepared to face without sentimentality the kind of action it is possible freely to perpetuate under conditions of utter respectability in an advanced, contemporary so-ciety, none of their assertions about the existence of moral norms will have much credibility."[10] Rubenstein knows, of course, that there are philosoph-ical arguments to defend "a higher moral law" and ethical principles that hold persons and even nations morally responsible for their actions. Yet the Holocaust, he contends, sadly shows that there is "little or no penalty for their violation. And, norms that can freely be violated are as good as none at all."[11]

Rubenstein's dilemma stalks me. It will continue to do so. I doubt that the "answer" to that dilemma, if there is one, will be found in some clinch-ing intellectual argument or irrefutable philosophical analysis, for the best responses to Rubenstein's dilemma are not that easy or simple. In the United States those responses involve sustained reflection on America's post-Holocaust encounters with the Holocaust: the post-Holocaust memo-ries we Americans should share, the emotions we should express, the beliefs we should hold, the decisions we should make about how to live after Auschwitz, and the questions that we ask about all of those aspects of our experience, individually and collectively.

Above all, study of the Holocaust should warn us in the United States how deadly it can be for racial thinking and racism to assert themselves; for hate, radical politics, and violence to continue their destructive work; for wealth or class to determine justice; and for might to make right. If such inquiry into the Holocaust does not have a high priority in American life, especially on college and university campuses, then not only will the Ho-locaust be too easily forgotten but also the quality of American life will be endangered even more than it is in the late twentieth century.

As my own experience testifies, no one knows in advance who might be permanently affected by an encounter with the Holocaust or how that im-pact might change a person's life. To a considerable degree such particu-larities remain matters of chance. But American higher education, especially, ought not to leave it to chance that such encounters will keep taking place. By ensuring that opportunities for sustained, face-to-face study of the Ho-locaust are central parts of their curriculum, the college and university can sensitize the conscience of individual Americans and thereby help to make the United States more conscientious. Failure to do so will mean that important questions will remain unasked, that silence in need of breaking will not be broken, that indifference will not be challenged enough, and that protest, resistance, and compassion will ignore or miss needs that should be served. Encounters with the Holocaust, including the challenges they entail, should keep stalking American souls. At least for some of us Americans, those encounters may move us—as nothing else can—to renew our national life and even to mend the world.

NOTES

1. Ida Fink, *A Scrap of Time and Other Stories*, trans. Madeline Levine and Francine Prose (New York: Schocken Books, 1987), 3.

2. See Richard L. Rubenstein, *After Auschwitz: History, Theology and Contemporary Judaism,* 2d ed. (Baltimore: Johns Hopkins University Press, 1992). This version of *After Auschwitz* is more a new book than a second edition. Nine of the original version's fifteen chapters have been eliminated. Those that remain have been substantially rewritten. Although earlier versions have appeared elsewhere, there are ten new chapters in the revised edition of the book.

3. Elie Wiesel, *The Accident,* trans. Anne Borchardt (New York: Avon Books, 1970), 96. This novel was published originally as *Le Jour* (Day) in 1961. The English translation appeared in 1962.

4. John K. Roth, "Tears and Elie Wiesel," *Princeton Seminary Bulletin* 65 (December 1972): 42.

5. I Kings 18:24.

6. Elie Wiesel, *Night,* trans. Stella Rodway (New York: Bantam Books, 1986), 3.

7. See Claude Lanzmann, *Shoah: An Oral History of the Holocaust* (New York: Pantheon Books, 1985), 70.

8. Elie Wiesel, foreword to *Shadows of Auschwitz: A Christian Response to the Holocaust*, by Harry James Cargas (New York: Crossroad, 1990), ix.

9. Richard L. Rubenstein, *The Cunning of History: The Holocaust and the American Future* (New York: Harper Torchbooks, 1987), 90.

10. Ibid., 67.

11. Ibid., 88.

Selected Bibliography

Chosen by the writers themselves, the books and articles listed below identify publications that each author places among his or her most significant contributions to Holocaust studies. Books and articles appear together, and each person's writings are listed chronologically.

Berenbaum, Michael. *The Vision of the Void: Theological Reflections on the Works of Elie Wiesel.* Middletown, Conn.: Wesleyan University Press, 1979. Reprinted as *Elie Wiesel: God, the Holocaust, and the Children of Israel.* West Orange, N.J.: Behrman House, 1994.

——— and John K. Roth, eds. *Holocaust: Religious and Philosophical Implications.* New York: Paragon House, 1989.

Berenbaum, Michael. *After Tragedy and Triumph: Modern Jewish Thought and the American Experience.* Cambridge: Cambridge University Press, 1990.

———. *The World Must Know: The History of the Holocaust as Told in the United States Holocaust Memorial Museum.* New York: Little, Brown and Company, 1993.

——— and Israel Gutman, eds. *Anatomy of the Auschwitz Death Camp.* Bloomington: Indiana University Press, 1994.

Berger, Alan L. *Crisis and Covenant: The Holocaust in American Jewish Fiction.* Albany: State University of New York Press, 1985.

———. "Bearing Witness: Second Generation Literature of the *Shoah.*" *Modern Judaism* 10 (February 1990).

———. "Elie Wiesel's Second Generation Witness: Passing the Torch of Remembrance." In Harry James Cargas, ed., *Telling the Tale: A Tribute to Elie Wiesel on the Occurrence of His 65th Birthday.* St. Louis: Time Being Books, 1993.

204 Selected Bibliography

———. "The Holocaust, Second-Generation Witness and the Voluntary Covenant in American Judaism." *Religion and American Culture* 5 (Winter 1995).
———. *Children of Job: American Second-Generation Witnesses to the Holocaust.* Albany: State University of New York Press, 1997.
Blumenthal, David R. "On Teaching the Holocaust." In J. Stein and H. Staub, eds., *Creative Jewish Education: A Reconstructionist Response.* New York: Rossell Books, 1985.
———. "Scholarly Approaches to the Holocaust." In David R. Blumenthal, ed., *Emory Studies on the Holocaust,* vol. 1. Atlanta: Emory University Press, 1985. Reprinted from *Shoah* 1 (1979): 21–27.
———, ed. *Emory Studies on the Holocaust,* vol. 1. Atlanta: Emory University Press, 1985.
———, *Emory Studies on the Holocaust,* vol. 2. Atlanta: Emory University Press, 1988.
Blumenthal, David R. *Facing the Abusing God: A Theology of Protest.* Louisville: Westminster/John Knox, 1993.
Cargas, Harry James. *Harry James Cargas in Conversation with Elie Wiesel.* New York: Paulist Press, 1976.
———. *Reflections of a Post-Auschwitz Christian.* Detroit: Wayne State University Press, 1989.
———. *Shadows of Auschwitz.* New York: Crossroad, 1990.
———. *Conversations with Elie Wiesel.* South Bend, Ind.: Justice Books, 1992.
———. *Voices from the Holocaust.* Lexington: University Press of Kentucky, 1993.
Eckardt, A. Roy. *Elder and Younger Brothers: The Encounter of Jews and Christians.* New York: Charles Scribner's Sons, 1967.
———. *For Righteousness' Sake: Contemporary Moral Philosophies.* Bloomington: Indiana University Press, 1987.
——— and Alice L. Eckardt. *Long Night's Journey into Day: A Revised Retrospective on the Holocaust.* Detroit: Wayne State University Press; Oxford: Pergamon Press, 1988.
Eckardt, A. Roy. *How to Tell God from the Devil: On the Way to Comedy.* New Brunswick, N.J.: Transaction Publishers, Rutgers University, 1995.
———. *On the Way to Death: Essays Toward a Comic Vision.* New Brunswick, N.J.: Transaction Publishers, Rutgers University, 1996.
Eckardt, Alice L. and A. Roy Eckardt. *Encounter with Israel: A Challenge to Conscience.* New York: Association Press, 1970.
———. *Long Night's Journey into Day: A Revised Retrospective on the Holocaust.* Detroit: Wayne State University Press, 1988; Oxford: Pergamon Press, 1988.
Eckardt, Alice L. "Forgiveness and Repentance: Some Contemporary Considerations and Questions." In Yehuda Bauer, Alice Eckardt, et al., eds., *Remembering for the Future.* New York: Pergamon Press, 1989.
———, ed. *Burning Memory: Times of Testing and Reckoning.* New York: Pergamon Press, 1993.
Eckardt, Alice L. "Suffering, Theology and the Shoah." In Steven L. Jacobs, ed., *Contemporary Christian Religious Responses to the Holocaust.* Lanham, Md.: University Press of America, 1993.
Fisher, Eugene J. *Faith Without Prejudice: Rebuilding Christian Attitudes Toward Judaism.* New York: Crossroad, 1993.

———. *Interwoven Destinies: Jews and Christians Through the Ages.* New York: Paulist Press, 1993.

———. *"Mysterium Tremendum:* Catholic Grapplings with the *Shoah* and Its Theological and Catechetical Implications." In Steven L. Jacobs, ed., *Contemporary Christian Responses to the Shoah.* Lanham, Md.: University Press of America, 1993.

———, ed. *Visions of the Other: Jewish and Christian Theologians Assess the Dialogue.* New York: Paulist Press, 1994.

——— and Leon Klenicki, eds. *Pope John Paul II, Spiritual Pilgrimage: Texts on Jews and Judaism, 1979–1995.* New York: Crossroad, 1995.

Fleischner, Eva. *The View of Judaism in German Christian Theology Since 1945.* Metuchen, N.J.: Scarecrow Press, 1975.

———, ed. *Auschwitz: Beginning of a New Era?* New York: KTAV, 1977.

Fleischner, Eva. "The Crucial Importance of the Holocaust for Christians." In Harry James Cargas, ed., *When God and Man Failed.* New York: Macmillan, 1981.

———. "Heschel's Significance for Jewish-Christian Relations." In John Merkle, ed., *Abraham Joshua Heschel: His Life and Thought.* New York: Macmillan, 1985.

———. "Mauriac's Preface to *Night*—Thirty Years Later." In Carol Rittner, ed., *Elie Wiesel: Between Memory and Hope.* New York: New York University Press, 1990.

Heschel, Susannah, ed. *On Being a Jewish Feminist: A Reader.* New York: Schocken Books, 1983. Published in a second edition with a new introduction by Schocken Books, 1995.

Heschel, Susannah. "Making Nazism a Christian Movement: The Development of a Christian Theology of Antisemitism during the Third Reich." In Betty Rogers Rubenstein and Michael Berenbaum, eds., *What Kind of God? Essays in Honor of Richard L. Rubenstein.* Lanham, Md.: University Press of America, 1995.

———, ed. *Moral Grandeur and Spiritual Audacity: Essays of Abraham Joshua Heschel.* New York: Farrar, Straus and Giroux, 1996.

——— and Robert P. Ericksen, eds. *The Churches in Nazi Germany.* Minneapolis: Augsburg-Fortress Press, forthcoming.

Heschel, Susannah, David Biale, and Michael Galchinsy, eds. *Multiculturalism and the Jews.* Berkeley: University of California Press, forthcoming.

Littell, Franklin H. and Hubert G. Locke, eds. *The German Church Struggle and the Holocaust.* Detroit: Wayne State University Press, 1974. Reprinted by the Edwin Mellen Press, 1990.

Littell, Franklin H. *The Crucifixion of the Jews.* New York: Harper & Row, 1975. Reprinted by Mercer University Press, 1986.

———. "Early Warning: An Essay." *Holocaust and Genocide Studies* 3 (1988): 483–90.

———. "The German Church Struggle and the Holocaust (1970–1990)." In Franklin H. Littell, Alan L. Berger, and Hubert G. Locke, eds., *What Have We Learned?—Telling the Story and Teaching the Lessons of the Holocaust.* Lewiston, N.Y.: Edwin Mellen Press, 1993.

———. "Inventing the Holocaust: A Christian's Retrospect." *Holocaust and Genocide Studies* 9 (1995): 173–91.

Pawlikowski, John T. *The Challenge of the Holocaust for Christian Theology,* revised edition. New York: Anti-Defamation League, 1982.

————. "The Auschwitz Convent Controversy: Mutual Misperceptions." In Carol Rittner and John K. Roth, eds., *Memory Offended: The Auschwitz Convent Controversy.* Westport, Conn.: Praeger, 1991.

————. "The *Shoah:* Continuing Theological Challenge for Christianity." In Steven
L. Jacobs, ed., *Contemporary Christian Religious Responses to the Shoah.*
Lanham, Md.: University Press of America, 1993.

————. "Christian Theological Concerns after the Holocaust." In Eugene J. Fisher,
ed., *Visions of the Other: Jewish and Christian Theologians Assess the Dialogue.* New York: Paulist Press, 1994.

————. "The Vatican and the Holocaust: Unresolved Issues." In Marvin Perry and
Frederick M. Schweitzer, eds., *Jewish-Christian Encounters Over the Centuries: Symbiosis, Prejudice, Holocaust, Dialogue.* New York: Peter Lang, 1994.

Peck, Abraham J., ed. *Jews and Christians after the Holocaust.* Philadelphia: Fortress
Press, 1982.

Peck, Abraham J. "The Children of Holocaust Survivors." In Allon Schoener, ed., *The
American Jewish Album: 1654 to the Present.* New York: Rizzoli Books, 1983.

————, ed. *The German-Jewish Legacy in America, 1938–1988: From Bildung to
the Bill of Rights.* Detroit: Wayne State University Press, 1989.

————, *Archives of the Holocaust: The Papers of the World Jewish Congress, 1939–
1950,* 2 vols. New York: Garland Publishing Company, 1990.

Peck, Abraham J. "A Continent in Chaos: Europe and the Displaced Persons." In
Liberation 1945. Washington, D.C.: United States Holocaust Memorial Museum, 1995.

Rittner, Carol and Sondra Myers, eds. *The Courage to Care: Rescuers of Jews during
the Holocaust.* New York: New York University Press, 1986.

Rittner, Carol, ed. *Elie Wiesel: Between Memory and Hope.* New York: New York
University Press, 1990.

———— and Leo Goldberger, eds. *The Rescue of the Danish Jews: A Primer.* New
York: Anti-Defamation League, 1993.

———— and John K. Roth, eds. *Different Voices: Women and the Holocaust.* New
York: Paragon House, 1993.

Rittner, Carol. *Beyond the Diary: Anne Frank in the World.* Derry, Northern Ireland:
YES! Publications, 1993. Revised and expanded in 1996.

Roth, John K. *A Consuming Fire: Encounters with Elie Wiesel and the Holocaust.*
Atlanta: John Knox Press, 1979.

———— and Richard L. Rubenstein. *Approaches to Auschwitz: The Holocaust and Its
Legacy.* Atlanta: John Knox Press, 1987.

———— and Michael Berenbaum, eds. *Holocaust: Religious and Philosophical Implications.* New York: Paragon House, 1989.

———— and Carol Rittner, eds. *Memory Offended: The Auschwitz Convent Controversy.* Westport, Conn.: Praeger, 1991.

————. *Different Voices: Women and the Holocaust.* New York: Paragon House,
1993.

Rubenstein, Richard L. *After Auschwitz: Radical Theology and Contemporary Judaism.* Indianapolis: Bobbs-Merrill, 1966. Revised and enlarged in a second
edition, *After Auschwitz: History, Theology and Contemporary Judaism.* Baltimore: Johns Hopkins University Press, 1992.

————. *The Religious Imagination: A Study in Psychoanalysis and Jewish Theology.*

Indianapolis: Bobbs-Merrill, 1968. Reprinted in a second edition. Lanham, Md.: Brown University Classics in Judaica Series, 1985.

————. *Power Struggle: An Autobiographical Confession.* New York: Charles Scribner's Sons, 1974.

————. *The Cunning of History: Mass Death and the American Future.* New York: Harper and Row, 1975. Also published as *The Cunning of History: The Holocaust and the American Future,* a paperback edition with an introduction by William Styron. New York: Harper Colophon Books, 1978.

————. *The Age of Triage: Fear and Hope in an Overcrowded World.* Boston: Beacon Press, 1983.

Index

About the Editors and Contributors

EDITORS

CAROL RITTNER was appointed the Ida E. King Distinguished Visiting Scholar of Holocaust Studies at The Richard Stockton College of New Jersey in 1994–95. She continues to teach there as Distinguished Professor of Religious Studies. In addition to her many Holocaust-related publications, Rittner has been the executive producer for two films: *The Triumph of Memory* and *The Courage to Care,* which focused on rescuers of Jews during the Holocaust. The latter received a 1986 Academy Award nomination in the Short Documentary Film category.

JOHN K. ROTH is the Russell K. Pitzer Professor of Philosophy at Claremont McKenna College. He has published more than twenty books and hundreds of articles, many of them focused on the Holocaust. In 1988 he was named U.S. Professor of the Year by the Council for Advancement and Support of Education and the Carnegie Foundation for the Advancement of Teaching. A member of the United States Holocaust Memorial Council, Roth is also the author of the text for the permanent exhibition at Holocaust Museum Houston, which opened in that Texas city in 1996.

CONTRIBUTORS

MICHAEL BERENBAUM, former director of the United States Holocaust Research Institute of the United States Holocaust Museum in Washington,

D.C., is the president and chief executive officer of the Survivors of the Shoah Visual History Foundation. The author of many books, scores of scholarly articles, and hundreds of journalistic pieces, Berenbaum has taught at Wesleyan University, Yale University, and Georgetown University.

ALAN L. BERGER, a specialist on Jewish and Holocaust literature, holds the Raddock Eminent Scholar Chair for Holocaust Studies at Florida Atlantic University. Before accepting that appointment, he was professor of religion at Syracuse University, where he founded and, for fifteen years, directed the Jewish studies program. In 1989 and 1990, Berger chaired the Annual Scholars' Conference on the Holocaust and the Churches.

DAVID R. BLUMENTHAL is the Jay and Leslie Cohen Professor of Judaic Studies at Emory University. In addition to his work in Holocaust studies and his influential reflections on how the study of Judaism fits within a university setting, Blumenthal has made significant contributions to three other fields in Jewish studies: medieval Jewish thought, the mystical tradition in Judaism, and contemporary Jewish theology.

HARRY JAMES CARGAS, professor of literature and language at Webster University, is well known for his important interviews with leading writers. He is the author or editor of more than thirty books, most of them focused on the Holocaust. The first Catholic appointed to the international advisory board of Yad Vashem, Israel's memorial to the Holocaust, Cargas is also vice-president of the Annual Scholars' Conference on the Holocaust and the Churches.

A. ROY ECKARDT, emeritus professor of religious studies at Lehigh University, has served as president of the American Academy of Religion, and for many years he was editor-in-chief of the *Journal of the American Academy of Religion*. A pioneer in Holocaust studies and a specialist on Jewish-Christian relations, Eckardt is the author of sixteen books, including two coauthored with Alice L. Eckardt, who is also a contributor to this volume.

ALICE L. ECKARDT, emerita professor of religious studies at Lehigh University, cofounded and codirected the Jewish studies program at Lehigh from 1967 to 1985. She is also a member of the executive editorial review board of *Holocaust and Genocide Studies*, associate editor of the *Journal of Ecumenical Studies*, and a member of the executive committee of "Remembering for the Future," which has organized major international conferences on the Holocaust.

EUGENE J. FISHER, long active in the field of Jewish-Christian dialogue, serves as associate director of the Secretariat for Ecumenical and Interreligious Affairs, National Conference of Catholic Bishops, in Washington, D.C. He is also a consultant to the Vatican Commission for Religious Relations with the Jews. The author and editor of many books, Fisher and his coeditor, Leon Klenicki, received the 1995 National Jewish Book Award in the category of Jewish-Christian relations for *Spiritual Pilgrimage: Texts on Jews and Judaism, 1975–95.*

EVA FLEISCHNER, Catholic theologian, teacher, lecturer, and author, served as professor of religion at Montclair State University from 1972 to 1991. She has also held visiting professorships at Colorado College, the College of St. Benedict, and Marquette University. She is a member of the advisory committee of the U.S. Catholic Bishops' Office of Catholic-Jewish Relations and the church relations subcommittee of the United States Holocaust Memorial Council.

SUSANNAH HESCHEL is the director of the Samuel Rosenthal Center for Jewish Studies at Case Western Reserve University, where she also holds the Abba Hillel Silver professorship in the Jewish studies program, which is part of Case Western's Department of Religion. The author of numerous studies on women and religion, Heschel has also done groundbreaking work on Christian-Jewish relations in Germany before and during the Nazi period.

FRANKLIN H. LITTELL, emeritus professor of religion at Temple University, cofounded the Annual Scholars' Conference on the Holocaust and the Churches in 1970. In 1989–91, he was the inaugural Ida E. King Distinguished Visiting Scholar of Holocaust Studies at The Richard Stockton College of New Jersey and in 1993–94 the Robert Foster Cherry Professor of Distinguished Teaching at Baylor University. Littell is also president of the Philadelphia Center on the Holocaust, Genocide and Human Rights.

JOHN T. PAWLIKOWSKI, professor of social ethics at the Catholic Theological Union in Chicago, has been a member of the United States Holocaust Memorial Council since 1980. He currently chairs the Council's subcommittee on church relations and serves on the Council's executive and community outreach committees as well. The author of many publications on the Holocaust and Christian-Jewish relations, Pawlikowski is also a member of the National Conference of Catholic Bishops' advisory committee on Catholic-Jewish relations.

ABRAHAM J. PECK, a lecturer in Judaic studies at the University of Cincinnati, is the administrative director of the American Jewish Archives. In addition to his extensive writings about the Holocaust, Peck frequently serves as a special consultant to the United States Holocaust Memorial Museum. He helped to develop the museum's 1995 exhibit on the liberation of the

Nazi camps and the experiences that Jews endured in the displaced persons'
(DP) camps after Nazi Germany's surrender in May 1945.

RICHARD L. RUBENSTEIN became president of the University of Bridgeport
in 1995. Prior to that appointment, he was the Robert O. Lawton Distinguished Professor of Religion at Florida State University, where he joined
the faculty in 1970 and directed the Center for the Study of Southern Religion and Culture from 1973 to 1982. From 1981 to 1992, Rubenstein served
as president of the Washington Institute for Values in Public Policy, a public
policy research institute in Washington, D.C. He is a pioneering scholar in
Holocaust studies whose books and essays have had a lasting impact on the
field.

ISBN 0-313-29683-9

9 780313 296833

90000>

HARDCOVER BAR CODE